Studying Abroad 2015

Studying Abroad 2015:
A guide for UK students

3rd edition

Cerys Evans

trotman | t

Studying Abroad: A Guide for UK Students 2015

This third edition published in 2014 by Trotman Publishing, a division of Crimson Publishing Ltd, The Tramshed, Walcot Street, Bath BAI 5BB

© Trotman Publishing 2014

Previous editions published in 2012, 2013

Author: Cerys Evans

British Library Cataloguing in Publication Data
A catalogue record for this book is available from the British Library

ISBN 978 1 84455 569 7

Typeset by IDSUK (DataConnection) Ltd

Printed and bound in Malta by Gutenberg Press Ltd, Malta

Acknowledgements

This book would not have been possible without the help of UK students at universities across the world who were happy to tell their stories. Many got involved in order to share their experience of a life-changing opportunity. Particular thanks go to Mark Huntington (A Star Future), Stefan Watts (Study Options), Jamie Dunn (US-UK Fulbright Commission) and the many university staff who took the time to talk to me and who put me in touch with their students.

Finally, Matt, Alice and Oscar deserve my heartfelt thanks for their understanding and support.

Contents

Contents

Contents

Contents

Contents

ROAD

nd, although there is a lot of information available
lenge is making sense of it, ensuring that it is
ng able to make meaningful comparisons between
tions available.

elp you to determine whether studying a degree
ght option for you. It will tackle the costs, risks
tudying abroad. It will enable you to compare the
nt countries and their education systems. You can
rials and the tribulations of a variety of students,
ng about their highlights of overseas study.
lp you to navigate the plethora of information
g you through the decision-making process by
rs to the essential questions.

the starting point of what could be a life-
onal and cultural adventure.

hange rates were used throughout the book
nber 2013).

(Euro)
(US Dollar)
9 (Canadian Dollar)
9 (Australian Dollar)
95 (New Zealand Dollar)
73 (Danish Krone)
.12 (Czech Koruna)
52 (Norwegian Krone)
.23 (Swedish Krona)
(Singapore Dollar)
.52 (Hong Kong Dollar)

global market a
online, the chal
genuine and be
the different op

Introducti

This book will h
abroad is the rig
and benefits of s
merits of differe
read about the tr
as well as learni
The book will he
available, guidin
providing answe

This book is only
changing educat

Britain has had a long trac
students to its universities
overseas to study. All that
much interest in the possi

The three-fold increase in
prompted some young pe
affordable ways to study.
degrees available to them
range of prices. Althoug
students from Wales and
comparably priced, and
those available at home.
available elsewhere in E
postgraduate level.

Note

The following exc
(sourced in Nover

But price alone is not e
A more competitive ma
leading students to ma
employers and studyin
produce a more dynan

- £1 to €1.17
- £1 to $1.61
- £1 to C$1.6
- £1 to A$1.6
- £1 to NZ$1.
- £1 to DKK8
- £1 to CZK3(
- £1 to NOK9
- £1 to SEK1(
- £1 to S$2.0(
- £1 to HK$12

However, choosing to
be made lightly. There
questions to ask befor

- £1 to ¥9.8.2 (Chinese Yuan Renminbi)
- £1 to JPY157.72 (Japanese Yen)
- £1 to ZAR15.90 (South African Rand)
- £1 to MYR5.06 (Malaysian Ringgit)
- £1 to JA$168 (Jamaican Dollar)
- £1 to SAR6.05 (Saudi Arabian Riyal)
- £1 to QAR5.87 (Qatari Riyal)
- £1 to BRL3.53 (Brazilian Real)

Student story
Simran Gill, Fontys University of Applied Sciences, Venlo, the Netherlands

Simran Gill is in the second year of a bachelor's degree in International Marketing. He originally decided to study outside England due to the high tuition fees, but he was also very keen on the added benefit of being able to experience life and study in Europe.

'The tuition fees in Holland are nearly €1800 (£1,540) a year, and the cost of living, including accommodation, is much cheaper than in the UK.'

His search for a university started at the Student World Fair. 'The Netherlands were well represented and knew how to cater for British students.' He later went on to visit his chosen institution and felt well supported throughout the research and application process. 'It was considerably easier than UCAS, but this could depend on the university. Fontys was extremely quick and helpful as and when questions needed to be answered. Studielink, Holland's equivalent of UCAS, is simple to navigate and free.

'The university assigned me a buddy who was a second-year student and who was able to guide me through the process of registration and also help in matters regarding student life in the city and university. When I have required information, Fontys has been extremely informative and when I needed help with accommodation the support given was fantastic.'

Simran's experience of studying has been positive, although there have been some adjustments that he has had to make. 'Well, there were several modules which I had not studied for since GCSE so when it came to statistics and maths, for example, it was difficult for me to adjust. The other subjects were challenging as I had to get used to a more concise way of writing, but it was more the workload that presented the real challenge for me. I did far more in my first few months in comparison to my friends at

UK-based universities. I was definitely worked hard for the money I spent, so it was worth it in that respect. I guess you are eased into it in the beginning but by the second month you are expected to be up to speed. Now that I'm in the second year, I would say that the course has become more focused, whereas last year it was rather generalised.

'The standard is extremely high. Learning is more personal and contact time with your lecturer is more than just a person standing in front of a hundred students. They know me by name and classes are no bigger than 30.'

He recommends starting early in your quest for somewhere to live. 'Be sure to look early and allow yourself to see the surroundings, as the environment where you live is also important.'

Now that he is a second year student, he's moved out of halls into a shared house with friends. 'I live with two other students, from Germany. Fontys is primarily populated by German students due to its location near the German border, which in turn has attracted many of them to study in the Netherlands. The rapport with them is great; they're very easy-going, yet focused when necessary. The university has an international influence which you can see by the many friends I have from all over the world.

'In regards to renting, there aren't many major differences from the UK. Deposits are small, and if you have friends in the year above who are moving out of their accommodation, it's easy just to continue the contract with the landlord once they have left, as I did.'

Simran didn't experience any major difficulties adjusting to his new way of life. 'Not at all, I relished the opportunity of living somewhere else and experiencing a new culture. The chance to live abroad does not always present itself, and at the age of 18 it's not common, so take it by both hands if available. Perhaps the hardest adjustment was having to slow down the pace of my English so my international peers could understand!

'Moving away from home is never easy wherever you go, but I get the chance to go back regularly, so missing friends and family has not been much of an issue.'

Simran's top tips

Living costs

'Living costs are relatively cheap. There are low-price supermarkets which offer a wide variety of products at good prices. Food is pretty much the same here as it is in the UK. Supermarkets are tremendously accessible; I live above one. I'd recommend setting a budget and making food in bulk, if necessary. Going out to party is not too expensive, as drinks are cheap in Venlo and I rarely spend over €80 (£68) a week.'

Insurance

'A European health card (EHIC) will cover anything under €200 (£170). I have also registered with the British Embassy in Holland, so in case anything happens support is provided for us.'

Working while studying

'Last year, I was the sole representative of the UK at Fontys International Business School. Partly due to my increasing involvement with the international relations team, we have gained four more new students from Britain this semester. I have subsequently earned a job with the university as an international relations consultant, working occasionally with the team to promote the university in the UK. They use my input and social media skills to help them recruit in the UK. One of the benefits of working for the university is that they are considerate of my timetable.'

Lifestyle and culture

'It's a wonderfully chilled and relaxed lifestyle, the people are friendly and their English is great. They have many celebrations at points of the year where one can become a part of their culture and tradition.'

Travel

'Travel is of no concern as bikes rule the roost in Holland, and my university is a five-minute ride away and the city centre is two minutes away. Train travel is speedy and on time and, with the county being relatively small, nothing is too far away. Germany is five minutes over the border, Belgium is 40 minutes distance and Paris is a four-hour drive.'

Options for after you finish your studies

'There are many graduate schemes which I can apply for. In my third year, a year in industry is required. Fontys has amazing connections with companies worldwide, so I feel that the option of pursuing a career in marketing is certainly attainable.

'My plans are to return to the UK with two new languages in my repertoire (Dutch and an understanding of German) and an experience which would rival that of any graduate from the UK. To become a marketing manager before 30 at a large company is the goal.'

Fontys University of Applied Sciences is the second largest institute of higher education in Holland with campuses in the south of the country.

You can follow Simran's progress in the Netherlands on his blog, http:// fromturbanstoclogs.blogspot.co.uk.

Chapter 1

Why study abroad?

UK students don't traditionally study abroad. Far more
international students come to the UK than leave its shores to
study. International study might be a new thing for UK students,
but across much of the world it is far more common. In fact, the
number of international students around the world just keeps
growing. The Organisation for Economic Co-operation and
Development (OECD) and United Nations Educational, Scientific
and Cultural Organization's (UNESCO) Institute for Statistics tell
us that nearly 4.3 million international students were enrolled in
higher education in 2011. The number of students going abroad to
study has almost doubled since 2000 and looks set to soar.

But how many of these are UK students? OECD reveals that 37,491
UK students were enrolled at overseas tertiary institutions in
2013. Although this figure is low compared to the global numbers,
it is worth knowing that the numbers have gone up 6% since
last year and almost 60% since 2006–2007. Things are certainly
changing.

If you mention studying abroad, a common response is that
we already have a world-class university system, so why look
elsewhere? But there are benefits of moving country to go
to university which is why UK students are starting to look
elsewhere, and in increasing numbers. There are plenty of reasons

why study abroad might be beneficial; maybe you want to avoid higher tuition fees, to have an amazing adventure or to gain a place at one of the top universities in the world.

Interest in overseas study has been steadily growing since the announcement of the fee increases in the UK. Studying abroad may be a hot topic, but is that enough of a reason to set sail for foreign shores? I don't think so. Things are changing so fast that it is hard to know what the economic, employment or educational landscape will look like in a year or two, while you might only be part-way through your overseas degree. So it makes sense to consider overseas study in far more depth as part of your wider and longer-term plans; you will need to look carefully at the pros and cons before you make your decision.

The global market

As you walk around schools and colleges in other European countries, it is normal to see international opportunities on the notice boards; summer schools, study exchanges and overseas degrees are far more commonplace than in the UK. Young people in many other countries have come to expect international experiences.

This is not always the case in the UK and this causes a problem, according to a recent report into the global skills gap. Three-quarters of board- and director-level executives and CEOs think that 'we are in danger of being left behind by emerging countries unless young people learn to think more globally'. A similar proportion (74%) are 'worried that many young people's horizons are not broad enough to operate in a globalised and multicultural economy'. (The Global Skills Gap: Preparing young people for the new global economy, Think Global and British Council, December 2011.)

The British Chambers of Commerce carried out a survey of over 8,000 UK businesses in 2012, exploring barriers to exporting and international trade. They came up with the following recommendation: 'It is important to ensure that the next generation of business owners are "born global" with language skills.'

Picture yourself having finished university and ready to look for work. If you consider the global marketplace for jobs, then you will not only be competing against UK graduates, but against the brightest and best from across the world. And while the number of graduates from western countries is starting to plateau, countries like China and India are producing more young graduates, many of whom choose international higher education. The market is starting to get even more crowded and competitive.

Many organisations now do business or seek clients in more than one country, so job applicants with international experience, and the increased cultural awareness that brings, have added value. Some students choose study abroad as the first step towards an international career. Those graduates who have spent a summer school in the States, an exchange to Sweden as part of their first degree followed by postgraduate study in Malaysia, have a head start.

A 2011 report from the Association of Graduate Recruiters (AGR), Council for Industry and Higher Education (CIHE) and CFE (research and consultancy specialists in employment and skills) examines how global graduates can be developed. 'Students have a role to play in acquiring global competencies and choosing appropriate pathways to enable them to develop a global mindset. Experience of working outside their home country and immersion in a different culture can catapult a graduate into being considered for rewarding and challenging roles.'

The report's authors worked with multinational employers based in the UK to identify the most important qualities a global graduate will need. 'Global graduates require a blend of knowledge, competencies and corresponding attributes spanning global mindset, cultural agility and relationship management and must be able to apply them flexibly.'

Studying abroad can not only give you the opportunity to study in a new country, but also to choose a degree with an international focus while studying alongside a group of students from across the world. Consider how all these aspects can help you to develop the global mindset that will prepare you for the international job market and the global economy.

> 66 I feel I am having a much more international experience here than I ever would have had in England. I am studying in a diverse environment which is reflected in the debates and classes that we take part in. My class has such a range of nationalities that makes the lessons more dynamic, but it also has a real effect on personal development. By being in these classes you develop a more tolerant attitude and change your outlook completely on some things. 99
>
> *Clare Higgins, The Hague University of*
> *Applied Sciences, the Netherlands*

Competition in the UK

Competition for university places

In 2013, over 180,000 students applied for university in the UK without gaining a place. For some of the most competitive courses in the UK, there are tens of applications per place. You have to be truly exceptional, and perhaps a little bit lucky, to get a place for medicine or veterinary science in the UK. Yet there are internationally recognised universities offering the same opportunities in the Caribbean and parts of Europe. Although you still need to demonstrate academic excellence and the right aptitude and attitude, the level of competition for places is not as extreme as in the UK. It is not surprising that applicants, frustrated by the limits in the UK, are looking for alternatives.

The UK operates a highly competitive system, where great importance is placed on predicted grades and high academic achievement. Competition for places is one of the reasons why entry criteria are shooting through the roof. A cap on the number of places available means that demand is currently outstripping supply, so the universities can pick and choose their candidates and ask for higher and higher requirements. More places are on offer to students achieving grades ABB and above; this has meant that students narrowly missing these grades have started to lose out. It has been announced that the cap will be abolished from 2015.

Other countries do things differently. Some countries will accept you provided that you have achieved three A levels (or equivalent) but are not so concerned about grades. This doesn't mean that they are less stringent in their entry processes; in some cases, they are more concerned with how you actually perform at university – if you don't achieve in your first year, they may ask you to leave.

A number of countries don't have a coordinated central application process like UCAS. On the downside, this may mean having to complete more application forms. On the positive side, it also

means that you aren't limited to the number of applications
you make, which can keep your options open. You can even
apply through UCAS at the same time as applying to overseas
universities; all the while gathering the information you
need to decide which option suits you best. Some students
use an international university as a back-up option to their
UK plans.

Competition for jobs

Many current students and recent graduates understand all too
clearly the effects of the upsurge in numbers in higher education
over the past decade. The increase in numbers of graduates,
exacerbated by the recent economic challenges, is creating a
crowded graduate job market. Yet the more graduates there are,
the more pressure there is to get a degree in order to compete. A
degree has become essential yet, conversely, a degree alone is not
enough. Students are looking for ways in which to stand out, to
make themselves different and to get an edge over the competition.
Studying abroad can be a way to achieve all these things.

As Dr Jo Beall of the British Council explained in 2012: 'The
good news is that people are beginning to recognise how vital
international skills are for enhancing their career. Research last
year revealed that more UK employers look for international
awareness and experience above academic qualifications. But
the bad news is that not enough people in the UK are taking
opportunities to gain international experience. That needs to
change if the UK will successfully compete in the global economy.
Our recent research showed that while almost two-thirds of
students felt they had an international outlook, they failed to see
the potential career advantages to be gained from international
experiences.'

> **❝** Global leaders need to be willing to work in different locations as an integral part of their career but many employers have difficulty recruiting graduates willing to travel or relocate. Employers felt that graduates with a global mindset would be more likely to embrace international immersion and relish the opportunity to work in different countries. It is essential that leaders are positioned where they are most needed and thus able to respond to market demands. **❞**
>
> *(Diamond, A., Walkley, L. et al., Global Graduates into Global Leaders, www.cihe.co.uk, [Online] accessed November 2012.)*

Financial benefits

From autumn 2012, tuition fees of up to £9,000 per year have been charged in England. Fees will continue to be charged at these rates for students starting university in 2014.

Welsh students are expected to contribute £3,685 per year in 2013, while fees in Northern Ireland (for students from Northern Ireland) are capped at £3,685. Studying in Scotland remains free for Scottish students, although students from the rest of the UK studying in Scotland will pay fees of up to £9,000 per year.

On top of the increasing fees, repayment options for student loans are also looking less appealing. In England and Wales an interest rate of RPI plus 3% (making a total of 6.3% at September 2013's rate) will be charged on your loan from day one, with variable rates charged once you graduate, depending on your earnings. The UK is not a cheap place to live at the moment either, with costs of food, energy bills and fuel particularly high. So, in addition to your hefty debts from fees, you might be looking at less reasonable terms on your loan and high costs of living.

Unsurprisingly, students and parents are now wondering whether there might be a more financially attractive proposition elsewhere. There are universities in countries like Sweden, Denmark, Norway and Finland that charge no fees to UK students. Many countries charge less than England, Wales and Northern Ireland – countries like Estonia and Ireland, for example. There are countries with considerably cheaper costs of living (the Czech Republic or Malaysia, for example) and there are universities with generous scholarships and sources of student financial support (for example, the USA and the Netherlands). Graduates from some overseas universities may come home with the ideal situation of no debt (or at least smaller debt), as well as many of the other benefits introduced in this chapter.

> 66 Belgium offered a world-renowned university at the heart of Europe for a fraction of the tuition price at American and British institutions. 99
>
> *Tom Aitken, KU Leuven, Belgium*

Academic benefits

There can be academic benefits to studying abroad, for example, the chance to try out a number of subjects before specialising; or how about the opportunity to study new subjects or specialist options not available in the UK? Some countries are world leaders in specific subjects; Australia, for example, is known for its geology and marine biology courses, among others. Other countries offer a different perspective on familiar subjects, like veterinary medicine or history. Or perhaps you relish the opportunity to study a subject in its natural setting, Arctic studies or American literature, for example.

> **❝** The style of learning is very similar to A levels in that you are taking multiple subjects at once. Because of this, each of my classes feels very interdisciplinary. For example, there is a Math major in my English class, who brings a different perspective to the texts compared to a History major, for example. **❞**
>
> *Stephanie Addenbrooke, Yale University, USA*

Studying abroad may give you a more realistic chance of studying at a world-class university or of taking one of the competitive subjects that is becoming increasingly difficult in the UK (see Competition for university places, page 11). Outside the UK, some of the best universities in the world can be more accessible in the grades they expect and in the scholarships they offer. Different countries place different importance on entrance exams, face-to-face interviews, exam results, and hobbies and interests. You may find that what is needed by other universities across the world plays to your strengths better than what the UK asks of you.

You will have the chance to experience a different academic environment, with access to different types of campus and university facilities. Some universities offer much smaller classes than in the UK, better tutor-contact time or high-profile internships; finding out exactly what is on offer is an important part of your research.

You may even find that the styles of teaching and learning outside the UK suit you better. For example, in Australia teaching is often more informal and lecturers are approachable and accessible; in Denmark, much is made of problem-based learning, while exams are required in all subjects.

Personal benefits

Studying abroad can be a great adventure, broadening your horizons and throwing up new challenges to be faced. It is hardly surprising that so many students come home from time overseas feeling confident, mature and independent. Understanding that there are different ways of doing things can make you more flexible. Learning to cope in an unfamiliar situation reinforces your adaptability and ability to use your initiative. Most universities arrange lots of events to let international students meet one another and get settled in, so your social skills will get some practice too.

> **❝** The values and memories that studying abroad gives you are always worth it and they equip you with skills to do it again or adapt to similar alien situations in the future.**❞**
>
> *Tom Aitken, KU Leuven, Belgium*

The list of personal benefits goes on and on. Many courses delivered in English attract a wide and varied mix of international students, not just those from English-speaking countries. The chance to make friends from across the world makes you more culturally aware, but also means a wider network of contacts for future life and work.

Even if you are being taught in English, studying in a non-English-speaking country means that you will need to develop your language skills in order to be able to communicate effectively. Most institutions will offer language courses to their students. Language skills can make you more employable; Britain lags behind the rest of Europe with its foreign-language skills and this might even be having an impact on our export market.

In a 2012 survey of over 8,000 businesses in the UK, the British Chambers of Commerce discovered that 'up to 96% of respondents had no foreign language ability for the markets they served, and the largest language deficits are for the fastest developing markets. For example, only 0.4% of business owners surveyed reported that they were able to speak Russian or Chinese well enough to conduct business deals in their buyers' language. Addressing the gaps in commercial exporting skills – including language skills – must be a priority to support the growth of Britain's export sector.'

Think how beneficial language skills could be to your future prospects.

> **66** My plan is to return to the UK with two new languages in my repertoire (Dutch and an understanding of German) and an experience which would rival that of any graduate from the UK. **99**
> *Simran Gill, Fontys University of Applied Sciences, the Netherlands*

Studying in another country can also give you access to lifestyle options that aren't accessible or affordable in the UK. If you fancy a sauna in your apartment building, try Finland. Or how about surfing before lectures in Australia? If you're looking for a great place to ski, parts of the USA or Canada have much to offer.

You might get the chance to work overseas too, perhaps part-time alongside your studies or as part of an internship, co-op programme or placement related to your subject. Essentially, you will get the chance to develop a global perspective or an international outlook, which is so important in today's global society.

The employer's view

When considering overseas study as part of a longer-term plan, you need to be sure of your prospects when you return to the UK. So what kinds of competencies could you develop through overseas study that would be attractive to employers back in the UK? Here are the views of some top employers.

> ❝ Cultural dexterity is important: an ability not to impose one's own culture on another one, to be sensitive to other cultures and how to do business in different environments. There are certain ways of working with clients in the Middle East that you wouldn't adopt in Japan. ❞
>
> *PWC*

> ❝ Adaptability and self-awareness are probably the two things that we find the toughest to find . . . we want our graduates to feel they fit with our culture and hit the ground running. ❞
>
> *HSBC*

> **❝** If you have people that can integrate with local teams, or who are able to move globally and take with them their experience in a seamless way, I think that can only help the business move forward. A lot of our work is very dependent on engaging with local governments [and] other local and national oil companies, and we need to be able to work with them effectively. **❞**
>
> *BP*

> **❝** You need the mindset that says, 'The person I'm talking to isn't like me and I need to understand what they are like and then work with them.' It isn't only about having the technical knowledge, it's also necessary to understand the values, customs, cultures and behaviours that are significant to them. **❞**
>
> *National Grid*
> *(Source: Diamond, A., Walkley, L. et al., Global Graduates into Global Leaders, www.cihe.co.uk, [Online] accessed November 2012.)*

A 2013 British Council report, *Culture at Work*, considered the views of recruitment specialists at 360 large organisations from nine countries, including the UK. The employers could clearly see the benefits that intercultural skills could bring to a company's earnings. They also identified the risks, including financial risk, of not having employees with these skills, which included:

- loss of clients
- damage to an organisation's reputation
- team conflict.

If you choose to study overseas, you should develop many of the qualities that these organisations are looking for, but you will still need to be sure that you can articulate these strengths to potential employers. Think about how you could sell your international experiences, your ability in foreign languages and your intercultural skills at interview.

Why not go?

Of course, studying abroad isn't the right choice for everyone and there are a number of reasons why you might not choose to take this option. Some of the reasons that make international study ideal for one person (the chance to have an adventure or take a leap into the unknown, for example) might make it an awful prospect for another.

YouGov and the British Council asked 1,000 undergraduates why they had not worked, lived or studied abroad and some of the most common responses were:

- 'It costs too much to do so.'
- 'My foreign language skills are not good enough.'
- 'I find the idea daunting.'
- 'I wouldn't know how to go about it.'

Source: British Council and YouGov, 2011. Next generation UK. [pdf] Available at: www.britishcouncil.org/scotland-news-next-generation-uk-research.htm [Accessed 4 September 2013]

You do need a certain amount of confidence to take this step. It is a braver move than simply following the crowd and it does have some risks. You are further from home if things go wrong, although many students overseas talk of the support network they build up of university staff, room-mates and fellow students.

The need for thorough preparation and research

Ideally, you need to be fully prepared to take this step. Getting a place through Clearing in the UK can be a stressful process and can lead to students feeling the pressure to accept courses or institutions for which they are not suited. Imagine how it feels when you end up in a different country. After A level results day in August there is often great interest in late opportunities overseas, but not always the time and space to make an informed decision. A rushed decision doesn't always end up being a negative one, but there are benefits from taking your time with this process.

> 66 The Dutch universities start earlier so I had not even enrolled, had no financial aid or plan, don't speak any Dutch and had no accommodation, so I felt very unprepared. 99
>
> *Clare Higgins, The Hague University of Applied Sciences, the Netherlands*

When considering an unfamiliar education system, you need to find out far more about the type and reputation of an institution, the way you will be taught and assessed, the qualifications you will gain, the grading system and so on; you can't assume that anything will be the same as in the UK.

Financial reasons

One of the downsides to overseas study is the lack of UK student financial support you can access. With no loans or grants from the UK government, you will need to find some money for fees and living costs before you go.

However, in 2014–2015, the Scottish government is piloting a scheme to open up opportunities to Scottish students by offering 500 students the same financial support whether they study at home or take their full degree at specific institutions in Europe:

- University of Maastricht, the Netherlands
- University of Groningen, the Netherlands
- RheinnWaal University of Applied Sciences, Germany
- University of Southern Denmark, Denmark
- Malmo University, Sweden.

You can find out more at the Student Awards Agency for Scotland at www.saas.gov.uk

If you're a UK student applying outside the EU and you need to apply for a visa, you will need to provide evidence that you have the money to study. Don't forget to factor in additional costs for application fees, travel, admissions tests, visa applications or insurance, for example.

> **❝** Remember that start-up costs are a lot. Whether it is desk lamps or mattresses, it soon spirals. Your first month's living costs will likely be twice as high as a normal month.**❞**
>
> *Tom Aitken, KU Leuven, Belgium*

There may be some opportunities for scholarships and occasionally even grants and loans from your host country. Even if you're lucky enough to get a scholarship or financial support from the country where you study, chances are that you'll need some money to supplement this, or in case of an emergency. If you plan to work to fund your studies, don't bank on getting work right away, particularly if you don't yet speak the language.

Language barrier

If you are studying in a country where English isn't an official language, even though your course may be taught in English, you will still need to manage away from the university. A rental agreement for accommodation or an application for a bank account, for example, will be in another language, so you will need to consider how you might cope. If most of your fellow students don't speak English as a first language, you may feel isolated in social situations.

Learning a new language is likely to be highly beneficial, but it is another commitment on top of your studies. If you are concerned about the language barrier, it is worth finding out how widely English is spoken in your chosen country and whether the institution takes many students from English-speaking countries.

Adjusting

You will need to be prepared to make adjustments if you decide to study abroad.

Education

Teaching and learning can be different (as you'll learn in Chapters 5 to 10). Expectations about what you should achieve in your first year can be very high, often determining whether you are allowed to stay on into the second year. The workload may be heavier than you would expect in the UK and terminology may be unfamiliar. It will be a steep learning curve, so you will need to use your initiative and seek help to avoid falling behind.

Lifestyle

Moving abroad means that your normal way of life will be thrown into disarray. The familiar and comforting will have disappeared, replaced by the new and strange, and the life you expect to lead at university may not always be realised. You may spend a disproportionate amount of time studying, adjusting to the new education system and working (rather than socialising). You may find that other home students from the host country are older or living at home. There will be cultural and social differences to the ways you spend your time and you will be far away from your normal support network of family and friends. In combination, these factors often lead to feelings of culture shock and homesickness. It is quite normal to feel this way, but it is an adjustment that you will need to consider.

> **66** There is a big restaurant scene in Doha, but a limited number of bars and they are all located in hotels. Much of student life when we are not working revolves around cultural events, socialising at the souqs, or going to the beach and malls. **99**
>
> *Benedict Leigh, UCL Qatar, Qatar*

Risks

Although many people love their experience of studying abroad, it is not risk-free. You might be concerned about whether you will get a visa, have fears about how you will manage financially and worry about the distance from family and friends. International study can bring flexibility, but there may be more restrictions in the choices that you make, particularly if you need a visa. It can be problematic to change institution or course once you start. It is not always possible to change your reason for being in a country, from studying to full-time work, for example, so you need to be fairly sure of your plans before you depart.

No matter how thoroughly you plan and research, you cannot know what you will be faced with when you come to leave university, so you cannot assume that the opportunities of today will still be there tomorrow. You may find that employers do not recognise or understand your degree, even if it is equivalent to those available in the UK. Even if you're attending a world-ranked university, UK employers may fail to recognise its status. Perhaps you were planning to stay on in a country, but economic conditions made that difficult. Courses that meet certain professional standards today might not fit the bill tomorrow, so it is worth considering a back-up plan, where possible.

> **66** Before you leave home, make sure you sort how your finances are going to work from your bank back home, and how you can withdraw money abroad.**99**
>
> *Tudor Etchells, IE University, Spain*

Finally, international education is big business, so there are people out there trying to make money from bogus institutions, low-quality provision and non-existent accommodation. Be on your guard and use some of the tips and reputable sources of information found in this book.

Having gathered and considered all the information that you need, you may just get the feeling that studying abroad is not the right option for you. If it isn't the right step right now, you don't necessarily need to rule it out for ever. You might want to consider alternatives to taking your full degree abroad (see page 77) or you might choose to study or work abroad at a later stage in life.

Many of the trailblazing students who have already taken the step of taking their full degree overseas have additional reasons for going. Some have already spent some time abroad, have family members who had lived overseas or have personal links to a country before they decide to study there. This is changing; as a degree overseas has started to become more common, more attractive and more understood in the UK, students are now making the move without those personal links beforehand.

If you're looking for . . .

- If you're looking for the cheapest fees, try Europe (Chapter 5).
- If you're looking for a similar student lifestyle to that of the UK, try Ireland (page 154), the Netherlands (page 162) and many of the US campus universities (Chapter 6).
- If you're looking for accelerated degrees or tailor-made education, try a private university (page 43).
- If you're looking for a low cost of living, try eastern Europe (Chapter 5), South Africa (page 285) or China (page 300).
- If you're looking for the best in the world, try the USA (Chapter 6).
- If you're looking for a different culture, try Qatar (page 305), Hong Kong (page 280) or Japan (page 307).
- If you're looking for no tuition fees, try the Nordic countries (Chapter 5) and parts of Germany (page 149).

- If you're looking for outdoor activities, try Canada (Chapter 7), Australia (Chapter 8) or New Zealand (Chapter 9).
- If you're looking for the opportunity to stay on after study, try Europe (page 127), Canada (page 232), Australia (page 255) or New Zealand (page 275).

Student story
Hannah Burrows, University of Southern Denmark Odense, Denmark

Hannah Burrows was already thinking globally when she headed off to Denmark to study for an MA in American Studies. 'After doing a law degree in Britain and qualifying as a lawyer in the USA, I decided that I wanted to study American Studies as a master's degree, which I felt would help me understand their system better. I looked at the courses on offer in Britain but I was daunted by the huge cost of tuition and disappointed that I did not have the opportunity to work or study abroad as part of any of the programmes. My boyfriend is Danish, and we were both looking at our options in the UK, the USA and Scandinavia. In the end, Denmark gave us both the best package of options.

'The best information resource for me was the university's Facebook page. That's how I learned the most about the university before going to see it in person. I looked through the photo albums of the local area, the videos of student testimonials, the pictures taken inside classes, and I asked questions to current students.

'The university I chose is the biggest in Denmark, and is the only one to offer a master's in American Studies. It's entirely in English, I study a full-time two-year programme to get a broad base of topics and get the opportunity to do internships and study abroad as part of the programme. The university offers accommodation for the full length of my degree, all of my teachers are recognised experts on America, and, best of all, there were no tuition fees whatsoever.

'I can work up to 15 hours a week and the Danish minimum wage is more than £13 an hour so that goes a long way to helping with living expenses. I had help from the university's career centre with finding a part-time job before I arrived in Denmark. You can also sometimes get help from the Danish government toward your rent and things like that.

'The application process was pretty simple. I applied directly to the university through their website. I had to send electronic copies of my CV, my transcript of grades from my undergraduate degree, and a copy of my diploma. I applied about a week after the applications opened, and I was accepted a month later.

'The university has an international office, so administrative aspects of moving to Denmark and general questions about being a student at the university went through them. They help with getting your social security number (in Denmark it's known as a CPR), for health insurance, for getting a bank account, for free Danish lessons, for your registration as a resident. That's probably the most complex thing I have dealt with in moving here.

'The university organises a buddy system for your arrival. They pick you up from the airport and help you move into your accommodation, and after that, they introduce you to people and help you to settle in to life in Denmark. My buddy has been one of my best friends since the day we met; the university matched us up really well. She was my shoulder to cry on when I got homesick at the very beginning!'

Hannah has had to get used to some differences in the Danish approach to education. 'The style of education is more laid back, they allow you to eat, drink and use your phone in class. Probably most strange is using first names, for your teacher right up to the vice-chancellor. It's a Danish thing, where they insist on the equality of first names.

'The teaching style is more like seminars than lectures, with a discussion by all students and the teacher together. For exams, the biggest shock for me was that you can choose your exam format. You can choose between an oral presentation, an essay or a written exam where you have access to your notes, books and the internet. They allow students a lot of independence, and in return expect you to take responsibility for your studies. If you want help, you can always get it from your teachers or the Study Board.'

Even with all the support available, there have been some adjustments for Hannah to make. 'It can be hard not speaking Danish at the beginning and you can feel left out if you don't understand what's going on. In my first week, the girls in my class would speak Danish together outside of class. I was too shy to ask them to switch to English so I could join in, but once I got the courage, they said it was no problem for them to speak in English.

'I suppose the biggest negative is that there is no Cadbury's chocolate here, and I have to wait for my mum to send it over in a package!'

Hannah's top tips

Accommodation

'You can arrange accommodation through the university. It's about £250 a month, with your utilities and internet included. You can arrange it privately with friends, but it might work out a little more expensive and be ready for all the paperwork to be in Danish!'

Food

'Food costs around the same at the supermarket as it does in England. Eating at restaurants is a bit more expensive, maybe 25% more than back home. Fast food costs roughly the same – a cheeseburger at McDonalds costs 10 kroner, just over a pound.'

Living costs

'The most expensive things about Denmark are buying alcohol, eating in restaurants and having a car. Always ask the place if they have a student discount, it's not always advertised but most places have something to offer. There are also tons of happy hour deals; because Danes start their nights out so late in the evening (after midnight), the bars generally offer free drinks if you get there between 9pm – 11pm, so you could bar-hop and get free drinks most of the night!'

Financial support for study

'There aren't that many scholarships for American Studies. There probably are for other subjects, especially if you're working in Engineering or Business, the university can match you up with a company who will sponsor your projects, research and internships, and give you a job at the end of your degree.'

Working while studying

'I can work up to 15 hours a week, and I have a job at the university proofreading English and posting on the university's Facebook page in English. If you're a native English speaker, it's not too hard to get a part-time job or two. Your first port of call in seeking work could always be the university.'

Making friends

'Denmark is a really social place that encourages a strong work–life balance, getting involved in groups and extra-curricular activities. They are big on sport teams, clubs and societies, and unions. In my first week, I ran for the board of a student society and to my amazement I was voted in! I also took up ballet classes to meet new people, started Danish classes with other students from the university and joined the Model United Nations.'

Lifestyle and culture

'The most common word you'll hear about the Danish lifestyle is "hygge" which means cosiness. They love to spend evenings together in bars, pubs, or having dinner and drinks at home. I have only been here a month, and already most of my classmates have invited me to theirs for a dinner party, or for drinks and games.

'During the day, Danes are pretty active: they're always on bikes and quite outdoorsy. They are definitely a nation of nature lovers. As for culture, this is the hometown of fairy tale author Hans Christian Andersen. His image is everywhere in the city. Pastries and hot dogs are like national symbols here, the locals will tell you that you haven't lived until you've tried the Danish version of each.'

Travel and transport

'Everyone in Denmark uses a bike. It's just unheard of not to own one! There are more bike paths than roads around Odense so it really is the best way to get around. They're safe and well lit. Just make sure you have a bike lock. You can get a student bus pass called a Wild Card as well, if you need to travel longer distances. The trains are clean, modern and on-time. Going home isn't too hard either – there are dozens of flights to several British cities every day for about £100.'

Options for after you finish your studies

'The university has a lot of links with big firms around Denmark like Lego, Nordea Bank, Novo Nordisk, Accenture and Danfoss, as well as government institutions, and you can easily get an internship organised with the help of the university.'

So, what next for Hannah? 'So far, my plan is to stay in Denmark. Although it's only been a month, I really love it here, and I could see myself applying to do a PhD at this university later on.'

And the best thing about studying overseas? 'The best thing is definitely that first step, when you see what opportunities you can get elsewhere by taking your focus away from Britain. The course in Denmark gives me several advantages over the equivalent in Britain, and I can even go further abroad for a semester without paying tuition fees as the university gives you a grant that pays you to study. I can't imagine getting the same level of benefits in an English course. A lot of degrees in Europe look to improve your employability prospects by putting you into work-like situations during your programme and getting hands-on experience in industry. When you're asked those questions in a job interview such as "when have you demonstrated leadership qualities . . .?", a degree from Denmark will give you many different instances with which you could answer, because it aims to simulate a cooperative work environment whilst doing academic study.'

University of Southern Denmark (www.sdu.dk/en) is a modern education and research institution with 20,000 students offering a range of bachelor's and master's degrees taught in English. It appears in the Times Higher Education World University Rankings Top 400 for 2013–2014.

Rotterdam Business School: Profile

Rotterdam Business School, the international business school of Rotterdam University of Applied Sciences, offers English-taught programmes at both bachelor and master levels.

Practical Experience

Education at Rotterdam Business School includes a mixture of knowledge accumulation, practical experience and personal development. All our bachelor's programmes include periods of work experience and study or placement abroad. Periods of practical training are also incorporated into our master's programmes. This allows students to gain both experience in their field and a taste of international business even before they graduate.

Learning from real life

Real-life business cases are at the heart of many courses. They challenge our students to learn to act quickly and decisively and to base their decisions on growing experience and healthy reflection.

International outlook

Just like in the world of business, our focus is fully international. We work closely with partners in the business and education communities around the world to enable our students to develop the global outlook they need. Over 40 different nationalities are represented in our student population: the ideal environment to prepare for an international career.

Our English-taught bachelor's programmes include:

- **International Business and Management Studies:** an English-taught management study programme focusing on all the major aspects of international business and management.
- **International Business and Languages:** a broad study programme focused on European languages and international marketing and communication.

- **Trade Management for Asia:** aims to produce future managers who are well versed in all aspects of international business, with a special focus on Asia.

We also offer 4 English taught master's programmes:

- **Master's in Consultancy and Entrepreneurship:** your stepping stone into the world of consultancy.
- **Master's in Logistics Management:** take your knowledge of Logistics and Supply Chain Management to the next level and transform your managerial and leadership skills.
- **Master's in Finance and Accounting:** will enable you to build the knowledge and analytical skills you need to design and implement the on-going management systems used to plan and control a corporation's performance.
- **Executive MBA (part-time):** designed to prepare participants for the management challenges of the 21st century.

Rotterdam

The dynamic harbour city of Rotterdam offers the perfect location to embark on an international study career. Home to the largest port in Europe, Rotterdam has global trade and transport links.

Both Rotterdam Airport (20 minutes away) and Schiphol Airport (45 minutes away) are within easy reach. There are also many options for train, bus, and ferry travel between Rotterdam and the UK.

For more information about our programmes and practical information about tuition fees and housing please contact our Global Recruitment and Student Support team (GR&SS):

Tel: +31 (0)10 794 62 50
Email: rbs@hr.nl
www.rotterdambusinessschool.nl

Rotterdam Business School: Case study

Tim Dixon, aged 22, from Yorkshire, England is a student in the Master in Finance and Accounting programme at Rotterdam Business School.

Why Rotterdam Business School?

While studying in England I was able to go on an Erasmus exchange to Rotterdam Business School (RBS). While at RBS I achieved good results and was challenged to perform to the best of my abilities. This was mainly due to the engaging and creative teachers. It was only natural that after such a good experience I wanted to see how else RBS could challenge me at Master's level.

Why did you choose the Master in Finance and Accounting?

While studying at undergraduate level I found accountancy and finance to be one of the most interesting fields in business specialisation. I have been surrounded by finance and accounting my whole life due to my parents' professions, so it was a natural progression of my interests to do a master's in the subject.

What do you like about studying at Rotterdam Business School?

I like studying at RBS for numerous reasons: great teaching staff, the international classroom and studying environment. Many of the lecturers have years of practical experience which really helps them put the theory into perspective for the students. I also find the varied testing and examination methods to be a well-balanced combination of tests, essays and group work. Working in groups with students from many different backgrounds and cultures can be a real challenge sometimes, but a very interesting and worthwhile one.

How do you like Rotterdam?

Rotterdam, while being a huge port city, is able to find that balance of business and pleasure; this makes it a very liveable city. The city also has a huge amount of public space, big lakes and parks. I find myself drawn to these places at the weekend to unwind.

How do you find the student experience in Rotterdam?

It's very easy to get by here as an international student. Many Dutch people speak at least some English. Rotterdam Business School also has a very active international student association which organises lots of events from nights out to football tournaments to weekend trips to cities like Paris or Berlin. There are plenty of ways to meet people and have fun.

Do you go back to the UK often?

I go back a few times a year for family events. It's very easy to do due to the ferry port and airports nearby.

University College Roosevelt: Profile

University College Roosevelt (UCR) is a small-scale international liberal arts and sciences college based in Middelburg in the south-west of the Netherlands. After three years of full-time studies, students receive their Bachelor of Arts (BA) or Bachelor of Science (BSc) degree from the renowned Utrecht University.

Among the special characteristics of UCR are:

- English as the official language, both in class and on campus at large
- small-scale classes (with no more than 25 students)
- highly interactive and intensive method of instruction
- residential college with inner-city campus
- international staff and faculty.

UCR's tight-knit academic community provides an environment that encourages intellectual exchange between students and professors in a friendly and informal atmosphere. The educational philosophy is based on the idea that a student benefits most from learning more about a variety of disciplines. This means that UCR students put together their own programmes with classes offered in the four departments: academic core, arts and humanities, social sciences, and science.

Classes offered range from a wide variety of disciplines, including anthropology, antiquity, chemistry, economics, French, German, geography, history, international law, life sciences, linguistics, mathematics, music and drama, philosophy, physics, political science, psychology, rhetoric, sociology, Spanish, and many more.

The tuition fee at UCR is set by the Dutch government each year. For the year 2014–2015, students pay €2,656 in tuition fees (about £2,200). A full year of studying and living at UCR is estimated to cost €10,000 (about £8,500).

For more information, see www.ucr.nl.

Chapter 2
What you need to know before you go

It is normal to have concerns and to feel some anxiety about whether studying abroad is the right step for you. As we have already seen in Chapter 1, common worries concern the cost of fees and access to finance; the prospect of leaving family and friends; concerns about getting a visa; whether your qualifications will be recognised when you return home; and fear of adjusting to another country, culture or language.

This chapter aims to put your mind at rest by addressing some of the questions you may have about making the move overseas.

Education

Don't assume that education overseas will be just like that in the UK. There are lots of questions to be asked. When does the academic year start? How long do bachelor's degrees take? How do I know if my university is genuine?

Length of study and academic year

When you start to look at the options for overseas study, it is important to understand that many countries operate a four-year bachelor's degree and a two-year master's degree. When comparing the academic experience and the cost of fees and living, an extra year can make a big difference.

Other countries may also have differences in when their academic year begins and when you can join a course. Many European universities start in early September. Some universities offer more than one start date during the year, which can save you having to wait a full year for the next intake.

Differences in teaching and learning

Education systems vary across the world, so you will encounter some differences when you study in another country. University in the UK requires independent study and critical thinking. In some countries (although less so in Europe and the western world) university education can be more tutor-led, following set texts. You need to know how education works in your chosen country (and institution, see Different types of institution on page 41) and how you will be taught and assessed. If you study in a country where every course is assessed by means of an exam, you need to be able to cope under exam pressure. Before you apply, you should check whether the style of education suits your style of learning. Finding out what to expect will help you prepare for any differences when you arrive. Your university will be able to tell you more.

> **❝❝** I would say that education in Brazil is much more tutor-led; Brazilian students have their hands held much more than in the UK.**❞❞**
>
> *Justin Axel-Berg, University of São Paulo, Brazil*
>
> **❝❝** The biggest shock for me was that you can choose your own exam format. You can choose between an

oral presentation of 45 minutes, or a 24-hour take-home essay, or a 3–4 hour written exam where you have access to your notes, books and the internet.**99**

Hannah Burrows, University of Southern Denmark

66 I have a very close relationship with all of my professors. Classes rarely, if ever, exceed 30 students.**99**

Joshua Jackson, SP Jain School of Global Management, Singapore and Australia

To prepare yourself and improve your chances of success, find out as much as you can about what to expect. Read through the course information and make a start on any recommended reading before you get there. See the chapters on 'Studying in . . .' for more details.

Different types of institution

Having local knowledge can be reassuring; in the UK, you may already understand which universities are considered to be the best, which have strong vocational backgrounds or which are seen to be weaker. It is much more difficult to make these comparisons on an international scale and where the education system is unfamiliar.

As you research your chosen countries, find out about the different types of institution and how they differ. In Finland, and in a number of other European countries, universities offer research-based education, while universities of applied science offer work-related education. In the USA, you can choose between university and community college. Reputation (but also cost and competitiveness) of the different types of institution may vary.

Although there are only a handful of private institutions with
UK degree-awarding powers, it is a different case overseas. The
USA has many private providers, and there are plenty to be
found across the rest of the world too. Private universities offer
a variety of different features; they tend to have higher fees, but
often offer more generous scholarships and financial aid. They
may offer a more supported or bespoke service, with accelerated
programmes, low student–teacher ratio and personalised tuition
and internships. Don't rule private universities out on a cost basis
alone; in some cases they might end up the better-value option,
because of the financial support available and the opportunities to
choose a tailor-made education.

University rankings

If you are seeking out a particular type of institution, you might
like to compare potential overseas universities to those that you
are familiar with in the UK. Use worldwide university rankings
to get an idea of how your chosen institutions fare on the world
stage and how they compare to institutions that you know from
the UK. Look at which international universities choose to work in
partnership with a familiar university back home; it is likely that
partner institutions will share some characteristics.

Here in the UK, the national league tables are familiar, but
you might not know so much about worldwide rankings. Pay
attention to worldwide league tables (Times Higher Education
World University Rankings, QS Top Universities, and Academic
Ranking of World Universities, for example) to check out how
your chosen UK university measures up to the global competition.
Although British universities are well-perceived, only a handful
of them regularly appear at the top of the world rankings. Many
universities that we might not recognise as household names
are beating UK universities hands down, for example, the
Karolinska Institute in Sweden, USA's Northwestern University

and the Swiss Federal Institute of Technology in Zurich are all rated more highly than University of Edinburgh and LSE in the Times Higher Education World University Rankings 2013–2014.

Try some of the following league tables:

- Times Higher Education World University Rankings www.timeshighereducation.co.uk/world-university-rankings
- Academic Ranking of World Universities (ARWU) www.shanghairanking.com
- QS Top Universities www.topuniversities.com/university-rankings
- *Financial Times* Business School Rankings http://rankings.ft.com/businessschoolrankings/rankings

If you are going to use league tables, make sure you don't use them in isolation and that you understand what they are measuring. A league table can't tell you whether a university is the right choice for you. The methods used to rank universities mean that large, research-based, English-speaking universities tend to do best. It is worth noting that many of the universities that don't make it into the top few hundred in the world can still offer you a good-quality education that might suit your needs perfectly.

UK equivalence

There are two aspects to consider under the equivalence of qualifications. Will your qualifications be accepted by your chosen overseas institution? And, when your studies are over, will a degree from your institution be recognised when you get back to the UK?

The International Baccalaureate and A levels tend to be well-recognised overseas and often meet the entry requirements of international universities. In some cases, they exceed the requirements. In the USA, for example, you may be able to join an associate degree course at a community college without A levels. You can find out more in Chapter 6, Studying in the USA.

Other qualifications, like Scottish Highers, or vocational qualifications, like BTEC Diplomas, may need to be verified by one of the centres of academic recognition. Overseas universities don't tend to include Highers or vocational qualifications within their published entry criteria, but you shouldn't assume that these qualifications won't be accepted. Each country has its own system of comparing international qualifications to those in the home country. Go to ENIC-NARIC (European Network of Information Centres – National Academic Recognition Information Centres in the EU) at www.enic-naric.net to find out about academic recognition in the country where you wish to study. For countries that are not listed, try their Ministry of Education.

For all of the countries listed within this book, degrees at undergraduate and postgraduate level taken at accredited universities are equivalent to the level offered in the UK; this means that you should be able to use them to access further study or graduate-level employment on your return to the UK. You will need to do further checks to ensure that your qualifications meet any professional requirements. See Professional recognition on page 45 for more explanation.

Although an honours degree is the norm in England, Wales and Northern Ireland, many countries outside the UK don't offer honours degrees as standard; they might offer an ordinary bachelor's degree instead. Where honours degrees are available, they might require additional work and the preparation of a dissertation. You will need to check whether your degree is classed as an honours degree or not, as this may have a bearing on your future plans, particularly for further study.

A number of the students featured in this book have decided to stay on in their chosen country or move to a new country for further study or work. If you decide to do the same, you may also need to check out how your qualification compares to academic standards in your new country of residence. You can do this through one of the national academic recognition information centres (NARIC); for a list of national centres, go to www.enic-naric.net. If your country isn't listed, your overseas university or the Ministry of Education in your chosen country will be able to advise further.

Professional recognition

If you intend to practise a particular profession on your return to the UK, or intend to take further study to fulfil this aim, it is essential that your qualification is accepted, otherwise you will have wasted precious time and money.

If you know that you want to move into a particular field, you should check with the relevant professional organisations in the country where you hope to practise. So, if you want to be a doctor in the UK, you could check with the General Medical Council, while prospective architects should contact the Architects Registration Board.

> **❝❝** The university course is exempt from PLAB by the General Medical Council (find out more at www. gmc-uk.org). While it will be very competitive, it should be fairly easy for British nationals to come and work in the UK.**❞❞**
>
> *Shakeel Shahid, Palacky University, Czech Republic*

The National Contact Point for Professional Qualifications in the UK (UKNCP) (www.ecctis.co.uk/uk%20ncp) aids the mobility of professionals across Europe. If you return to the UK with a professional qualification, UKNCP can advise you on regulations in your profession and outline the steps you will need to take before finding employment. They can also link you to the relevant authorities in other countries across Europe. To find professional bodies outside Europe, you should speak to your overseas university's careers service.

UK-regulated professions and contact details for the professional bodies can be found on the UKNCP website. These bodies should have clear guidelines on acceptable qualifications. Check before you go and then keep checking as you continue your studies. There is a risk that changes may be made to these guidelines while you are midway through your studies; some students have been affected in this way. Should this happen, there can be options for further study to make up any shortfall in knowledge or expertise.

Quality and reputation

One natural concern for many students is about the quality of the education they will receive overseas. The UK has its own systems for checking quality, but how can you be sure that international universities meet the same stringent standards? When you are making decisions from a distance, how can you be sure that your university even exists, let alone that it is a genuine provider of quality education?

There is money to be made from international students, so you need to be aware of potential scams and of discrepancies between what an institution says it will offer and what it actually delivers. You want to be sure that any money you spend is going towards a good-quality education that will deliver what you expect.

Use www.enic-naric.net to find a list of recognised universities from over 50 countries, as well as information on the various education systems. You can verify that your institution is recognised with education authorities or similar government bodies in your chosen country. Bear in mind that if you need to apply for a visa, there may well be a requirement that you are attending a recognised university. You are safer and better protected within an accredited and recognised university.

Ask your university about how it is inspected or checked for quality. Most countries will have national (or regional) organisations making sure that universities meet required standards. You may be able to read their inspection reports online. You can find further information on the quality assurance systems for higher education at www.enic-naric.net.

Using reliable and official websites, such as those included in this book, should help you to find your way to accredited and quality-assured universities. Use common sense when trawling through information and be suspicious of some of the following points:

- a purportedly official website full of errors, adverts or broken links
- an institution offering courses at rock-bottom prices
- if entry requirements are much lower than comparable institutions
- if you are being offered the chance to gain a qualification much more quickly than normal.

How to apply

Most countries don't have the equivalent of UCAS, a centralised admissions system, so give yourself time to fill out more than one application. You may have to apply on paper, rather than online, so allow time for the application to be delivered (and take copies,

Fees are not the only consideration. Some countries have high fees, but extensive financial support systems (particularly for those with academic excellence or low-income background). Other countries have high fees but a lower cost of living. Some countries with a generally lower cost of living may still have variations within pricing, perhaps high prices for accommodation, internet access or even alcohol. If you had to pay three or four months' rent to secure accommodation, as you do in some countries, how would it affect your finances? Other costs include visas, travel and costs of application. Consider all these factors when calculating the cost of study and remember that exchange-rate fluctuations can have a great impact on any cost calculations.

Paying for your studies

One of the challenges for a student choosing to study overseas is how to fund it. The UK system of loans and grants can only be utilised in the UK. Although the terms of UK student loans are no longer as attractive as they once were, they do solve the problem of having to find the money to pay for tuition fees up front.

Any financial support when studying overseas will need to come from:

- financial support from the host country
- scholarships
- savings
- earnings.

In most cases, international students have to fund themselves. Scholarships are often highly competitive. Jobs may be hard to come by, particularly if you don't yet speak the language, and some visas may restrict or deny you the opportunity to work. If you are applying for a visa, you are likely to have to prove that you have the necessary funds; you need to consider how you

will fund yourself before you apply. See page 55 for information
on visas.

Even if you are staying in the EU, it is recommended to have some
money saved. Mark Huntington, of A Star Future, advises young
people on overseas study. 'We recommend that even those who plan
to work while abroad should have at least a semester's worth of
living expenses covered before they go.'

Whilst those living costs and tuition fees might not always be as high
as they are in the UK, they still have to be paid for. International
students often use a combination of sources to pay for their studies:
savings or personal loans, income from work, and scholarships.

Financial support from the host country

In EU countries, ask the Ministry of Education or your chosen
institution about any opportunities for grants or other benefits to
students. In the Netherlands and Estonia, for example, there are
study allowances and grants that UK students can access. In some
countries, fees may include a free or discounted travel pass or free
language lessons.

Scholarships

Scholarships are available, although competition can be fierce.
Scholarship funding tends to be more widely available for
postgraduate rather than undergraduate study. You should
apply early, often a year in advance, following all instructions to
the letter. Bear in mind that many applicants are unsuccessful
in gaining scholarships and, even if you are successful, many
scholarships do not cover the full costs of study, so consider how
you will cover any shortfall.

The Ministry of Education or embassy should have information
about government scholarships, while your institution is the

best source of information for local sources of funding. See
Chapters 5 to 10 for more information. You can also search for
scholarships through websites like www.scholarshipportal.eu,
www.hotcoursesabroad.com/study/international-scholarships.html
and www.iefa.org.

Other sources of funding include:

- US-UK Fulbright Commission: www.fulbright.org.uk
- Marie Curie scheme (EU doctoral students): www.ukro.
  ac.uk/mariecurie/Pages/index.aspx
- Commonwealth Scholarships: http://cscuk.dfid.gov.uk/
  apply/scholarships-uk-citizens
- Erasmus Mundus: www.britishcouncil.org/erasmus-
  programmes-erasmus-mundus.htm
- The Leverhulme Trust: www.leverhulme.ac.uk/funding/
  funding.cfm
- UK Research Council: www.rcuk.ac.uk
- UNESCO Fellowships: www.unesco.org/new/en/
  fellowships

Charities and trusts

In the UK, a range of charities and trusts offer funding in various
amounts. Each has their own eligibility criteria, deadlines and
application procedures. You could start with the Educational
Grants Services, search at www.family-action.org.uk/section.
aspx?id=21211.

If you are looking for postgraduate funding, approach your
university, which should have a copy of the Grants Register, a
worldwide guide to postgraduate funding. If not, try your local
careers service or local library.

The Association of Charitable Foundations (www.acf.org.uk/
seekingfunding/index.aspx?id=70) has a useful guide to applying
to charitable trusts and foundations.

Career development loans

If you are studying overseas because your course is not available
closer to home and you intend to return to the UK, EU or EEA to
work after your studies, it may be possible to get a Professional
and Career Development loan. Your institution overseas will
need to register your chosen course with the Skills Funding
Agency in the UK before you can apply for your loan, unless
they have already done so for another student. Repayments start
once you complete your course, regardless of your situation.
You can borrow up to £10,000 for up to two years of study, so it
would be more appropriate for postgraduate students. For more
information, go to www.gov.uk/career-development-loans/overview.

Life overseas

Whether you will be 100 or 10,000 miles away from home, it is
important to know that you will be supported. Finding out the
basics before you go can help to ease the adjustment process.
Who's going to be there to help you out? What are the essentials
you need to know about moving and living overseas?

Support available

The international office at your chosen university is likely to be
your first, and probably your best, source of support throughout
the process: from when and how to apply for a visa to finding
the cheapest place to buy groceries. They should support you
throughout the research and application process and will also be
there for you once you arrive.

information on a visa application; if discovered, your application will be declined and future attempts to apply will be affected. Some health conditions (TB, for example) and key criminal convictions (violent offences or drugs charges, for example) can also affect your chances.

Visa applications can be complex, but it is essential to follow each step to the letter, ensuring that you provide all the evidence required.

> **❝** The process of applying for a visa was quick, but a little bit complicated. Firstly you must register and complete a form on the federal police's website before booking an appointment at the consulate. Unfortunately, my university acceptance letter was caught in a postal strike so I was rather delayed in getting documents sorted, but once I got to the consulate they were friendly and helpful and the whole process took well under a week from giving them my passport to receiving my visa.**❞**
>
> *Justin Axel-Berg, University of São Paulo, Brazil*

Registering within Europe

Although the EU allows its citizens free movement, there may be some red tape to go through when you first move to another European country. In many cases, EU citizens have to register with a local government office. Normally you should do this within the first week or two of arrival. Your university will explain what you need to do.

> ❝ My application for foreign residency, which is
> necessary after three months of living here, was all
> sorted by the university. ❞
>
> *Jacob Matthias Kummer, IE University, Spain*

EU countries

Austria, Belgium, Bulgaria, Croatia, Republic of Cyprus,
Czech Republic, Denmark, Estonia, Finland, France,
Germany, Greece, Hungary, Ireland, Italy, Latvia, Lithuania,
Luxembourg, Malta, the Netherlands, Poland, Portugal,
Romania, Slovakia, Slovenia, Spain, Sweden, UK.

EEA countries

The EEA is made up of the all the countries in the EU plus
Iceland, Liechtenstein and Norway. Although not within the
EEA, Switzerland offers some rights to EEA citizens.

Accommodation

Safe and acceptable accommodation is essential to enable you to
settle in and start adjusting to life overseas. The good news is
that most universities with international students do their utmost
to place them in suitable housing, often giving them priority. To
enhance your chances of finding accommodation, remember to:

- apply well in advance
- be realistic about the rent you are prepared to pay
- be flexible about where you are prepared to live.

Most students want good quality, affordable accommodation in
a convenient location; you may find that there is not enough to

go round, so it is worth considering what you are prepared to compromise on.

Types of student accommodation

If you're counting on university-run halls of residence, you may be surprised; some countries don't offer this option for accommodation. Some universities have campus-based halls run by private companies, while others have no accommodation at all. Alternatives on offer include temporary or short-term accommodation, rental property or home-stay with a local host family.

> ❝ The university cannot guarantee accommodation because of the size of the student body, but private sector provision is excellent and catered towards students in either 'republicas' (shared houses) or individual kitchenettes or studio flats both next to the campus and further into the city. It'll be very hard to sort anything out before you arrive though, so plan on starting in a hostel for a couple of weeks. ❞
>
> *Justin Axel-Berg, University of São Paulo, Brazil*

> ❝ The university provided a database for housing and the opportunity to apply for halls. Whilst halls primarily go to undergraduates, there is always a chance for postgraduate students. Housing in Leuven is a mixture of studios, rooms and shared apartments. The database is made up of registered landlords who sign up to a university-drafted contract, giving you full support if anything was to go wrong. ❞
>
> *Tom Aitken, KU Leuven, Belgium*

Finding accommodation from the UK

In some university towns there is a shortage of student accommodation, so some international students, particularly late applicants, find themselves in the position of leaving the UK without long-term accommodation. Arranging private accommodation from a distance can be risky. You shouldn't pay a deposit to a private landlord for unseen property.

Seek the advice of your university's international or accommodation office on the safest options when finding accommodation from the UK. They might discuss reputable short-term options with you, perhaps bed and breakfast, a local hostel or home-stay. Home-stay involves living with a local family; it can be a great way to give you time to adjust and help you to learn about life in your chosen country, as well as boosting your language skills. Securing short-term accommodation like this should then give you time to find suitable longer-term accommodation when you get there.

Check what's included

Whichever accommodation option you choose, remember to clarify what will and won't be included in your rent (water, electricity, gas, any kind of local rates, internet) and factor in travel costs; that way you can make a more meaningful comparison between properties. Check whether you will need to buy things like cooking utensils and bedding when you get there.

Practicalities

As you prepare to make the big move, you're going to need to know about the cheapest ways to phone home; how to open a bank account; how to navigate the area by public transport; the system for paying tax on your earnings; and much more. Talk to your university's international office or check out expat websites like Just Landed, www.justlanded.com. You can also ask questions on online message boards for prospective students, some of which are filled with information about accommodation, buying bikes and so on.

Once you arrive, you can start to use the network of friends that you make. This is where the local students, and those who've already studied there for a while, become invaluable. Most people are more than happy to help.

Insurance: health and belongings

It is important to make sure that you and your belongings are adequately insured from the time you leave the UK until your return.

If you are studying within the EEA or Switzerland, take out a European Health Insurance Card or EHIC. It is free and easily obtainable, normally arriving within seven days of application. It entitles you to the same treatment as a resident of the host country, but doesn't cover additional costs, like ongoing treatment or returning you to the UK in the event of an accident (www.ehic.org.uk). Conditions vary depending on your country of study, so be sure to check any time limits or restrictions carefully on the EHIC country-by-country guide.

You will need to take out additional insurance for travel and health to cover you whilst you are away. A number of UK providers offer study-abroad insurance policies, including Endsleigh (www.endsleigh.co.uk/Travel/Pages/study-abroad-insurance.aspx) and STA Travel (www.statravel.co.uk/study-abroad-travel-insurance.htm). Alternatively, you could take out a policy in your host country. If you are working alongside your studies you may be required to purchase additional insurance to cover you. Your international office should be able to advise you further.

There may be vaccinations or preventive measures, like malaria tablets, that you need to take before you travel. Talk to your GP and see the Travel Health pages of the Foreign and Commonwealth Office (www.fco.gov.uk). You may need to demonstrate that you are fit and well in order to gain a visa; this may involve a medical examination.

> 66 Our school provided us with health insurance policies in both Singapore and Sydney. In Sydney it was mandatory to have health insurance to get the visa. 99
>
> *Joshua Jackson, SP Jain School of Global*
> *Management, Singapore and Australia*

Personal safety

Although studying abroad is not, in itself, a dangerous activity, visiting different countries carries different risks. The Foreign and Commonwealth Office has useful information for Britons travelling and living overseas, including travel advice by country. Find out about safety and security, health issues, local laws and customs or natural disasters before you go. The Foreign and Commonwealth Office also has a useful travel checklist to follow: see www.fco.gov.uk/en/travel-and-living-abroad/staying-safe/checklist.

Follow the advice of your international office; they have a vested interest in keeping you safe and have an understanding of the risks in the local area. However, you do have to take responsibility for your own safety, much as you would if you were leaving home to study in the UK.

> **❝❝** Pickpocketing, having food stolen while on a train and witnessing mass brawls have all occurred in the two years I have spent in China. However, providing you are aware of risks and use some common sense you should be fine. On the whole, China is probably the country that I have felt safest in for travelling, living and walking home late at night. **❞❞**
>
> *Lewis McCarthy, University of Shanghai Jiao Tong, China*

> **❝❝** Despite São Paulo's violent reputation, it's really quite a safe place. I've lived here for three years now, travelling all over the city at all times of night and day and never come to harm anywhere. **❞❞**
>
> *Justin Axel-Berg, University of São Paulo, Brazil*

According to a 2012 British Council survey of students from over 80 countries, some of the safest places to study include Canada, USA, Germany, New Zealand and Singapore.

Top tips for staying safe include the following.

- Get to know your local area.
- Don't flash valuables and cash.
- Drink sensibly.
- Don't take unnecessary risks.
- Stay alert.
- Tell people where you are going.
- Keep in contact.

Language and cultural issues

However much you prepare yourself and find out about what to expect, there are going to be some adjustments to make when you move abroad. Differences in language, lifestyle, culture and cuisine may bring unexpected challenges.

> 66 Embrace the lifestyle and culture. Live it. I admit I take a fair few siestas here in Spain and have whole meals of tapas! 99
>
> *Tudor Etchells, IE University, Spain*

> 66 The lifestyle in Singapore is very metropolitan, busy, and Asian; they are more traditional, hierarchical and family oriented. It is definitely a hybrid between typical Western and Eastern lifestyles, a good stepping stone between England and Malaysia, for example. 99
>
> *Joshua Jackson, SP Jain School of Global Management, Singapore and Australia*

Culture shock is a common side effect of spending time overseas, away from family, friends and the ease of your own culture. It takes time to adjust and you will need to be open-minded and flexible as you get used to the changes a new country brings.

Your university will provide orientation events to help you to adjust and make new friends. Most universities have a range of support services (student welfare staff, counsellors, health professionals and so on) to help you if you find the adjustment process particularly challenging. If you look after yourself, by eating well, taking exercise and sleeping well, you will feel in a stronger position to tackle any challenges.

Other tips to help you deal with culture shock include the following.

- Keep in touch with family and friends back home.
- Get involved with familiar activities, like sports or cultural activities you enjoy.
- Display personal items and mementoes to make your room feel homely.
- Make an effort to meet other international students, who may be feeling like you.
- Get to know students from the host country so you can find out about your new home.

Staying on after study

After spending three or four years in your host country, you may start to wonder whether you want to return to grey old Britain. So which countries offer the most attractive welcome for students who want to stay on? Canada, Australia and New Zealand give extra points in their immigration system to students who have studied at their universities; this can make it easier to apply to stay on for work or even permanently. In many other countries, working-visa and temporary-residence systems have been simplified for international students; you may find that you have the right to stay on and work for a period of time, for example.

Other options that can aid integration include opportunities to learn the local language, work permits and internship opportunities. See the 'Studying in . . .' chapters for more information on staying on after study.

Returning to the UK

Coming back to the UK after your new experiences is not always as positive as you might anticipate. Reverse culture shock can be an unexpected side effect of spending time away. It can impact on the way you relate to friends and family and affect the way you adjust back to life at home. Try to remember how you managed to adjust to your new life overseas; you may well need to use these same skills to adjust to your return. Don't assume that returning home will be seamless; allow yourself time to come to terms with the changes.

You will need to consider how to highlight the benefits of your experience and how to sell yourself to potential employers (or educational establishments). Think about how you might articulate what you can now offer an employer, what you have learned and the skills you have developed. Consider how you could explain to an employer the type of institution you attended and how your degree compares to those on offer in the UK (or your chosen destination country). You can work with your university's careers service to prepare for this long before you leave university. Use their support to search for job vacancies and other schemes for graduates or postgraduates. Make sure that you get hold of references from teaching staff and from employers; it is much easier to do this before you leave.

There will be some loose ends to tie up before you leave, such as giving notice to your landlord, notifying your utilities' suppliers and reclaiming any deposits you have paid. Let your bank know that you are leaving and close your account; this might take a couple of weeks to finalise.

A break in residency?

If you return to the UK having been overseas for several years, this could be considered to be a break in UK residency, which can prevent you from accessing certain services like education and benefits on your return. However, if your departure is considered to be temporary and if you maintain strong links or a base in the UK, your break may be considered a temporary absence. Advice centres, like Citizens Advice Bureau (www.citizensadvice.org.uk), will be able to advise further, as this can be a complicated subject with legal implications.

Tax

Whether your absence is considered temporary or not will also affect the tax you will need to pay. If you leave the UK permanently and are not classed as a UK resident, then, on your return, you only pay UK tax on UK income. If you are returning after a temporary period of absence (the more likely scenario if you are only going for the purposes of study), you may have to pay UK tax on some foreign income if you bring it with you to the UK; this doesn't include income from employment but might include income from things like investments. Some countries have treaties preventing the need to pay double tax. This information can be complex and is subject to change, so you should make contact with HM Revenue and Customs at www.hmrc.gov.uk for current information.

You are also likely to be taxed by your host country on any money earned whilst overseas. To find out the rules on tax and whether you should be paying it, talk to your overseas university; they should be able to direct you to any specialist advice you need.

Support and networking after you leave

If you want to keep in touch with your wider network of friends from university, you could join an alumni organisation. This should also keep you up to date with events and developments. Other university services may still be available to you after you leave, including careers services.

Student story
Shakeel Shahid, Palacky University,
Czech Republic

The challenge of getting into medicine in the UK, as well as the cost, led Shakeel Shahid to the Czech Republic. 'I just wanted to do medicine, regardless of location. There aren't a lot of opportunities for someone who has already obtained a degree to get into a medicine programme either, which makes it even harder for someone who is either thinking of a career change, such as myself, or someone who was either not able to get into medicine directly after their A levels.

'I decided on Palacky University mainly due to good reviews from people who had already attended the university. Before I applied, I talked to students who had attended this university, and their reviews were very good compared to other places I had looked at such as Romania or Italy.

'The university staff at Palacky are very helpful and prompt in answering questions. It is located in a university town, so it's an ideal location in terms of settling down and getting used to living in a foreign place. It's also only a couple of hours flight from Manchester and London.

'The cost of living is significantly cheaper than the UK. Food, transport and even the accommodation is cheaper than what I would pay in the UK. For example, I was paying £6,000 a year for student accommodation in UK, but here I am paying £2,400, including rent, utilities and very fast internet. Food costs for me in the UK were £200 a month, and now it's half that for two people in Czech Republic where I live with my brother.

'The fees, however, are £9,000, just like the UK. For students wanting to go to somewhere cheap, but decent, Romania is another option.

'The application process was very smooth. The staff were very helpful and made the process easier. Of course, it's nothing like UCAS. You have to be bit more proactive here. You have to keep in contact with the university staff in terms of following up on your application and learning about any deadlines and any required documents.

'Before arrival, the university gave us directions to the city from Prague, and then explained how to find the university in the city itself. When it came to things that were required, like books, the university did tell us about it, but I felt like it was at the last moment. I would have preferred it if they'd let us know that information earlier so I could have been more prepared.

'Since I've been here, one good thing is that the students that are already studying here are very helpful, so I haven't found the need to ask much of the university staff.

'Other than moving to a new place, and all the apprehensions and stresses that come with it, there haven't been any difficulties. You are so caught up in the work right away that you don't really have time to think about any difficulties.

'The education is not that difficult, but the teaching it is very different because English is not everyone's first language. The dates of the exams are not set. They are taken orally, which is very different from the UK. There are tests that have to be taken every week, in order to sit the final examination. So we have to work every single day ensuring we keep up. There is no respite!'

Shakeel's top tips

Accommodation

'University accommodation rooms are usually shared with someone else but you can ask the university in advance if you want to share your room with a friend. If you want to rent your own flat, you can easily find good quality accommodation in the city centre for around £448 for two people, including bills and utilities. But you have to be very proactive and confident, because people here don't always know much English, and you have to make sure that you're very careful in checking out the accommodation because all the agreements are in the local language. It's better to take someone who knows the language to help you out when signing the contract.'

Food

'There are high quality restaurants if you're into dining. There are all kinds of cuisines here, like Italian, Chinese or Mexican. You can always try out the local food as well. There are a lot of grocery stores, including a Tesco. Groceries are very cheap here.'

Living costs

'Make sure you keep a record of your spending, that way you can keep track of costs and not waste money. If you spend sensibly the monthly costs are not that high – £100 for two people in my experience so far.'

Working while studying

'Unless you know the local language really well, there is no point working. And even if you know the language you won't have any time to work because of the workload.'

Making friends

'Join Facebook groups. Get to know the people that are going to start with you. You can get to know a lot of people even before you arrive in the country. Living in the university accommodation helps make friends easier than living in private. But, from personal experience, you have to be confident and talk to people. It's not really hard making new friends as everyone else is in the same boat as you so you find a lot in common. A lot of the older students will volunteer to help you around in the city, so take that opportunity to meet new people.'

Lifestyle and culture

'The people are extremely friendly. Everyone is very respectful of other cultures, and it's a very Christian but secular city at the same time.'

Travel and transport

'Trains and taxis are extremely cheap here. For travel within the city it's advisable to get a tram card. It's about £7 for three months.'

Options for after you finish your studies

'If you really like the place, you can always stay here. But for British students, it's very easy to go back to the UK. The university course is exempt from PLAB by the General Medical Council (find out more at www.gmc-uk.org). While it will be very competitive, it should be fairly easy for British nationals to come and work in the UK. I plan to go back to the UK and finish my Foundation training there.'

In addition to the opportunity to study medicine, Shakeel has experienced a number of benefits of studying abroad. 'You get to meet a lot of different people from other countries that you would not otherwise meet. You get to learn a new language. You get to experience a new culture. You get to travel. And living on your own for five years is a very good life learning experience.'

Palacky University (www.medicineinolomouc.com) is one of a number of European universities offering degrees in medicine and dentistry taught in English.

University of Twente: Profile

The University of Twente is a young, entrepreneurial research university with proven excellence in the field of new technologies and their impact on society and humanity. We develop technologies that shape the future and are unique in our capacity to transcend the boundaries between disciplines.

The interface between technologies; that's where important and intriguing innovations occur. Twente's key research areas include nanotechnology, biomedical technology, ICT, sustainable energy and governance. We do not approach new technologies in isolation, but in relation to behavioural, social, and management sciences; combining high tech with a human touch. As a modern, entrepreneurial university, Twente is renowned for its engineering ability in supporting industry and commerce, and its creation of new innovative businesses. In our 50-year history, over 700 spin-off companies have been launched onto the market.

The University of Twente is the only campus university in the Netherlands. Here 9,300 students and 3,300 employees study, work and unwind in the beautiful green grounds. The attractive campus, built on a country estate just outside the city of Enschede, provides an academic, social and safe setting where students quickly become active members of a thriving community. The university has state-of-the-art facilities for teaching and research, an excellent library, a wide range of sports facilities, a medical centre, counselling facilities, a hotel, worship facilities and much more.

How does the University of Twente rank worldwide?

- The University of Twente is a reputable and highly ranked member of the European and Dutch university sector. The university is ranked 170th of universities worldwide according to the Times Higher Education (THE) World University rankings 2013–2014. The university scores particularly highly on the international mix category. According to the Academic

Ranking of World Universities, the university ranks even among the top 150 universities in the academic field of chemistry.

- In addition, survey results from I-graduate show that the University of Twente ranks among the top-10 universities worldwide on technology, IT support, and internet access.
- The University of Twente brings innovations on the market by over 700 spin-off companies. This is a very high number compared to other universities around the world. Entrepreneurship is stimulated among students, staff and graduates.

Bachelor of Science degree programmes

The University of Twente offers bachelor's programmes in fields ranging from engineering and natural sciences to behavioural and management sciences. Each of our six English taught bachelor's degree programmes is accredited by the Accreditation Organisation of the Netherlands and Flanders; on graduation, students are entitled to call themselves Bachelor of Science. The Netherlands enjoys international acclaim for its problem-based learning methods, for training students to analyse and solve practical problems independently, and for emphasizing self-study and self-discipline. By emphasising these principles, we will give the students the best possible preparation for a challenging and exciting career.

Innovative education and a nose for business

At the University of Twente, we offer the opportunity to break through existing academic boundaries, combining technological and social disciplines. Our study programmes are highly innovative, with a strong emphasis on helping the students to apply their knowledge to real, practical issues. In addition to that, we have a nose for business: our entrepreneurial spirit has helped many graduate students to channel their research into commercially viable enterprises.

Project-based education

The so-called Twente Educational Model of the University of Twente offers an innovative approach to academic training. It is all about challenging students to get the best out of themselves. The academic year is divided into modules of 10 weeks each. In each module, all of the classes, practical assignments and projects are centred on a single theme. In projects, students are challenged to use their knowledge for solving real problems, often related to current issues. It is a great way of making sure students have acquired all the necessary knowledge related to that particular theme. The themes in the programmes usually touch on a range of different disciplines. The advantage is that students get a broad foundation and will be able to operate successfully in a lot of different fields later.

Three key profiles

All of our programmes have been developed to match specific strengths and preferences of students and are structured according to three profiles. In the course of the bachelor's programme, we will help students to find out which of these three best suits them:

- *Researcher:* an expert who critically judges existing scientific knowledge and adds to the development of new scientific knowledge
- *Designer:* an expert who integrates scientific knowledge with the systematic development of new solutions for complex problems
- *Organiser:* an expert who combines knowledge from various scientific fields with the aim of implementing new solutions in a complex societal environment.

Bachelor of science programmes

ATLAS: University College

ATLAS is the Netherlands' first technology-driven liberal arts and sciences programme. ATLAS stands for the Academy of Technology and Liberal Arts & Sciences. It is a highly demanding, interdisciplinary honours programme integrating social, technical, behavioural and design perspectives. At ATLAS, we help pre-selected international students get the best out of themselves and each other – and use it to contribute to a better world.

Unlike other Liberal Arts colleges, ATLAS has a unique technological profile. Drawing from a diversity of academic fields – from psychology and politics to engineering and physics – our curriculums are centered on real-life themes and project-based education. Moreover, a part of your curriculum is a 'personal pursuit' that focuses on developing your personal interest: music, sports, a second language, development work or attending an international summer school. As a result, you will acquire a solid foundation in both engineering and social science concepts, as well as develop your creativity, flexibility, leadership and communication skills to become an academic all-rounder.

Our aim at ATLAS is, therefore, not just to deliver academic champions, but influencers, leaders, drivers of change – holistic problem solvers, who understand what society needs and can bring about the kind of change that will make the world a better place. Besides, with an ATLAS BSc honours degree you will be eligible for prestigious technical or social science master's programmes in the Netherlands or abroad.

> **66** I couldn't choose one discipline that I wanted to study. The balance between freedom and guidance within ATLAS is already helping me discover subjects that I want to commit to and study in depth.**99**
> *Nick Gregory, ATLAS University College student*

Advanced Technology

Advanced Technology is a unique three-year technical bachelor of science degree programme offered only at the University of Twente. It is a young and practice-based programme with an eye for societal needs. In order to come up with truly creative solutions you need a wide scope without being 'trapped' in one single discipline. That is why you will combine knowledge from different domains, such as electrical engineering, chemical engineering, applied physics, mathematics, mechanical engineering and business administration. Advanced Technology provides access to many master of science degree programmes both within the Netherlands and internationally.

Creative Technology

Creative Technology will equip you to become a designer with technical expertise and a sensitivity to social developments. You will be challenged to use the latest technologies to develop interactive applications aimed at users' health, convenience and enjoyment. In addition to design, smart sensor and new media technologies, you will also gain insights from behavioural science, communication science and business. You will become adept at understanding technological trends and collaborating with experts to turn your inventions into successful products. As a creative technologist, you will distinguish yourself through your level of technical expertise and knowledge of design, creative processes and how technology affects human beings.

Electrical Engineering

Electrical Engineering will challenge you to develop and improve electronics-based systems. The programme teaches you how modern technology works and how we can use it to further improve, accelerate or scale down electronics-based systems. Your work and commitment will result in high-tech applications based on nanotechnology, robotics, electronics and communication technology. Programme-specific developments include lab-on-a-chip, methods for building faster and better computers, chips that can be used to carry out a pregnancy test and sensors for application in communication. As an electrical engineer, you are highly employable and able to apply your knowledge and skills in almost all technological areas.

European Public Administration

The European Public Administration bachelor's programme will familiarise you with Europe's multilevel governance, equipping you to connect European policies with local and global realities. With its multidisciplinary nature, linking four vital academic fields – economics, politics, sociology and law – our programme will prepare you to play your part in the complex, fascinating setting of international policy. The programme is taught entirely in English – the working language in most international organisations – and students are required to have strong (English) communication skills. Therefore this bachelor's programme will offer you a head start in your aspirations.

International Business Administration

International Business Administration is an English-taught bachelor's programme designed to equip you for a successful career in the complex and demanding world of international business. It will familiarise you with business theories, while simultaneously helping you to develop your business skills and academic thinking. It covers key disciplines like finance, staffing, purchasing, development, strategy and marketing – all in the specific context of the cross-border business and multinational corporations that typically dominate today's world of trade and industry. The link between theory and practice, combined with your strong communication skills, will give you the opportunity to enter the job market with excellent international career opportunities.

Master of science programmes

Once a student has acquired a bachelor's degree, he/she will have the option of continuing with a master of science degree programme. The key research areas of the master's programmes include nanotechnology, biomedical technology, ICT, sustainable energy and governance.

More information?

www.utwente.nl

Chapter 3
Alternative options

If you feel that a full degree overseas is not right for you, you need not necessarily rule out all of the benefits of education outside your home country. Whatever the reasons swaying you against taking a full degree abroad, there may be an alternative choice for you to consider.

'I don't feel ready to take my full degree overseas'

Studying for a full degree overseas is a big step, but have you considered taking part of your UK degree course overseas instead? There are a range of schemes offering you the chance to study abroad without always lengthening your degree; some of these choices even bring their own financial benefits.

> I love to travel and I have always wanted to see the world. I chose my university partly based on whether they offered study abroad or exchange opportunities as I knew that I would like to go abroad for part of my degree. I enjoy experiencing new cultures and going to new places, and studying overseas just makes it convenient.
>
> *Angela Minvalla, exchange student at*
> *RMIT University, Australia*

As you research UK universities, look into the types of study-abroad option they offer. Perhaps you like the look of the University of Exeter's BSc Archaeology with Forensic Science degree, which features half of the second or third year in South Dakota, USA; LLB English Law and Hong Kong Law split between London and Hong Kong through King's College London; or maybe a BA in Social Anthropology and Arabic at the School of Oriental and African Studies (SOAS) with a year abroad. It is important to find out whether your degree course will be lengthened by this experience and which years of study count towards your final degree classification.

More and more UK universities now have overseas campuses offering courses taught in English and mirroring some of the courses available back in the UK. The latest figures from the UK Higher Education International Unit suggest that around half a million students are studying for a UK degree overseas. These campuses are often set up to attract international students, but an added benefit for UK students could be the chance to study for a semester or a year at the international campus.

Check out which courses and in which countries you can study this way. University College London (UCL) has campuses in Qatar and Australia, while Newcastle University, University of Southampton and University of Reading all have a presence in EduCity, Malaysia. University of Wolverhampton has a campus in Mauritius, and University of Liverpool has a base in China. The UK government is keen to see UK universities establish teaching outposts abroad, so there may be even more choice for UK students in the future.

If you prefer the familiarity of a UK university name on your degree certificate, you could always opt for a full degree course at a UK overseas campus. Fees might be the same or a little lower than you'd expect at home, but the costs of living are often considerably less. In some cases, you might even gain a degree from the UK and from the country you will be studying in.

> **❝** My tutor at University of Birmingham will come out to visit after a few months to see if we are happy with the work and our lifestyles. He also asks for a summary update every couple of months. **❞**
>
> *Madeleine Prince, Cawthron Institute*
> *(professional placement abroad), New Zealand*

What will I pay?

If you are studying overseas for part of your course, you will often continue to pay tuition fees to your university at home, rather than to your overseas university. If you choose to spend a year at certain US universities, for example, this may mean studying at a fraction of the full cost of tuition. If you are studying for a full year overseas, your UK tuition fees should be reduced. The rules vary from country to country, with a maximum of 15% charged in England and up to half fees payable in Wales. Your UK university will be able to tell you more.

You will still be able to access the normal UK system of grants and loans, with a higher overseas rate of loan for living costs available. In some cases, you may be able to apply for a travel grant to assist with the costs of travel, medical insurance, visas and so on. There may be additional bursaries or scholarships which you can apply for. For example, the British Universities Translatlantic Exchange Association (BUTEX) offers awards to students studying in the USA or Canada for at least one semester, www.butex.ac.uk. Third Year Abroad suggests some other sources of funding: www.thirdyearabroad.com/before-you-go/money-matters/item/1431.html

Find out more from your UK university or from your national organisation for student finance:

- Student Finance England (www.gov.uk/student-finance/overview)
- Student Awards Agency for Scotland (www.saas.gov.uk)
- Student Finance Wales (www.studentfinancewales.co.uk)
- Student Finance NI (www.studentfinanceni.co.uk).

> **❝** As tuition in Scotland is free, the cost of tuition on my year abroad was covered by the Scottish government. Living costs proved to be far less expensive in the south, so the only real expense was the flights (as well as all the travelling I did in the USA). **❞**
> *Rosie Hodgart, University of South Carolina (exchange), USA*

If you are studying outside Europe, you are still likely to need a visa in the same way as if you were taking your full degree course; your university will be able to get you started with this process.

With these options, you can gain a degree from a familiar university along with the benefits of international experience, but without so many of the risks. You may get some financial support throughout the process, with the benefit of personal support from both institutions too. It should be reasonably straightforward to transfer any credits achieved internationally back to the UK; your university should have planned for this to happen.

Erasmus

Through the European Union Erasmus scheme, you have the opportunity to study in another European country for between three and twelve months. This is completed as a part of your course, so counts towards your degree.

You will receive an Erasmus grant to put towards the additional costs of studying abroad, but you will still be expected to find your own living costs. For 2013/2014, an Erasmus grant of €275–€370 (£235–£320) per month is available. Additional one-off funding of €400 (£340) is also on offer in 2013/2014 for those choosing a less-visited country – Bulgaria, Croatia, Cyprus, Czech Republic, Estonia, Greece, Hungary, Latvia, Lithuania, Malta, Poland, Romania, Slovakia, Slovenia and Turkey. If you fall into the category of widening participation, there is an extra €500 (£427) available.

You will not be expected to pay fees to your host university and shouldn't have to pay more than 50% of tuition fees back home. In some cases, if you opt for a full year overseas you won't pay tuition fees at all, although this ruling varies from year to year. Some universities offer additional bursaries to students opting for an Erasmus placement.

For more information, talk to your UK university's study-abroad or international office and go to www.britishcouncil.org/erasmus-about-erasmus.htm.

The Erasmus Mundus scheme allows students to study joint programmes in multiple countries, some outside the EU, at postgraduate level. Scholarships are available. Find out more at Erasmus Mundus, www.britishcouncil.org/erasmus-programmes-erasmus-mundus.htm

> **"** The Erasmus scheme is really big in Denmark – they have a market where previous international students sell their furniture or Danish-plug electronic items, and they organise trips to see tourist attractions around Denmark. **"**
> *Hannah Burrows, University of Southern Denmark*

English-language assistant

Once you have two years' worth of higher education under your belt, you could consider working as an English-language assistant. These opportunities are normally open to language students in the UK, giving them the chance to work in an overseas school for a year (and get paid).

You should pay reduced tuition fees to your UK institution, or sometimes no fees at all, and may qualify for the overseas rate of maintenance loan. If you choose to stay in the EU, these opportunities can attract Erasmus funding.

This option would lengthen your study by a year, but should give you some valuable experience of education and life overseas. Your university's study-abroad office should be able to tell you more. Third Year Abroad at www.thirdyearabroad.com has lots of useful information.

Short-term study overseas

Shorter options to study overseas include summer schools and short placements. You could spend a summer learning a language or testing out international education, to see if you are ready to commit to further study abroad. Check out the costs and visa requirements well in advance of making final arrangements.

Opportunities include:

- Study China: a two to three week programme for existing undergraduate or foundation-degree students, www.studychina.org.uk
- INTO China: Chinese language summer programmes, www.intohigher.com/china

- IAESTE: summer placements for full-time HE (Higher Education) science, technology and engineering students, www.iaeste.org/students
- pre-university summer schools at US universities like Harvard and Stanford, www.fulbright.org.uk
- short-term exchanges in the USA, www.educationusa. info/5_steps_to_study/short_term_programs_step_1_ research_your_options.php

Talk to staff at the study-abroad office at your university to find out more.

'I want to gain a degree from an international university without leaving the UK'

There are a couple of choices if you want to gain an international degree from within the UK: either distance learning; or choosing a UK-based overseas university.

Distance learning

Online and distance learning is on the increase. With thousands of international universities offering degrees by distance learning, you need not set a foot out of the house to gain an international education. Of course, you will need to be disciplined and focused, and you won't gain the experience of living in another country, but you may end up with a degree from a top university at a fraction of the cost. It is worth noting that not all universities allow you to complete a full degree by distance education; they might offer blended learning, a combination of distance and face-to-face learning.

The benefits of distance learning are affordability, convenience, flexibility, choice and support (from tutors and classmates). On the other hand, you need to be truly disciplined and aware of the fact that you will lose the face-to-face interaction that you would get on campus. It can be more difficult to assess whether distance-learning providers are reliable, without a physical presence to assess them by.

How do I know that my distance-learning provider is genuine?

You need to be even more thorough when researching a distance-learning provider. See page 46 for some questions to ask of potential institutions. Remember, if it sounds too good to be true, it probably is.

There may be some warning signs to look out for when checking out a distance-learning institution's website. If the organisation only provides a PO Box address, if it has a similar name to other well-respected institutions or if you can gain a higher-education qualification purely on the basis of previous experience, you might need to dig a bit deeper to ascertain whether it is genuine and accredited.

You may find it easier to be sure of the provenance of your qualifications from a traditional university that happens to offer distance-learning courses. Many traditional, accredited universities across the world, and as many as 90% in the USA (according to EducationUSA), offer distance-learning provision. If the institution claims to be accredited, double-check this with the accrediting organisation. You can find out more at the Ministry of Education of the country you hope to gain your qualification from. Check out these websites too.

- International Council for Open and Distance Education (ICDE), www.icde.org
- Study Portals (search for a distance-learning course in Europe), www.studyportals.eu

- Distance Education and Training Council (USA), www.detc.org/search_schools.php.

Free online international education is on the increase. Prestigious universities including Harvard and the Massachusetts Institute of Technology (MIT) have set up edX (www.edx.org), while Stanford, Princeton and others have set up Coursera (www.coursera.org). Both offer online and interactive learning and the chance to gain university credits with no entry requirements and currently with no fees. Although it might be a slow process to achieve all the credits needed for a bachelor's degree, it could give you the chance to experience US-style teaching and check out your interest in particular subjects.

UK-based overseas universities

Campuses for a number of overseas universities can be found in the UK, most commonly in London. A number of these are American universities, offering US degrees. Although these universities recruit students from all over the world, only a small percentage currently attend from within the UK. This may change, with the fee hike in parts of the UK now making the fees at these universities appear much more reasonable.

In the case of Richmond, the American International University in London, you can gain a dual degree from the UK and USA, while experiencing an international university and accessing the UK system of loans and grants. With undergraduate fees set at £9,000 for 2013–2014, costs are comparable to most of the top UK universities although, as these are private institutions, your maximum tuition-fee loan will be capped at £6,000.

International universities with a campus in the UK include the following.

- Richmond, American International University
  www.richmond.ac.uk
- Hult International Business School
  www.hult.edu/en/Campuses/London/About-London
- Azad University, Oxford
  www.auox.org.uk
- Limkokwing University of Technology
  www.limkokwing.net/united_kingdom.

You can find out more about courses, fees and how to apply on their websites.

Student story
Rosie Hodgart, University of South Carolina, USA (exchange)

Rosie Hodgart has always had an interest in the USA. 'Rather than wanting to study overseas, I always knew I wanted to study in the USA specifically and spend a significant amount of time there. I knew that the huge benefits of studying overseas, both educationally and culturally, would change my life forever and decided I had to take a leap of faith. I also wanted a break from my home institution. In Scotland, we do four years of university rather than three and that is far too long to spend in one place.'

Rosie was studying Geography and American Studies at University of Dundee, but an exchange wasn't a compulsory part of her course. 'I had to proactively apply to study abroad in the USA. I got the list of my university's exchange partners in the USA and looked at each university, its location, as well as the website, to see which seemed the best fit for me. I chose the University of South Carolina because I was extremely interested in southern culture, and wanted to truly immerse myself in it. I also wanted the big-college experience with football teams, big societies etc. that is so often portrayed in films and popular culture, and it seemed the south was the place to go for that.

'As tuition in Scotland is free, the cost of tuition on my year abroad was covered by the Scottish government. Living costs proved to be far less expensive in the south, so the only real expense was the flights (as well as all the travelling I did in the USA).

'Applying for a visa was a tricky process, made harder by the fact I received little support from the international office at my home university. There was a lot of paperwork, payments to make, things to send off, so it was hard to keep track. I'd heard a lot of horror stories about the visa interview as well. Although the interview itself was quick and easy, I had to wait for three to four hours before being seen. I would advise students to bring a book.

'I received plenty of support from the University of South Carolina. I emailed them non-stop with question after question and they always got back to me in a timely manner with lots of information. They told us who we were sharing rooms with and gave us the students' emails so we could make contact before arriving in the USA. This was great and made me far less nervous about moving in with strangers. They arranged orientation and mixers and socials for the new study-abroad students, which was also extremely helpful and made the transition to the USA much easier.

'Once I got there, I was too busy to feel homesick at any point. I knew a few people who had moments of homesickness, but as a group of international students we were there as support for anyone who felt a bit down. It took time to get used to the culture and really understand South Carolina, but it was by no means a difficult process.'

Rosie encountered some big differences in the US education system. 'The Liberal Arts system allows for a unique understanding of a breadth of courses. Rather than just Geography and American Studies courses, I was allowed to choose from any courses related to these fields. I took classes in African American Psychology, South Carolina History, Sociology, Anthropology, Geography of the Middle East etc. I looked forward to attending class each day and learned so much in my one year in the States.

'Teaching also differs hugely. Rather than the UK system focused on independent study and big final exams and essays, there was much more class-based learning, class interaction and frequent small tests and essays. It was also possible to complete extra credit assignments to boost your grade and, in some classes, attendance even counted as part of the grade.'

Rosie's top tips

Accommodation

'Find out if the accommodation of the university you're applying to will be shared rooms. I had to share a room with another girl which seemed extremely daunting but turned out to be great. We luckily got on very well and still keep in touch. Also be aware of whether your accommodation is catered or self-catered. The meal plans can be extremely expensive with not very nice food.'

Food

'Be aware of regional differences in food. The south had fantastic cuisine but few organic or fresh-produce stores; mainly just massive Wal-Marts outside of the town. Make sure you try your state's famous dishes. While in the south, I sampled everything southern cuisine has to offer, from grits to gumbo.'

Living costs

'Living costs were extremely cheap. Accommodation was cheaper for me in the USA than it was in Dundee, and day-to-day costs of food, drink and meals out were cheaper. There were also many perks in going to a big college in the USA, as students pay so much to go there. We had a free cinema with free popcorn every Monday night showing the latest releases; the gym (and outdoor pool) was completely free; free football tickets to the Gamecocks' matches; and free student tickets to big events like R'n'B artist, Usher, performing at the university's stadium.'

Finding out about the USA

'I found the best sources of information to be the US-UK Fulbright website (www.fulbright.org.uk), individual university websites, Wikipedia for information on the specific town or region, and independent blogs and forums.'

Working while studying

'I thought I might get a job second semester on campus to help support myself but I didn't have time. I travelled so frequently and was making the most of my time there that working seemed to be the furthest thing from my mind. I knew one or two people who did and it is a great way to meet more American students and earn some extra cash but make sure it doesn't hold you back from making the most of your time abroad.'

Lifestyle and culture

'There was definitely a period of culture shock for me on arrival. The south is perhaps the least European place in the USA – the politics and culture of the whole region was eye-opening. It's important to keep that in mind when choosing a university, especially in America. Each state is so different, with such different cultural beliefs. My area of study at my home university focused primarily on the US south, so I had some knowledge on what I was getting myself into, and I was eager to learn more about that region. Also for me, I wanted a place entirely different from the UK, where I could learn a whole new way of life, so it was the best decision I made.'

Travel

'I travelled a lot during my year abroad. Every few weekends my friends and I would go to a different town in South Carolina or a neighbouring state. I managed to see most of the south and east coast all the way up to Pennsylvania and New York State. We also jumped on a flight over to California for a long weekend. I would recommend travelling as much as possible. Internal travel in the USA is fairly cheap, especially if you book in advance, and I'd recommend having a British driving licence before going abroad, so you're able to rent cars and travel.'

Rosie's time in the USA was life-changing. 'My year abroad has formed the direction I have chosen my career to take. I am so passionate about US–UK relations and educational exchange that, since returning to the UK, I have had many jobs in this field. I worked with the US-UK Fulbright Commission, then as Internship Coordinator for a company that places US students in London for internships, and I am about to begin my new role as Educational Advisor, again with Fulbright. However, if your area of interest does not lie in promoting educational exchange, your year abroad will still be extremely beneficial to any direction your career will take. It sets you apart from the crowd and will encourage employers to pick your CV out of a pile. It has provided me with a number of great opportunities that simply would not have been available to me if I had stayed in the UK.

'If I had not gone abroad I may have never had the confidence to move away from home so easily, or fallen into such a fantastic job. Living and studying in a completely different culture, the ability to travel within the country you're studying in, it really does change your outlook on your own life; it helped me figure out what I wanted to do for my future career.'

University of South Carolina (www.sc.edu) is a public research university which was founded in 1801. It appears in the Times Higher Education World University Rankings Top 400 2013–2014.

HKU: University of the Arts Utrecht: Profile

The art of HKU: University of the Arts Utrecht (NL)

The City of Utrecht is the fourth-largest city in the Netherlands. HKU: University of the Arts Utrecht is at the heart of Utrecht's cultural and student life. With over 4,000 students, HKU is one of the largest universities of art in Europe. HKU offers bachelor and master programmes and research degrees in fine art, design, media, games and interaction, music, theatre and arts management.

Courage is something HKU appreciates and fosters – the courage to keep a critical eye on the content and boundaries of your own work. What HKU asks of you is an explorative attitude, an enterprising spirit and the will to pursue your individual passion. HKU offers you the chance to discover and develop your talent.

As an HKU student, you are given the opportunity during your course to work on projects for customers in the work field. These may be commercial companies, non-profit organisations or cultural initiatives. That way, you learn hands-on where your strengths lie and what you can offer the world as a designer, lecturer, producer or performer. HKU produces creative professionals and entrepreneurs with initiative who know where their chances lie, both nationally and internationally. HKU works with renowned art and cultural educational institutions all over the world, so you have a wide choice of opportunities for exploring international developments in your discipline.

It's important for you to learn to present your work in a professional setting. HKU has its own Academy Theatre, concert halls and an Academy Gallery in Utrecht's city centre. Experimenting in presenting your work in these venues during your course gives you the opportunity to evolve yourself into a professional.

www.hku.nl/english

University of Groningen: Case study

Name **Christian Garrard**
University **University of Groningen**
Course **LLB International and European Law**
Which year you are in **Third Year**
Home Town in UK **Canterbury**

I chose to study abroad as well as in the UK because it is something I always wanted to do. Furthermore, going to the Netherlands would be a particularly useful experience for me since I'm studying International Law. Here, I study with international students and gain an amazing international experience. The course I am taking at the University of Groningen is unique: no university in the UK offers a programme like this.

Before arriving in Groningen, the university put me in touch with an organisation that provides accommodation, similar to the halls in the UK. The application process for my course was very simple and the university supported me in different ways, for example by advising me about my budget. When I got to the city, there were many organisations that introduced me to different aspects of student life in Groningen. There was no problem getting help when I needed it.

I would definitely recommend students in the sixth form to consider going to Groningen to study. You can always apply for both Dutch and British universities at the same time if you are not sure right away. At the moment, there is no financial assistance from the UK, unfortunately, but doing a university degree here in the Netherlands is so much cheaper than back home. In addition, the quality of teaching is just as good if not better than at many universities in the UK. The vast majority of the lecturers have a high level of English, so communication is never a problem either.

Before coming here, I hadn't exactly known what to expect. The biggest surprise for me was how soon I felt at home.

Chapter 4
Researching your options

There are so many questions to ask about yourself, your chosen country and your chosen university before you even apply. In the early stages, it is even hard to know what those questions should be. If you thought that narrowing down your UCAS choices to five was tricky, imagine choosing from the whole world. If that all sounds like too much hard work, consider that somewhere out there may be the perfect course for you at the perfect price; it's got to be worth a little bit of work to find it.

Getting started

With almost the whole world to choose from, the first step should be to research the countries that you are interested in. The chapters on studying in various countries will give you an overview of the different education systems, costs and financial support, how to apply and the visa system. Each chapter will also feature the most useful and reliable websites where you can find out more. This should help you start to compare what is on offer and how it fits in with your plans.

Where to study

This book focuses on opportunities taught in English, so the Republic of Ireland, USA, Canada, Australia and New Zealand are likely to have the largest choice of courses. Many other Commonwealth countries use English, including Singapore, Malaysia and certain Caribbean, Pacific and African nations. Find out more at the Association of Commonwealth Universities, www. acu.ac.uk.

Universities in many overseas countries are now actively starting to recruit UK students in a way that was unheard of only five years ago. Events like The Student World Fair feature university exhibitors from all over the world, as far apart as Malaysia, Grenada and Canada, all keen to attract UK students. You might have seen the news stories about universities in the Netherlands, in particular, and the increase in applications from UK students. Although the introduction of courses taught in English was originally aimed at international students from other countries, many UK students are now starting to take advantage. Some universities overseas have even started to teach all their courses in English.

In a number of countries where English isn't widely spoken, the government or the institutions are keen to recruit international students so offer a high proportion of courses taught in English. These countries include:

- the Netherlands
- Denmark
- Sweden
- Finland.

According to the OECD's Education at a Glance 2013, there will be some courses taught in English available in countries such as:

- Belgium (Flemish)
- the Czech Republic
- France
- Germany
- Hungary
- Iceland
- Japan
- Korea
- Norway
- Poland
- Portugal
- the Slovak Republic
- Switzerland
- Turkey.

The OECD tells us that very few programmes are taught in English in:

- Austria
- Belgium (French)
- Brazil
- Chile
- Greece
- Israel
- Italy
- Luxembourg
- Mexico
- the Russian Federation
- Spain.

However, it is worth noting that even these countries will feature private or international universities with a curriculum in English. Others may well be moving towards recruiting more international students, so watch this space.

How to choose

Many people choose a country for emotional, rather than practical, reasons. Maybe you have always longed to spend time in a particular country or you've fallen in love with a place that you've visited. Perhaps your family or friends have links with an area of the world or you have a boyfriend or girlfriend who lives overseas.

In other cases, the decisions are much more measured and logical. Some have a particular type of course in mind and their decision is driven by the availability of that course. Others have a set of requirements, in terms of prestige, entry requirements or world university rankings.

Others don't even choose a specific country, but make a shortlist of institutions that meet their particular criteria. John Magee, now studying in Norway, took a very structured approach to his search for opportunities across Europe.

> **66** Firstly, the schools had to be ranked on the *Financial Times* European Business School Rankings, so they were internationally recognisable to future employers. Secondly, the schools had to offer my desired degree, an MSc in International Business/ International Management. Thirdly, a more selfish criterion of being situated in a mountainous country that offered easy access to alpine activities. Lastly, it was preferable if the

> course offered an exchange semester, to help me secure the
> maximum amount of international experience. **99**
>
> *John Magee, BI Norwegian Business School, Norway*

In many cases, access to student financial support or scholarships
is a deciding factor.

> **66** The full cost of study would be about US$20,000
> (£12,400) a year, as much as the most expensive
> courses in England. I have a 100% scholarship on my tuition
> fees but pay for accommodation. This is conditional on the
> basis that I get within the top 25% of the class throughout
> the year. **99**
>
> *Joshua Jackson, SP Jain School of Global Management,*
> *Singapore and Australia*

It is also worth considering the cost of living, how welcoming
the country is to international students (for example, how easy
it will be to get a visa and whether there are opportunities to
gain employment afterwards) and how well your degree will be
recognised when you return to the UK.

Essentially, you need to determine what matters to you and what
your priorities are. Consider some of the following factors and
weigh up how important each one is to you:

- subject availability
- length of study
- professional recognition of qualifications
- university ranking
- type of institution

- size of university
- style of teaching and assessment
- specialist options (for example, internships or specialist subjects available)
- drop-out rates
- pass rates
- destinations of ex-students
- cost of tuition fees
- cost of living
- availability of loans or grants
- availability of scholarships
- opportunities to stay on and work after completion of studies
- interest in specific countries
- opportunity to learn particular languages
- lifestyle factors
- distance from home.

What type of university will suit you best?

Whether you see yourself as an academic aiming for postgraduate study or you want a route straight to work, you'll find a university to suit you. Many countries have polytechnics, community colleges or Universities of Applied Sciences where you'll be taught with a more vocational, work-related focus; these institutions share some characteristics with the post-1992 universities in the UK. If you are looking for a more traditional style of teaching from lecturers with a research background, try a research-based or research-intensive university. Make sure that you always find out what type of university you are applying to; it could have a big impact on what you get out of your university experience and which doors will be open to you when you finish.

Carefully considering what matters to you, much as John Magee did, helps to focus on the essential and desirable criteria. A final list of criteria might look something like the following.

- Essential: a city-centre, research-based university in the Times Higher Education Top 200, offering low cost of living and the possibility of a scholarship.
- Desirable: flight time of less than eight hours, opportunity to stay on and work.

What we describe as a course in the UK might be called a programme or program in some countries, with course used to refer to the modules you study as part of your degree.

Researching the options

There is no wrong or right way to choose where you want to spend the next few years. Just make sure that you discover the realities of life there, not just the pictures from the glossy brochure. It is not unusual to see universities overstating their position to international students, so make sure that you look for a secondary source of evidence (particularly if a university is telling you that they are among the best in the world).

Just as in the UK, courses with the same title may be really diverse. You should ask about course content, course structure, how you will be assessed and so on. You might find that the course you are looking for doesn't exist in your chosen country; there are limited history or English literature courses taught in English in continental Europe, for example. Courses where your learning relates specifically to practice in a particular country don't always travel well so they might not be available: social work or teaching, for example. Titles may vary from country to country; whereas UK university courses often have quite broad academic titles like biology or mechanical engineering, vocational universities in other countries might use titles that are more specific and job-related. Look out for courses in econometrics, interaction design or human ageing.

Ask the universities about additional factors, such as the ratio of students to lecturers, drop-out rates, student-success rates, library services and internet access. If you have the opportunity to visit a country or campus, take it. This can be a great chance to find out more, meet the staff and ask questions. Many students talk about the feeling they get from being on a particular campus and it is hard to 'virtually' recreate this if you have very little contact with the university before making your choices.

There are other ways of finding out more. If a visit isn't possible (and let's face it, it often isn't), try visiting recruitment events in the UK. There are a number of big events that take place in the UK: the Student World Fair, USA College Day, QS World Grad School Tour, Hot Courses Global Student Fair and the Study Options Expo. At these events, you can meet representatives from universities who are actively seeking UK students. To make best use of these events, find out the exhibitors beforehand, highlight whom you want to speak to and take your list of essential questions to ask. Note down or record any responses you get, so you can consider them later.

Don't want to restrict yourself to just one country? Can't decide between Los Angeles, Hong Kong or Milan? There are a number of options where you can study in two, three or even four different countries and even gain more than one degree. Take a look at the World Bachelor in Business partnership (http://wbb.usc.edu), SKEMA's EAI Bachelor (www.skema.edu/international/eai-transfers) or SP Jain's

Bachelor of Business Administration (www.spjain.org/BBA), for example.

Online research

A reliable place to start your online research is at the British Council's UK Students Abroad website (www.britishcouncil.org/higher-education/uk-students-abroad). This site has information on where you can study, funding and a section for parents. You'll also find links to recognised sources of information in countries around the world.

Most of the countries interested in attracting international students have their own official websites; you can find these in the 'Studying in . . .' chapters. For information on European opportunities, start at www.ec.europa.eu/education/study-in-europe.

All universities looking to attract international students will have their own websites with English content. Many universities have a number of other ways to engage with their potential students via social media like Facebook, Twitter or YouTube, where you can search directly for the universities you are interested in.

Following some key organisations on Facebook or Twitter when you start your research helps to keep you up to date with new developments, events and key deadline dates. You can also attend virtual student fairs and web chats from the comfort of your own home. Hobsons Virtual Student Fairs at www.hobsonsevents.com is one example; although it is not specifically aimed at UK students, it should still provide some useful information on study in the USA. Other websites, like the Student Room (www.thestudentroom.co.uk), have discussions on international study. Bear in mind that information from chat rooms can be useful, but isn't always correct, so you need to double-check any facts you get from sources like this.

Course search

The 'Studying in . . .' chapters include some of the best websites to search for courses and institutions in a specific country. If you want to search for courses before you decide on a country, try websites like Study Portals (www.studyportals.eu), EUNICAS (www.eunicas.co.uk), A Star Future (www.astarfuture.co.uk/what_to_study.html) or Hot Courses Abroad (www.hotcoursesabroad.com).

Is the website you need opening up in another language? Look out for the Union flag or the letters EN to select the English version. If not, try a translation website like Google Translate, www.translate.google.com.

Organisations to like on Facebook

- EducationUSA
- US-UK Fulbright Commission
- The Student World
- A Star Future for Brits Studying Abroad
- Dutch Degrees
- Study in Holland
- Maastricht Students
- Study Options
- CUCAS-Study in China
- CampusFrance Paris
- New Zealand Educated
- Study in Finland
- Study in Australia
- Study in Estonia
- Study in the Czech Republic

- Study in Germany
- Study in Sweden
- Study in Norway
- Study in Denmark
- INTO China
- EUNICAS
- Hotcourses Abroad
- Textbooks and Passports.

Organisations to follow on Twitter

- @CUCAS_CHINA
- @TheStudentWorld
- @astarfuture
- @StudyOptions
- @CampusFrance
- @StudyInHolland
- @StudyinNorway
- @StudyinSweden
- @EdUSAupdates
- @USUKFulbright
- @studyinde
- @EduIreland
- @StudyinDenmark
- @nzeducated
- @FutureUnlimited
- @studyinestonia
- @INTO_CHINA.

There are some great blogs and diaries out there too. Take a look at some of these:

- Third Year Abroad, The Mole Diaries: www.thirdyearabroad. com/before-you-go/the-mole-diaries.html
- Textbooks and Passports: www.textbooksandpassports.com

- Samuel Knight in Groningen: www.samstudyingabroad.tumblr.com
- From Turbans to Clogs: http://fromturbanstoclogs.blogspot.co.uk
- Maastricht Students: www.maastricht-students.com
- The University of Nottingham in North America: http://universityofnottinghamnorthamerica.blogspot.co.uk
- The Student World Blog: www.thestudentworld.com/blog
- Leon's Overseas Adventures and Muddled Thoughts: http://hungryleon.blogspot.co.uk

Websites like iAgora (www.iagora.com/studies) allow international students to rate their experiences at an institution based on categories for housing, student life, academic, costs and so on. SteXX, the Student Experience Exchange (www.stexx.eu), allows students to review and rate European universities. Use sites like these to get a student perspective on your chosen institution. Perhaps you will decide to rate your experiences too, after studying overseas.

Many schools, colleges, universities and public libraries have access to Venture (formerly known as Exodus), an international careers-information database. The online database features lots of useful information on studying overseas, including country profiles. Ask your UK institution for a username and password.

Students interested in postgraduate study or research should find the Prospects website useful, as it features profiles of over 50 countries (www.prospects.ac.uk/country_profiles.htm).

Using an agent

Some applicants choose to use the service of an agent or an educational consultant to help them navigate the plethora of information out there. Many like the reassurance of working with an organisation that understands the education, application and visa system of a particular country or countries. Check whether you have to pay for the service they provide and what you will get in return. Some organisations charge no fees. It is always worth asking about the affiliations of any organisation: whether they are linked to specific universities, for example.

There are a number of organisations operating in the UK, all offering different types of support and service. Some of these are listed here.

- A Star Future: www.astarfuture.co.uk
- Study Options: www.studyoptions.com
- EUNICAS: www.eunicas.co.uk
- PFL Education: www.preparationforlife.com
- Degrees Ahead: www.degreesahead.co.uk
- Mayflower Education Consultants: www.mayflowereducation.co.uk
- M & D Europe: www.readmedicine.com
- Outreach Education: www.outreacheducation.co.uk
- Study International: www.studygo.co.uk
- Pass 4 Soccer Scholarships: www.pass4soccer.com.

> 66 After results day, my teacher recommended that I get in touch with A Star Future because she knew that I would be really interested in their information on clearing places at foreign universities. 99
>
> *Clare Higgins, The Hague University of Applied Sciences, the Netherlands*

> 66 I applied through Study Options. They were fantastic and made the process so easy. They copied all of my transcripts for my A level results and sent off passport, results, organised the visa, the course, everything! 99
>
> *Kadie O'Byrne, Murdoch University, Australia*

Getting a different perspective

Of course, the websites listed here barely scratch the surface of the information out there. The students I spoke to share some great ways to get a different perspective.

> 66 I did some rather intense research, checking out the university website, the city website and the online literature available. I also used more creative methods such as searching for YouTube videos of the campus and the city, listening to the local radio station online and reading the local paper online to try to get a better grip of what my future life might be like. 99
>
> *Simon McCabe, University of Missouri, USA*

Finalising your choices

Let's recap the steps to finalising your choices.

- Consider your priorities.
- Write a list of essential and desirable criteria.
- Write a list of questions to ask each institution.
- Start to research in more detail.
- If you're struggling, write a pros-and-cons list.
- Narrow down your choices to a shortlist of five or six.

It is important to contact the university direct, talking to admissions staff as well as course leaders or professors. When you come to apply, this can have the additional benefit of making your name known to the recruiting staff, as well as improving your understanding of what those staff are looking for.

You should clarify the application process, documentation required and the visa requirements, as well as establishing a timescale for the process. The university should then send you the necessary paperwork or a link to the information online.

Try to apply to a number of institutions, while still considering the work required to produce a good-quality application, as well as any associated costs. Applying to a number of institutions gives you a better chance of a selection of offers to choose from.

Student story
Jacob Matthias Kummer, IE
University, Segovia, Spain

'I have always had, and most likely always will have, a desire to travel. I think there is a big world out there, which of course one can explore travelling, but travelling does not always mean experiencing another culture. Not wanting to take a gap year to travel, but still with a need to get out of the UK and experience something different, I decided to pack my bags, to live and study abroad.

'I chose Spain for many reasons. Firstly, I had a strong basis in the language, which certainly helps. Secondly, having travelled through Spain a lot in my life, I had only seen the tourist side of it. I had fallen in love with the country, and certainly had a desire to experience it from a more local level. Also, it wasn't too far from home, in case I had to return for emergencies, or if it didn't work out.

'One day, three months before I was supposed to start at Nottingham Trent University, having just returned from a language exchange trip to Santa Cruz de Tenerife, I had a slight panic. I realised that there was something more. I had experienced certain aspects of student life, and also everyday life in Spain, and I wanted more. Suddenly, the thought of moving up to Nottingham was one which I did not want to make a reality. The following day, I went online and googled "international university Spain". As it turned out, IE was the first result. Obviously, further research into the institution was carried out afterwards to make sure it was a good fit, but a week later, I had booked my flights to come and visit.'

Once he had decided to apply for a bachelor's degree in Architecture, Jake didn't have any difficulties with the process. 'It was very simple and straightforward. I downloaded the application form from the university website, whilst in constant email contact with the admissions department, which helped me out step by step. It involved completion of an application, submission of a portfolio, and then an interview, which I did over the telephone. Then, I had to wait for my exam results. Shortly after the results came out, I received confirmation that I was accepted. I then applied for financial aid, and found out the result a couple of months later.

'The fees are €18,000 (£15,380), but I am on scholarship of 50%, making it €9,000 (£7,690), which actually works out to be a similar price to universities in the UK nowadays. I do not have a loan, which I would get in the UK, but I am fortunate enough to be able to survive without. Living costs in Segovia are a lot cheaper than back in the UK.'

Jake felt that he got lots of support from his institution before he arrived. 'Every question under the sun was answered by email, with quick replies. The admissions department are great at IE. They really take you step by step through the process. It made the process a lot smoother than I thought it would be. Also, upon arrival at an open day, I was welcomed with open arms, despite arriving four hours late. They accommodated me with a campus tour, even though the open day was over!'

The support has continued now that he is a student. 'Professors and heads of departments are available frequently to discuss any problems, so really, whenever there is a problem, it is always addressed in a short period of time. Also, there is a student office which offers help with other problems unrelated to academics. They are always a huge help and offer great support. My application for foreign residency, which is necessary after three months of living here, was all sorted by the university.'

Jacob's top tips

Educational differences
'In IE University, the teaching is more personal. Professors and staff know who you are, and they really help you to succeed. You are not just a number.'

Adjusting to life overseas
'I have never been homesick, apart from when I have been ill. It is a different culture, and the norms of life will soon come to be second nature. I think after a period of four months, you tend to feel quite settled.'

Accommodation

'Plan ahead. If you can get there to visit flats, do it at least two months before, or get yourself into a residence.'

Food

'Most places in Spain provide great food, although it is always worth learning some of the vocabulary for food so you know what you're eating!'

Working while studying

'Whether you can work while you study depends on the course. If you have time, then do it. It's a great way to get into the local community.'

Options for after you finish your studies

'Hopefully, after I finish my studies, I'll take a few months to relax and maybe travel. Then I hope to find a job or internship either in Spain or abroad elsewhere, and then consider graduate study options.'

Jake certainly doesn't regret choosing an international university for his bachelor's degree. 'The best thing about studying overseas is the people you meet. Meeting people from different backgrounds really changes the way you think, on both a personal and professional level. International contacts are always a big plus. Do it! You can always return home if you don't like it!'

IE University (www.ie.edu) is a private university offering its students tailor-made education with an international, humanistic and entrepreneurial perspective.

Norwegian School of Economics: Profile

NHH

NORWEGIAN SCHOOL OF ECONOMICS

NHH is an elite institution, which recruits only the best students from both within and outside Norway to its various study programmes. NHH offers three master programmes for international students within the Master of Science in Economics and Business Administration. Read more at www.nhh.no.

Master in Energy, Natural Resources and the Environment

The goal of the Energy, Natural Resources and the Environment programme (ENE) is to educate the next generation of interdisciplinary managers in the study of energy and natural resource development and environmental impact.

Master in International Business

The International Business programme (MIB) at NHH aims to equip students with the right mix of analytical and practical skills for a career within multinational companies, international organisations or smaller firms whose activities involve a substantial degree of international business.

Master in Marketing and Brand Management

The Marketing and Brand Management (MBM) programme is aimed at students that want to lead and make decisions in the marketing department of a company, including positions such as brand manager, marketing analyst or head of marketing.

Active student life

The NHH Student Union (NHHS) is the most active student organisation in Norway. The school encourages students to start new groups that cater to the multifaceted and varied interests of students; such as the telemark ski club, finance group, student choir and the entrepreneur organisation.

The difference is Bergen and Norway

Bergen is a very charming city with a relaxed atmosphere and vibrant student life. It is located within the magnificent landscapes of Norway and proves to be a very special place to live, study and work.

Admission

We accept applications from November for the following fall semester. Deadline for receipt of applications: 15 February.

Further practical information

As a student at NHH you are also guaranteed accommodation in student housing and granted work permission.

Norwegian School of Economics: Case study

'The teaching at NHH is based on the most up-to-date and timely case studies, which gives me the feeling of being part of the contemporary world energy business.'
Maria Korotkova, Russia

'The professors and guest lecturers share with us their valuable experiences, which is better than textbook-based discussions.'
Sarah Raquipiso, Philippines

'At NHH I received a world-class education; a solid grounding in economics and exposure to specialised subjects such as oil and gas. My time at NHH and in CEMS allowed me to build a diverse international network of friends and colleagues. I find NHH students to be people who are very competent in their subjects, analytically superb, but also with a keen sense of initiative.'
Isikan Aysev, Turkey

'I did my master thesis in collaboration with Chanel, about how women use and perceive luxury cosmetics. My present job at Chanel covers tasks as PR, growth strategy, marketing and distribution management. Being able to leverage the skills I obtained at NHH, while being constantly challenged, make my job at Chanel truly exciting.'
Melissa Malka, Norway

'Bergen's beautiful sceneries and atmosphere makes an ordinary day exciting. Simply exploring the city, hiking the surrounding mountains, or enjoying the night life makes my day feel adventurous.'
Anna Sariceva, Latvia

'NHH is truly global, both in terms of the course subject matter as well as the student body. Accordingly, students at NHH have well-rounded international perspectives.'
Emma Micklem, South Africa

Inholland University of Applied Sciences: Profile

Inholland University of Applied Sciences offers a wide range of Bachelor programmes on five main campuses across the west of the country. These include English-taught programmes in the fields of International Business Innovation, Media & Entertainment, Tourism and Engineering, offered in the cities of Amsterdam/Diemen, Delft, Haarlem or The Hague.

Small-scale, international and practical experience, are key characteristics of Inholland's learning environment. We welcome and support a substantial number of international students, whom we offer a safe and open learning environment in which they are known and can feel at home. Students receive a lot of attention, have direct and personal contact with professional lecturers, and get a balanced education in terms of theoretical background and practical experience.

Students take part in project-based activities where they learn how to interact, communicate and collaborate with their fellow international students. Project assignments involve real-life situations and contribute to the professional development of the students. In their third year students go on a work placement for a full semester, putting their knowledge and skills to the test in a real company, as real employees. The fourth and final year includes a large-scale applied research project culminating in the student's bachelor thesis. Upon graduation, students of our international programmes are well-equipped to operate as professionals in a multicultural and international work environment, anywhere in the world.

Students can use Inholland's extensive digital library, modern ICT facilities and all sorts of guidance and advice (e.g. counsellors, coaches). The International Office and the International Recruitment Office can assist students in non-study-related issues.

Inholland offers the following English-taught programmes:

- International Business Innovation Studies
- International Media and Entertainment Management
- International Music Management
- Tourism Management
- Aeronautical Engineering
- Mathematics and Applications (Information Technology)

Practical Information:

- Tuition fees for the 2014–2015 academic year have yet to be set, but will not exceed €2,000.
- UK students are eligible to receive financial support from the Dutch government if they meet the specified requirements.
- No visa requirements for UK students.
- Inholland offers appropriate living accommodation on or in the vicinity of the campus at reasonable prices.
- UK students are required to provide two A levels and minimum of four GCSE certificates to be admissible.
- Depending on the programme of choice, students may be requested to take part in an intake test and an interview.
- Due to the high number of international students, the application procedure is relatively long. Students are advised to start their application around April/May to ensure a place for the September intake. If you receive your diploma late in the summer, please contact us for further assistance.

For questions about the application procedure, please contact:

international@inholland.nl

Inholland University of Applied Sciences: Case study

Robin Davies, Wales, 27

'Inholland was recommended to me by a friend who was already studying here. Visiting the university during an open day, I immediately felt the friendly and welcoming atmosphere. The students were enthusiastic about school and they seemed to enjoy it very much so I decided to enrol.

'I really like the atmosphere. People are sociable, classes are interactive and they really teach you how to become a good professional. The school provides a great number of facilities; you can work in the cafeteria or in the lobbies and you can also find at any time a free computer around school for group or individual work.

'The level of education is worthy and most of the teachers are passionate and they have a good attitude. They have an open door policy allowing you to go to them when you have any problems and they are happy to help. The work in projects teaches you how to work with people from different cultures and being more hands on than in traditional research universities. Meeting new people and developing a professional network is easy and with determination and passion you can achieve your goals.

'I feel that I am a lot more confident now in my social life and at school, especially because we had to do a lot of presentations. Even if I found it scary at first, now I am quite good at it, because the teachers motivate you to do it.

'The opportunities come in various forms and are numerous. I can work in an international company in the Netherlands or abroad and even open my own business because the university offers me the necessary knowledge to do that.'

Chapter 5

Studying in Europe

UK students are lucky to have such a diverse range of countries right on their doorstep. Flights to some European cities can be as cheap or as quick as a train journey within the UK. European study brings the benefit of cultural and language differences, without having to travel too far.

One myth about studying in Europe is the need to have brilliant language skills. Increasingly, European universities are offering entire courses in English. Of course, living in a different country will also enable you to immerse yourself in the language, thereby developing new language skills as a bonus. Some universities will offer you the chance to take language lessons alongside your studies.

This chapter focuses on EU (European Union) or EEA (European Economic Area) countries where UK students are charged the same fees as those for home students. The countries featured offer a range of courses available in English. The European countries that aren't listed in this chapter will still have opportunities for study in English (most European countries do) but you may find that some are more limited, perhaps restricted to private or international institutions.

In the Times Higher Education World University Rankings 2013–2014, a listing of the top 200 universities in the world, you will find universities from many European countries – Switzerland, France, Germany, Ireland, Sweden, Finland, the Netherlands, Belgium, Denmark, Spain, Norway and Austria are all represented.

Compatibility in the education system

Although there are differences in the education systems across Europe, a system known as the Bologna process has helped to make higher education more compatible and comparable across much of the continent. With transparent, mutually recognised systems and a clear credit framework, studying across Europe is now much simpler.

The Bologna process covers the European Higher Education Area (EHEA), an area much wider than the EU or EEA. It includes some countries applying for EU membership (Montenegro and Turkey, for example) and some post-Soviet states (Armenia, Ukraine and Azerbaijan, for example).

The process of studying for an entire degree abroad is sometimes known as 'diploma mobility'.

Bachelor's degrees, master's degrees and doctorates in these countries are all comparable in level. The European Credit Transfer System (ECTS) is used to measure workload and allows comparison between degrees in different countries. This makes it fairly straightforward to study a first degree in one European country and a postgraduate degree in another; some students even move part-way through their studies. Credit can be awarded for academic study, relevant placements and research, as long as they are part of the programme of study. Sixty credits equate to one full-time academic year. You may see bachelor's degrees of 180 or 240 credits, for example.

Another benefit of the coordinated system is the diploma supplement, a detailed transcript used across Europe and the EHEA which outlines any studies you complete and gives full details of the level, content and status of your achievements. It is particularly helpful if you intend to work or study in another country as it provides a recognisable context to any attainments.

The coordination of quality assurance standards means that higher education across all these countries has to meet minimum requirements. It is important to note that this doesn't remove the need for thorough research into what you will receive at your European university. You will find a range of different types of opportunity on offer. Just as in the UK, universities across Europe vary in their prestige, research, teaching and facilities. Ensuring that you find a good match to your needs is a key part of the research that you undertake

It is important to note that most bachelor's degrees outside the UK are not classed as honours degrees as standard; extra study is normally required to gain an honours degree.

Finding a course and institution

A Star Future (www.astarfuture.co.uk/what_to_study.html) and EUNICAS (www.eunicas.co.uk) feature course listings specifically for undergraduate courses taught in English. Another option is to use the Study Portal websites, www.bachelorsportal.eu, www.mastersportal.eu and www.phdportal.eu, but make sure that you select English as the language of instruction. You can use PLOTEUS (Portal on Learning Opportunities throughout the European Space) at www.ec.europa.eu/ploteus/home-en.htm. Try the advanced search on GES Database (www.study-info.eu/index. htm). EURAXESS has a database of research opportunities across Europe (www.ec.europa.eu/euraxess).

Different websites often bring up a different range of courses, so it is worth searching more than one website. Although these websites are a good starting point, the information on application deadlines and fees can sometimes be incorrect, so you should turn to the institutions for the latest information; you will be able to clarify any details with them.

ENIC-NARIC (European Network of Information Centres – National Academic Recognition Information Centres) has information on the education system of 54 countries, within Europe and beyond. The website also lists higher-education institutions for each country, so you can be sure that your chosen institution is recognised (www.enic-naric.net).

Entry requirements

Entry requirements vary between countries and between institutions. Similarly, competition for places varies as well. Most European countries do not have such a competitive system as we have in the UK, where the cap on numbers means some students won't gain a place, even when they have the academic ability to cope with the course. Many European countries ask that you have completed A level study, without asking for specific grades; they are often more concerned with your performance at university than beforehand, so some students will lose their place after the first year if they cannot cope with the academic demands. It should be noted that the drop-out rate amongst international students tends to be considerably lower than from home students.

Some European countries expect a wider range of subjects than UK students would normally take. It is standard practice in some countries to ask for a qualification in maths or a foreign language at A level standard. If you haven't studied these subjects, look closely at the entry requirements to be sure that you will be considered.

Certain courses in some countries are subject to selective recruitment; look out for the terms *numerus clausus* or *numerus fixus*, which might indicate a competitive system for restricted places. Your nationality should not prevent you from accessing education in any EU country, although you will need to ensure that you meet any entry requirements.

What is your UK qualification equivalent to?

Unless you have taken an internationally recognised qualification, like the International Baccalaureate, it is possible that your UK qualifications will need to be compared to the qualifications in the country where you wish to study. A levels tend to be understood overseas, but many other UK qualifications will require further evaluation. Each country has its own system for ensuring the adequate comparison of academic qualifications. Your chosen institution will be able to advise you further on any information that they require, so it is best to speak to them initially. You may later need to contact the ENIC-NARIC organisation in your host country for formal comparison of your qualifications (www.enic-naric.net). There will be a fee for this service.

Applying

Each European country has its own system and timescale for application. In some countries this is centralised, a bit like

UCAS, but in other cases you have to apply individually to each university. The country guides will give you an idea of the different systems and deadline dates for application.

Registering your stay

Although UK students studying in the EU or the EEA will not require a visa, you will need to register your stay if you are going to be in the country for longer than three months. In most countries, you simply need to take your passport to a police station or immigration department. It is advisable to do this early; in some cases it must be done in the first week of your stay. Some countries charge a small fee for this service. Your university's international office will be able to tell you more.

Costs and help with finances

For course fees, UK nationals studying at public universities in other EU countries are treated in the same way as home students from that particular country. That means that they pay the same fees as those for home students.

While England's tuition fees are now the highest in Europe, many countries charge no tuition fees to full-time EU students, including:

- Austria
- Cyprus (bachelor's degrees)
- Denmark
- Finland
- Germany
- Malta (bachelor's degrees)
- Norway
- Sweden.

Tuition fee loans may also be available to EU students, in the countries where they are offered to home students. There is no requirement to offer maintenance grants and loans to EU students, although some countries choose to do so. Your university should be able to tell you more about the possibility of a loan or grant and any conditions you might need to meet.

The Netherlands is one of the few countries offering grants and loans to EU students, although you will need to be in work to access the grants. Loans are also available, but you will need to be under the age of 30. For more details, see the country profile for the Netherlands on page 162. Changes to the rules in Denmark means that EU students who work 10 to 12 hours per week may now be eligible for grants and loans. For more information on studying in Denmark, see page 134. Recent news coming out of Bulgaria suggests that EU students aged under 35 are eligible to apply for tuition fee loans. To find out more, use some of the websites listed in the European country profiles or get in touch with staff in the international office of your chosen university.

There are public and private universities across the EU and EEA. Public universities are more likely to have a standardised system of tuition fees. In France, for example, courses at public universities tend to cost the same, regardless of subject or institution. In other countries, different courses or universities can charge varying amounts. Private institutions will charge a broader range of fees, often based on what they believe the market (i.e. the student) is prepared to pay. On the other hand, private institutions may well have additional opportunities for scholarships and favourable financial support, so it is worth investigating further.

Cultural differences

Although you may be familiar with some of the European countries on the UK's doorstep, there will still be cultural differences to come to terms with. Different countries and their inhabitants have their own distinctive characteristics that you will need to get used to if you are to adjust properly. Although the language barrier may not impact on your ability to study (when courses are taught in English), it can add to your isolation outside the university environment. Taking advantage of language classes can be an important factor when trying to settle in.

In some countries, many students stay in their local area and part-time study is common, while elsewhere students traditionally go to university when they are older; all this will impact on your university experience, so it is important to look into this before you decide on your venue for study.

> ❝ It's a wonderfully chilled and relaxed lifestyle, the people are friendly and their English is of great quality. They have many celebrations at points of the year where one can become a part of their culture and tradition. ❞
>
> *Simran Gill, Fontys University of Applied Sciences,*
> *the Netherlands*

Talk to your university's international office or try to make contact with other UK students in preparation for the cultural differences you will face.

Working while studying

The opportunities to work will vary from country to country, often based on the number of local job opportunities for those with skills in English. In some countries, your opportunities will be limited so, to be on the safe side, you should plan your finances with the expectation that you will not find work.

If you need to work to get access to student grants and loans, as in the Netherlands, it may be worth moving to your new country a little earlier to begin the search. Alternatively, you can search for job opportunities through the European Job Mobility Portal (EURES) at www.ec.europa.eu/eures/home.jsp?lang=en. Your university may also have job shops advertising student-job vacancies.

If you hope to work in Europe, either during or after your studies, it may be useful to prepare a Europass CV, which comprises a standard CV template used widely across Europe; it should make your educational background and work experience more easily understood. Find out more at www.europass.cedefop.europa.eu.

> **❝** I have a job at the university proofreading English and posting on the university's Facebook page in English. If you're a native English speaker, it's not too hard to get a part-time job or two. Your first port of call could always be the university in seeking work. **❞**
> *Hannah Burrows, University of Southern Denmark*

Staying on after study

As a free mover in Europe, staying on after study should not be restricted by legislation, although it may be limited by local opportunities. Competence in the local language, economic issues and local job opportunities may determine whether you choose to stay on for further study or work. Even if they don't remain in their university town or country, most students talk about the realisation that there is a whole world of opportunities out there for them.

> **❝** I'd like to travel the world. I don't want to be fixed. I want to see the world and make a difference. I won't be going back to the UK, that's for sure. Being abroad has caught on like a bug. **❞**
>
> *Rebecca Jackson, Stenden University of*
> *Applied Sciences, the Netherlands*

Country-specific information

Note

A number of European countries are very limited in the undergraduate courses they offer taught in English at public institutions. The list includes Austria, Belgium, France, Iceland, Italy, Spain and Norway. However, private providers and international universities in these countries do offer a range of undergraduate degrees taught in English; they will be more expensive than the public institutions, but might still end up being cheaper than the UK options due to a more generous package of scholarships or financial support.

Belgium

There are 310 UK students enrolled in higher education in Belgium, according to OECD, Education at a Glance 2013.

Higher education in Belgium

The Flemish and French communities each have their own education system. Most higher-education opportunities in Belgium require Flemish- or French-language skills, but there are some courses taught in English. These are more often at postgraduate level, with quite limited options for undergraduate study.

> ❝ I decided to study in Belgium due to the opportunities to intern in Brussels alongside studying. KU Leuven fitted the bill perfectly; it has the best reputation both in Belgium and within EU institutions. ❞
>
> *Tom Aitken, KU Leuven, Belgium*

Applying

Applications need to be in quite early with some September-start courses showing deadlines of mid-September the previous academic year. Apply directly to your chosen university.

Costs

Tuition is free, although there are registration fees which can be up to €835 (£713) per year. See the You could study . . . section below for examples. The cost of living in Belgium is comparable to that in Finland and Ireland, which makes it slightly more expensive than the UK. It is ranked at number 13 out of 102 countries on the Numbeo 2013 Cost of Living Index at www.numbeo.com.

> ❝ The cost was marginal in comparison to the UK: €2,800 (£2,400) for an Advanced Master's; €610.60 (£520) for Initial Master's. Most master's degrees at Russell Group Universities in the UK cost £7,000 plus. ❞
>
> *Tom Aitken, KU Leuven, Belgium*

Five of Belgium's universities can be found in the Times Higher Education World University Rankings Top 200 for 2013–2014.

You could study . . .

Business Administration BA
Hogeschool-Universiteit Brussel
Three years
Apply by 1 June
Annual fees €610 (£520)
Monthly living costs €800 (£680)

MSc Electrical Engineering
University of Leuven
Two years
Apply by 1 March
Annual fees €610 (£520)
Monthly living costs €850 (£726)

PhD Computer Sciences
Hasselt University
Four years
Apply by 15 September
Annual fees €270 (£230)
Monthly living costs €610–€770 (£520–£660)

Useful websites
www.highereducation.be (Flemish community)
www.studyinbelgium.be (French community)

Also worth considering . . .

Luxembourg could provide an alternative venue to Belgium, although any opportunities taught in English are likely to require additional skills in French, German or Luxembourgish. The only university is the University of Luxembourg (www. en.uni.lu), although there are a couple of international campuses there too. Find out more at ENIC-NARIC's Luxembourg page, www.enic-naric.net/index.aspx?c=Luxembourg.

Czech Republic

The Czech Republic has a long tradition of higher education and is home to the oldest university in central Europe. It offers a range of courses in English, and low living costs. According to OECD, Education at a Glance 2013, 418 UK students are already studying in the Czech Republic.

Higher education in the Czech Republic

Courses in the Czech Republic are based at public universities and private colleges, some of which are international. They run a two-semester system, with courses starting in October or February.

Undergraduate studies tend to take three to four years, with master's degrees taking two to three years, and doctorates from three years.

There are opportunities to study for competitive courses like medicine, dentistry and veterinary science in the Czech Republic and in other countries in eastern Europe.

Applying

Applications are made directly to your chosen university, before a deadline often in late February or March. Additional requirements might include academic transcripts and certificates, a letter of motivation, an admissions test and interview. Your university's international office will advise further on all aspects of the application process.

You can search for courses through the database on Higher Education Studies at www.naric.cz/HigherDB/index.php?Sezn=S1, as well as through PLOTEUS and the Study Portals listed on pages 121–2.

Costs

Although courses taught in Czech are free, you will be charged tuition fees for courses taught in English. The universities set their own tuition fees for such courses and there is no maximum limit. Fees usually start at around €2,000 (£1,700) but can be as much as €15,000 (£12,820) for a degree in medicine or dentistry. Scholarships may be available; you can find out more at the Ministry of Education, Youth and Sports (www.msmt.cz) or from your university.

For its cost of living in 2013, the Czech Republic is ranked 57 out of 102 countries according to Numbeo (www.numbeo.com), which is considerably lower than western Europe and the Nordic countries. Study in the Czech Republic (www.studyin.cz) suggests allowing for living costs of around US$350–US$750 (£200–£465) per month.

You could study . . .

BSc Economics and Finance
Charles University, Prague
Three years
Apply by 15 April
Annual fees €6,000 (£5,130)
Monthly living costs CZK8,500 (£280)

MA Business and Law in International Markets

Anglo-American University, Prague

Two years

Apply throughout the year

Annual fees €5,340 (£4,560)

Monthly living costs not provided

PhD Chemistry and Food Technology

Tomas Bata University, Zlin

Four years

Apply by 28 June

Annual fees €2,500 (£2,136)

Monthly living costs CZK2,810 (£94)

Useful websites

www.studyin.cz

Also worth considering . . .

If you're interested in opportunities in eastern Europe, have you considered Bulgaria, Croatia, Hungary, Poland, Romania, Slovakia or Slovenia? Find out more at:

- ENIC-NARIC country page for Bulgaria, www.enic-naric.net/index.aspx?c=Bulgaria
- Study in Croatia, www.studyincroatia.hr
- Study Hungary, www.studyhungary.hu
- Study in Poland, www.studyinpoland.pl
- ENIC-NARIC country page for Romania, www.enic-naric.net/index.aspx?c=Romania
- Study in Slovakia, www.studyin.sk
- Slovenia, www.slovenia.si/en/study.

Denmark

According to annual figures from OECD Education at a Glance 2013, 615 UK students have already made the move to study in Denmark. You will find that education in Denmark centres on problem-based learning, developing your ability to present creative solutions to complex problems. The country has a strong tradition of public universities and, best of all, there are no tuition fees. At PhD level, there are even fully funded, salaried opportunities in English.

> **❝** The university I chose is the biggest in Denmark, and the course gave me the best opportunity of all of the ones I looked at. It's entirely in English and I study a full-time two year programme to get a broad base of topics. I get the opportunity to do internships and study abroad as part of the programme. I can have a part-time English-speaking student job alongside studying. The university offers accommodation for the full length of my degree, all of my teachers are recognised experts on America, and, best of all, there were no tuition fees whatsoever. **❞**
>
> *Hannah Burrows, University of Southern Denmark*

Higher education in Denmark

Denmark offers over 500 higher-education programmes taught in English. You can study at research universities (*universitet*) at undergraduate and postgraduate level; it takes at least three years to complete a bachelor's degree, two years for a master's, and three or four for a doctorate. Programmes at university colleges (*professionshøjskole*) are more professional in nature, leading to three-year to four-year professional undergraduate degrees in areas like engineering, teaching or business. Academies of professional higher education (*erhvervsakademier*) offer degrees in partnership with universities and two-year academy professional degrees (AP); an AP can be topped up to a professional bachelor's degree with further study.

The academic year runs from September to June, with the possibility of February intake too. Some courses are competitive and have additional requirements beyond the completion of A level-standard qualifications.

All courses in Denmark are assessed by oral or written exams.

> ❝ The teaching style is more like seminars than lectures, with a discussion by all students and teacher together. You have a lot of group work in class, and sometimes homework can be preparing a Powerpoint presentation with two other students. ❞
>
> *Hannah Burrows, University of Southern Denmark*

Applying

At undergraduate level, applications can be made through the Danish Co-ordinated Application System (KOT) at www.optagelse. dk/admission/index.html. Danish students can apply online but UK students will need to send their forms by post. Applications can also be obtained from your chosen institution. Forms are available around two months before the application deadline.

Through KOT, you can choose up to eight courses and can opt for a quota 1 or quota 2 application; the option you choose depends on the qualification you are applying with – your chosen university will advise you as to which one is most suitable. The application deadline is mid-March for undergraduate courses starting in

August and September, with a deadline of 1 September for the limited courses starting in January or February.

Students applying through KOT also have the option to be put on standby: this means being added to a waiting list if you are not admitted initially. If you get a standby offer, you may be contacted about a place as late as two weeks into the semester; if you get a standby offer that doesn't become a study place, you will be guaranteed a place for the following year.

Direct application is required at postgraduate level, with deadlines varying; your chosen university will be able to advise you further.

Costs

Danish students are eligible for State Educational Support (SU) in the form of a grant of DKK5,753 (£658) per month and access to loans of DKK2,943 (£337) per month. Under a recent EU court ruling, students from other EU countries should qualify for this support as long as they are working 10 to 12 hours per week. However, as this is a new development, it remains to be seen how eligibility for SU funding will work in practice. For further explanation, see the Ministry of Education website, www.su.dk/English/Sider/foreign.aspx. Some scholarships may be available. See Study in Denmark (www.studyindenmark.dk) for details.

Denmark is an expensive country to live in. It comes in at number five in the cost-of-living rankings 2013 (www.numbeo.com), but with no fees and with wages of around £13 per hour for students, it is still possible to have a reasonable standard of living. Students with no Danish language may be able to find jobs in English-speaking bars and cafés, for example, although jobs for non-Danish speakers might become harder to find if the changes to SU attract more EU students to Denmark.

The Technical University of Denmark (ranked 117), Aarhus University (ranked 138) and University of Copenhagen (150) are all in the Times Higher Education World University Rankings Top 200 for 2013–2014. UK universities with comparable rankings are University of St Andrews, University of Leeds and University of Birmingham.

You could study . . .

AP Service, Hospitality and Tourism Management

Copenhagen Business Academy

Two years

Apply by 15 March

Tuition fees DKK0

Monthly living costs from DKK6,000 (£670)

BEng Global Management and Manufacturing

University of Southern Denmark, Odense

Three and a half years

Apply by 15 March

Tuition fees DKK0

Monthly living costs DKK4,400–DKK7,000 (£500–£800)

MA Film and Media Studies

University of Copenhagen

Two years

Apply by 1 February

Tuition fees DKK0

Monthly living costs DKK7,500–DKK9,500 (£860–£1,088)

Useful websites

www.studyindenmark.dk

www.en.iu.dk/education-in-denmark

Estonia

Estonia offers good value for money and a vibrant student life. As many as 90% of international students say that Estonia is a good place to study (International Student Barometer™ 2011) but, so far, there aren't many UK students based there.

Higher education in Estonia

The country is keen to attract international students and is expanding its courses taught in English; it currently offers more than 100 recognised degrees taught in English. These programmes are accredited and are available at the following institutions:

- Estonian Academy of Arts: www.artun.ee
- Estonian Academy of Music and Theatre: www. studyinestonia.ee/study/institutions/international-degree-programmes/estonian-academy-of-music-and-theatre
- Estonian University of Life Sciences: www.emu.ee
- Tallinn University: www.tlu.ee
- Tallinn University of Technology: www.ttu.ee/en
- University of Tartu: www.ut.ee
- Estonian Business School: www.ebs.ee.
- Estonian School of Hotel and Tourism Management: http://estonianhotelschool.com
- Estonian Entrepreneurship University of Applied Sciences: www.euas.eu

Other higher-education institutions may offer alternative options taught in English, including modules for exchange students or short courses.

Education in Estonia takes place in public universities, private universities and professional higher-education institutions. The academic year starts in September and is divided into two semesters. Generally, you would be looking at a three-year academic bachelor's degree, a one-year to two-year master's qualification, and a three-year to four-year doctorate. Programmes in medicine, dentistry, pharmacy, veterinary science, architecture and civil engineering take five to six years.

All courses include exams which take place at the end of each semester. Grades are standardised, ranging from A (or 5) to E (or 1). Grade F (or 0) means that the assessment has not been passed.

Applying

Some institutions have started to accept online applications through Dream Apply (https://estonia.dreamapply.com) with others expected to follow suit. For all institutions, the first step should be to contact your chosen institution for advice on the correct procedure to follow. Deadline dates are set by the individual institutions and range from May to August for courses starting in September. Some doctorates are open to applications all year round.

Costs

According to Study in Estonia, fees range from €1,023 to €7,350 (£870 to £6,280) per year. Medicine, law, business administration, and social sciences are often more expensive. PhD students should not have to pay fees.

Estonia is one of the few countries offering some form of financial support to EU students, although this is going through some changes. From 2013–2014, the government will offer a need-based study allowance if a student's average monthly income is below €280 (£239) per family member. Students could be entitled to an allowance of between €75 and €220 (£64–£188) per month. There is also the possibility of applying for a study loan.

Doctoral students with a state-funded study place have the right to receive an allowance of €383.47 (£327) per month.

Some scholarships are available, primarily for postgraduate study; ask your university for more information.

Livings costs in Estonia are reasonable. You should allow a minimum of €160–€225 (£136–£192) per month for living costs, excluding accommodation. Expect to pay from €96 (£82) per month for a room in a dormitory and up to €450 (£384) for a private flat. Estonia is ranked at number 43 out of 102 countries on the cost-of-living rankings for 2013; this is considerably lower than the UK and much of western Europe.

You could study . . .

Bachelor of Liberal Arts in Humanities
Tallinn University of Technology, Tallinn
Three years
Direct application by 1 July
Annual fees €3,000 (£2,564)
Monthly living costs €500 (£427)

MSc Financial Mathematics
University of Tartu
One year
Direct application by 16 April
Annual fees €3,200 (£2,735)
Monthly living costs €550 (£470)

PhD Zoology and Hydrobiology
University of Tartu
Four years
Direct application by 31 March (contact potential supervisors in advance)
Annual fees €0
Monthly living costs €500 (£427)

Useful websites

www.studyinestonia.ee

Also worth considering . . .

If you're interested in opportunities in the Baltic states, have
you considered Latvia and Lithuania? Find out more at Study
in Latvia, www.studyinlatvia.lv and Study in Lithuania,
www.lietuva.lt/en/education_sience/study_lithuania and
the Lithuanian Centre for Quality Assessment in Higher
Education, www.skvc.lt/en/content.asp?id=235.

Finland

Finland is considered to be a safe and forward-looking nation with
a high-quality education system. Temperatures can range from
+30°C to –20°C and the sun never sets in parts of the country in
June and early July. The academic year runs from August to the
end of May; it is split into two semesters, August to December,
and January to May. Most students start in August, with limited
opportunities to join in January.

The latest figures from OECD Education at a Glance 2013 show us
that 216 UK students were studying in Finland at the last count.

Higher education in Finland

Higher education in Finland takes places in research-based
universities or vocationally focused polytechnics (or Universities
of Applied Sciences). In the universities, few programmes are
taught in English at undergraduate level, although master's and
doctoral degrees are more widely available. It is the opposite in
the polytechnics, where there are plenty of programmes taught
in English at undergraduate level, with a smaller number of UAS
master's programmes. (Doctoral qualifications are not available

in the polytechnics, only in the universities.) To access a UAS master's programme, you will need to have had three years of relevant experience, in addition to any academic requirements. To search for programmes, go to the Study in Finland database at www.studyinfinland.fi/study_options/study_programmes_database.

The degrees vary in length as follows:

- bachelor's degree: three years (university); three-and-a-half to four years (polytechnic/university of applied sciences)
- master's degree: two years (university); one-and-a-half to two years (polytechnic/university of applied sciences)
- doctoral degree: three to four years (university); not available at polytechnic/university of applied sciences.

Applying

Applications tend to be online, although the application process and timescale are split between the universities and polytechnics.

At universities, undergraduate applications are direct. Applications to master's programmes can be made direct or via www.universityadmissions.fi; ask your university which way to proceed. In most cases, you should apply for bachelor's and master's degrees between November and January. Doctoral programmes require direct application; the application timescale varies between institutions: some accept applications at any time, while others have specific timescales in which to apply. Speak to the international office or the relevant faculty at your chosen university.

At polytechnics, undergraduate applications should be made in January or February via www.admissions.fi. For a UAS master's degree, you should apply direct to the polytechnic at the time they specify; you can find out more on your chosen institution's website.

As the academic year begins in August shortly after A level results come out, there is normally insufficient time to confirm a place, so applicants might need to consider a gap year.

Undergraduate admissions procedures normally require an entrance test. This tends to be a written test, but may be an audition or portfolio for certain art, drama or music programmes. Most university tests are taken in Finland, but some polytechnic entrance tests can be taken outside the country. Make sure that you prepare fully, following any instructions provided by the institution.

> If you get your school grades and meet the admissions criteria, they put you through to the entrance exam, which includes an English exam. The next step is a group aptitude test and then an interview This definitely ensures that all the students are serious about studying at this university.
>
> *Fiona Higgins, HAAGA-HELIA, University of Applied Sciences, Finland*

Costs

Higher education in Finland is free to EU students at all levels of higher education. There is no entitlement to grants or loans.

Overall, Finland is slightly more expensive than the UK, coming 14th (to the UK's 18th) in the cost-of-living rankings for 2013 (www.numbeo.com). It comes in lower than Norway, Denmark,

Ireland and Australia. The average monthly living costs are between €700 and €900 (£600 and £770); expect to pay more in Helsinki than in smaller towns and cities. Student housing is reasonably priced; your university will support you in finding accommodation. As an EU citizen, you have the right to work in Finland, although language issues and a fairly heavy workload at university mean that this is unlikely.

> **"** The housing is very cheap (cheaper than the UK) and relatively decent. The only thing that costs a lot is the food and the alcohol, but as long as you are aware of money, then it should work out! **"**
>
> *Fiona Higgins, HAAGA-HELIA,*
> *University of Applied Sciences, Finland*

Most scholarships are for doctoral study or research, although institutions may have limited scholarships for students on other levels of study. Speak to your institution about this possibility. For more details, see the 'Scholarships' section at Study in Finland, www.studyinfinland.fi/tuition_and_scholarships/other_possibilities.

You could study . . .

Bachelor of Hospitality Management
Saimaa University of Applied Sciences, Imatra
Three and a half years
Apply by 11 February
Tuition fees €0
Monthly living costs €700–€900 (£600–£770)

MSc Software Development
University of Tampere
Two years

Apply by 31 January

Tuition fees €0

Monthly living costs €700–€900 (£600–£770)

PhD in Marketing

Hanken School of Economics, Helsinki

Four years

Apply by 8 April for autumn start, 30 September for January start

Tuition fees €0

Monthly living costs €700–€900 (£600–£770)

Useful websites

www.studyinfinland.fi

Also worth considering . . .

If you're interested in the Nordic countries, perhaps you would be interested in studying in Iceland. To find out more, go to Study in Iceland at www.studyiniceland.is and the ENIC-NARIC country page for Iceland at www.enic-naric.nct/index.aspx?c=Iceland.

France

France is the UK's closest continental neighbour, offering good-quality education with a strong international reputation. It attracts 6.2% of all international students at university level, but has limited English-medium options at undergraduate level in its public universities. This may well change over the coming years, as the rules about teaching in English at public universities are being amended. According to OECD Education at a Glance 2013, 2,992 UK students are studying in France.

France has four universities in the Times Higher Education World University Rankings Top 200 Universities 2013–2014.

Higher education in France

Higher education takes place in universities, grandes écoles and institutes of technology. The grandes écoles focus on science, engineering and business courses. They are the most prestigious and selective institutions. They charge higher fees and require a competitive exam for entry, which students may spend two years working towards (after achieving A level-standard qualifications).

There may be some opportunities for the best international students at these institutions, perhaps after initial study at another university. You are advised to contact them to discuss their requirements, but you are likely to need proficiency in the French language.

The academic year starts in September or October and ends in May or June, much as in the UK.

> **“** The class size is around 30–40 students, and there is an emphasis on group work. Furthermore, the professors are always willing to help students individually, and often give up their spare time in order to ensure that each student is on the same level. **”**
>
> *Alican Spafford, Rouen Business School, France*

Applying

Applications for courses taught in English should be made through the international office of your chosen institution. There is a centralised application process known as APB or Admission post-bac for courses taught in French. You can normally make direct applications from around November. Application deadline dates vary between spring and summer, but you should apply as early as you are able. Some institutions have a rolling programme of application and recruitment, which goes on throughout the year.

In addition to your application form and application fee, you may need to include some of the following documents:

- academic transcript
- certificates
- personal statement, to include motivation for studying and future career goals
- letters of recommendation (normally two)
- research proposal (for postgraduate research)
- copy of passport.

The master's degree you choose depends on your future plans; choose a professional master's degree as a route to employment, and a research master's degree as a route to a doctorate.

Costs

France invests in education; it spends an average €10,000 (£8,500) per student per year. One result of this is the low price for degrees from public universities, which are generally under €500 (£427) per year for most undergraduate and postgraduate study. Fees at public universities are set by law, while private institutions are more expensive, ranging from €3,000 to €10,000 (£2,500 to £8,500) or more per year.

The fees listed below are those set for 2013–2014.

- Bachelor's degree or licence: three years, annual tuition fees of €183 (£156).

- Master's degree: two years, annual tuition fees of €254 (£217).
- Doctoral degree or doctorate: three years, annual tuition fees of €388 (£331).

France is a fairly expensive place to live, ranked number 17 of 102 countries in the cost-of-living index (www.numbeo.com), just one place above the UK. CNOUS, the National Centre for University and Student Welfare, suggests that students would need around €700–€850 (£600–£725) per month for living costs. Costs in Paris are considerably higher. You'll find lots of useful information on student costs, and student life in general at www.cnous.fr.

Grants may be available to some international students through the French Ministry of Foreign and European Affairs. Entente Cordiale scholarships are awarded for postgraduate-level study. Information on these and other scholarships can be found at CampusBourses (www.campusfrance.org/fria/bourse), while CNOUS (www.cnous.fr) has more information on the system of grants and loans. Note that application deadlines for funding may fall earlier than course application deadlines.

If you are looking for work, the nearest CROUS centre will offer a temporary-student-employment service, although any vacancies are in high demand. Search on the CNOUS site for your regional CROUS office (www.cnous.fr/_vie_59.htm).

You could study . . .

BA in Arts
College Universitaire de Sciences Po, Reims (private)
Apply by spring (date TBC)
Three years

HIGH T■CH HUMAN TOU■H

you're looking for a challenging, inspiring academic environment in which to pursue your ■udies whilst enjoying a foreign adventure, the University of Twente is an option you can't ■ford to miss. We are a leading Dutch residential university with a high global ranking. Scan ■e QR codes below to enter the exciting ■orld of 'High Tech Human Touch'...

UNIVERSITY OF TWENTE.

ATLAS:
ONLY THE BEST

ATLAS, or the Academy of Technology and Liberal Arts & Sciences, is a brand new, international programme for honours students with a passion for technology and social change. Like you?

INTERACTIVE
CAMPUS VIDEO

We offer you the only Dutch university with its own campus - an attractively landscaped, colourful micro-world and a gateway to student life at its very best. Take the interactive video tour now!

ENTER A
VIRTUAL WORLD

Our Virtual Reality Lab is as high-tech is it gets! Join students from many backgrounds to explore, investigate and develop, using product simulation, holography or motion capturing. It's all there.

WAKE UP
AND GO GREEN!

Esther Verburg developed a 'green' vision when studying Industrial Engineering. Today, she is out to change the world as a social entrepreneur. She's also one of our senior lecturers.

university of groningen
2014 | 400 years

> **20 English-taught Bachelor Degrees**
> **110 English-taught Master Degrees**

f /universityofgroningen

t /prospectivesRUG

GOLD
Award 2013
International
Student Satisfaction
The Netherlands
studyportals

founded in 1614

www.rug.nl /opendays

Annual fees €9,800 (£8,376), depending on family income

Monthly living costs €580 (£495)

MSc in Public Health

EHESP School of Public Health, Paris

Apply by 16 February

Two years

Annual fees €254 (£217)

Monthly living costs approximately €800 (£683)

PhD Neutronics

National Institute of Nuclear Sciences and Engineering (INSTN), Gif-sur-Yvette

Apply by 11 March

Three years

Annual fees €0

Monthly living costs not provided, thesis allowances available

Useful websites

www.campusfrance.org/en

Germany

Germany offers a world-class education with low or no tuition fees in a country with the largest economy in Europe. 2,057 UK students already study there (OECD Education at a Glance 2013).

Higher education in Germany

In Germany, higher education is run by each of the 16 states, rather than by one central Ministry of Education. You can choose between universities, universities of applied sciences and specialist colleges of art, film or music. Universities offer the more academic options up to doctoral level, with universities of applied sciences taking a more practical approach, but only to master's level. Colleges of art, film and music offer creative or design-based

- academic reference
- educational transcript
- SAT or ACT (American College Test) scores (see College Board for further details, www.sat.collegeboard.org/register/sat-international-dates)
- research proposal.

Most application processes are open between October and June or July (for an autumn start), although you should check individual deadline dates and apply in good time.

Costs

Fees for undergraduate-level study at public institutions will have been phased out completely by *Wintersemester* 2014. However, higher-education institutions across the country make a charge for semester contributions; this covers certain administration charges and should entitle you to student discounts and free public transport. The cost varies between institutions; you should budget for around €200 (£170) per semester.

Where fees are charged for postgraduate study, they range from around €650 (£555) to as much as €10,000 (£8,500) per semester. You can expect to pay higher fees at private universities and colleges, at both undergraduate and postgraduate level, in some cases as much as €30,000 (£25,640) per year.

If you're lucky enough to get a scholarship, it is unlikely to cover all costs. Scholarships are particularly limited for undergraduate study. Search on the DAAD Scholarship Database and ask your university about their opportunities, www.daad.de/deutschland/stipendium/datenbank/en/12359-scholarship-database.

Living costs vary depending on where you study and the type of lifestyle you enjoy. According to student estimates on the DAAD website, costs vary between €350 and €1,000 (£300 and £854) per month. Cities like Chemnitz, Dresden and Jena come out cheapest, with Munich, Hamburg, Cologne and Frankfurt the most expensive cities.

Germany is ranked number 25 of 102 countries on a 2013 cost-of-living ranking (www.numbeo.com), so living there should be not only cheaper than the UK, but also cheaper than New Zealand, the Netherlands and Singapore.

You could study . . .

BA Tourism and Travel
Worms University of Applied Sciences
Three years
Direct application by 15 July
Tuition fees €0
Monthly living costs €800 (£683)

Master's degree in Advanced Construction and Building Technology
Technical University of Munich
Two years
Direct application by 31 May
Tuition fees €0
Monthly living costs €830 (£710) in Munich

PhD Political Science
Graduate School of Economics and Social Sciences, University of Mannheim
Three years
Direct application by 15 April (early application by 15 January)
Tuition fees €0, plus grants awarded
Monthly living costs €600–€700 (£512–£600)

Useful websites
www.study-in.de/en

Also worth considering . . .

Alternatives to Germany might include Austria, Liechtenstein or Switzerland. Discover education in Austria at OeAD (Austrian Agency for International Mobility), www.oead.at/welcome_to_austria/education_research/EN. You can research opportunities in Liechtenstein through ENIC-NARIC, www.enic-naric.net/index.aspx?c=Liechtenstein. Find out more about higher education in Switzerland at www. swissuniversity.ch or the Rectors' Conference of the Swiss Universities at www.crus.ch/information-programme/study-in-switzerland.html?L=2.

Republic of Ireland

The Republic of Ireland is close to home and English-speaking, with a higher-education system that has much in common with the UK system. It is therefore a popular choice among UK students, with 3,987 UK students based there at the last count (OECD Education at a Glance 2013).

Higher education in Republic of Ireland

Degrees can be awarded by universities and by a number of institutes of technology. Other higher-education institutions exist, where qualifications are awarded through HETAC, the Higher Education and Training Awards Council (www.hetac.ie). A number of the higher-education institutions in Ireland are private. For a list, see the Education in Ireland website, www. educationinireland.com/en/Where-can-I-study-/View-all-Private-Higher-Education-Institutions.

For general information on education in Ireland, go to the Irish Council for International Students website, www.icosirl.ie.

Trinity College Dublin tops the two Irish universities on the Times Higher Education World University Rankings Top 200 2013–2014. It is ranked number 129 (just above the universities of Lancaster and Leeds). University College Dublin also features, at number 161, above Leicester and Liverpool.

The qualifications on offer differ slightly from those in England, Wales and Northern Ireland in that a three-year ordinary degree is available, as well as a three-year or four-year honours degree (Scotland offers a similar choice). The grading system (first, upper second, lower second and so on) echoes the UK. Taught and research master's degrees should take one to two years, with doctorates taking a minimum of three years' research.

You can search for undergraduate and postgraduate courses through the Qualifax Course Finder (www.qualifax.ie). Postgraduate options can be found through Postgrad Ireland (www.postgradireland.com).

Entry requirements

The A level requirements for most degrees can make Irish universities a challenge to enter. This contrasts with many other European countries where the completion of A level-standard qualifications is sufficient and specific grades aren't always necessary. Irish universities tend to be looking for academic subjects that echo those taken at school in Ireland. If you are applying with different qualifications, you should speak to the university's international office or admissions office in advance; they may need to evaluate your qualifications before you apply.

Most degree-level programmes ask for three Cs at A level, or equivalent, as a minimum requirement. At universities and associated colleges, your best four A levels (or three, plus an AS in a different subject) will be considered up to a maximum of 600 points. In the scoring system for A levels, grade A* at A level is worth 150 points, and grade E is worth 40. (For full details, see the Central Applications Office website at www.cao.ie/index.php?page=scoring&s=gce.) Some institutions will consider different combinations of A level and AS level grades, so may be accessible for those without four A levels. For the more competitive courses, like medicine, the need for particularly high grades can make four A levels a necessity.

Entry to medicine

For entry to medicine, applicants must have at least 480 points (which can be obtained from four Bs at A level, for example), plus any minimum requirements from their university. Both exam results and HPAT scores will be considered when offering a place. See Undergraduate Entry to Medicine brochure for more details, (www.cao.ie/downloads/documents/UGMedEntry2014.pdf).

The Health Professions Admission Test (HPAT, www.hpat-ireland.acer.edu.au) is required for undergraduate entry to medicine, while the Graduate Medical School Admissions Test (GAMSAT, www.gamsat.acer.edu.au/gamsat-ireland) is needed for applications to postgraduate medicine. Application dates are often early and examination dates may be restricted to a single day.

Applying

While the academic year is in line with the UK, running from September to June, the application system has its differences.

Undergraduate applications are based on actual grades (and an admissions test, in some cases) and little else, so offers aren't made until results come out.

You can apply online or on paper from 5 November through the Central Applications Office (CAO) at www.cao.ie. Applications should be made by 1 February or earlier, particularly for restricted-entry courses, although there is a late closing date for other courses of 1 May. In most cases, there is no need for references or a personal statement. A fee is charged for processing.

Postgraduate applications

Postgraduate applications can be made direct to your chosen university, often via the international office. Some institutions use the Postgraduate Applications Centre (PAC) at www.pac.ie. Closing dates vary, even within a single institution. In most cases, a minimum of a 2:2 grade in an undergraduate honours degree is required for a master's degree.

In addition to the application form and fee, you may need to include an academic transcript, references, a CV, a research proposal (where relevant) and a statement of interest, explaining your motivation, commitment and what you hope to achieve.

> Postgraduate research at Trinity College Dublin can be applied for at any time. Each programme of taught postgraduate study has an individual deadline; many programmes require applications by 30 June, but you should check for your chosen course.

Costs

UK students on their first full-time undergraduate degree should not have to pay tuition fees. However, you will be required to pay a student contribution or registration fee of a maximum €2,500 (£2,137) in 2013/2014. This will increase to €2,750 (£2,350) in 2014/2015 and €3,000 (£2,564) in 2015/2016.

According to Postgrad Ireland, you can expect postgraduate fees of over €4,000 (£3,418) for research degrees, with taught programmes ranging from under €4,000 (£3,418) to as much as €29,500 (£25,213) for an MBA.

At number 11 out of 102 countries on a 2013 cost-of-living ranking, Ireland is a little more expensive than the UK (see www. numbeo.com for more details). Dublin is the most expensive place to live, with estimated living costs of around €275 (£235) per week. Education in Ireland estimates that, on average, a student can expect to spend between €5,000 and €10,000 (£4,273, and £8,547) per year; of course, this will depend on where you live and the lifestyle you choose.

You could study . . .

BArch in Architecture
University of Limerick
Five years
Apply through CAO by 1 February
Registration fee €2,500 (£2,136)
Monthly living costs €1,000 (£854)

MA Celtic Civilisation
University College Cork
One year
Apply by 18 November
Annual fees €5,400 (£4,615)
Monthly living costs €1,145–€1,495 (£978–£1,277)

PhD Agriculture and Food Science

University College Dublin

Three years

No application deadline date

Annual fees €5,800 (£4,957)

Monthly living costs €1,050 (£897)

Useful websites

www.educationireland.ie

Italy

Very few public universities in Italy teach their courses in English. Even so, the latest figures show us that 250 UK students are studying in the country (OECD Education at a Glance 2013). Italy also remains a popular destination for students on Erasmus exchanges.

Higher education in Italy

The majority of universities in Italy are state-funded, although there is a range of alternative provision including non-state universities, universities for foreigners (focusing on Italian language, literature and culture), specialist postgraduate schools, and telematic (or distance learning) universities. Most programmes are taught in Italian; English-medium opportunities in Italy are most often found at private universities and colleges.

There are a number of options to study medicine in Italy, taught in English and often at a cost of below €3,000 per year:

- University of Bari: www.uniba.it/offerta-formativa/english-medical-curriculum
- University of Milan: www.mimed.it/unimi.shtml
- University of Pavia: http://nfs.unipv.it/medicinecourse/school/school.html
- Sapienza University of Rome: http://en.uniroma1.it/structures/faculties–0/medicine-and-dentistry

- Tor Vergata University of Rome: http://med.uniroma2.it/node/4114
- Second University of Naples: www.medicina.unina2.it

Competition can be intense and you will need to learn Italian to cope with patient contact as the course progresses. The IMAT test is often a key part of the selection process; you can find out more at Admissions Testing Service (www.admissionstestingservice.org).

> All the teaching is done through large lectures (130 students per class) but the professors do have office hours and are reachable by email. There are no seminars and classes aren't compulsory: a big bonus.
>
> *James Wheeler, Bocconi University, Italy*

The academic year runs from September or October until July. The qualifications on offer are a three-year *laurea* which is the Italian bachelor's degree, the two-year *laurea specialistica* which is comparable to a master's degree, while the *dottore magistrale* is comparable to a doctorate. Much of the assessment in Italian higher education is exam-based.

The Politecnico di Milano announced plans last year to deliver most of its degree courses and all of its postgraduate courses in English from 2014; it is facing opposition from its faculty members and now a court ruling may limit its plans.

Applying

Provided that you meet the general entry requirements for higher education in the UK and have completed 12 years of education, you can be considered for undergraduate study in Italy. If you have a bachelor's degree, you can be considered for a master's degree, and if you have a master's degree, you can consider applying for a doctorate. You should apply direct to individual institutions, which may set their own additional entry requirements. You can discuss the process and timescale with your university's international office before you apply.

Costs

Fees are set by the individual institutions. You should expect to pay up to €1,000 (£854) per year for undergraduate study in the public institutions, although some institutions will charge more for courses taught entirely in English. Fees at private institutions are higher again, although these might still end up costing less than many of the courses in the UK. Postgraduate fees start at around €700 to €800 (598 to £683) per year. For living costs, Italy comes out a little cheaper than the UK. It is ranked 19th (to the UK's 18th) in the cost-of-living rankings for 2013 at www.numbeo.com.

You could study . . .

Laurea (Bachelor's) degree in Computer Engineering
Politecnico di Torino, Turin
Three years
Apply by 31 July
Annual fees €2,459 (£2,101)
Monthly living costs €600–€800 (£512–£683)

Master's degree in Economics and Political Science
University of Milan, Milan
Two years
Apply between April and September (competitive application)
Annual fees €2,992 (£2,557)
Monthly living costs of up to €1,000 (£854)

PhD Modern Languages, Cultures, Societies and Linguistics
Ca' Foscari University of Venice
Three years

Apply by 27 May

Annual fees €1,140 (£974)

Monthly living costs from €750 (£641)

Useful websites

www.study-in-italy.it

Also worth considering . . .

If you're looking for higher education near Italy, then how about Malta? There are no tuition fees (even for medical courses) and the island attracts a number of UK students every year. Find out more at the ENIC–NARIC country page for Malta: www.enic-naric.net/index.aspx?cMalta. Malta only has one university; the website for the University of Malta is at www.um.edu.mt.

Greece could also provide an alternative to Italy, although few international students choose Greece for their studies. You can find out more at the Greek Ministry of Education (www.minedu.gov.gr).

The Netherlands

Interest in the Netherlands as a study venue has been growing steadily, with its cheaper fees and hundreds of programmes taught entirely in English. Dutch universities are keen to attract international students and have been actively recruiting in the UK by visiting schools and attending education fairs. According to the latest figures, some 1,004 UK students are studying in the Netherlands. That's an increase of 144 students since last year, with the universities also reporting an increase in applications.

The Netherlands has an impressive 12 universities in the Times Higher Education World University Rankings 2013–2014 Top 200.

The country finds itself in third position, after the US and UK, for the number of institutions in the top 200.

Higher education in the Netherlands

The style of teaching in the Netherlands is interactive and student-centred, with tutorials and seminars taking place in smaller groups than you would expect in many UK institutions. The academic year runs from early September to late June.

You can opt to study at a research-based university (WO) or a University of Applied Sciences (HBO), which offers more vocational options. An academic or research-oriented bachelor's degree (WO) takes three years, while the applied alternative (HBO) would take four years, with the chance of a work placement and often a study-abroad opportunity. Associate degrees take two years, with the option to move on to an applied bachelor's degree.

If you are not ready to specialise in a single subject, a number of institutions in the Netherlands offer liberal arts programmes where you can opt from a number of subject options before deciding on a final major subject.

> 66 We're taught in a classroom. There are no lectures. The classes are very practical and laid back. I find the teaching style very personal as there are only up to 30 people in a class. We're really aided and guided. 99
>
> *Rebecca Jackson, Stenden University*
> *of Applied Sciences, the Netherlands*

At master's level, you again have the choice of either a research-based degree (WO) or the applied route (HBO), both of which take one to two years. In contrast, doctorates are only available through the research universities (WO).

To find a course, you can browse the NUFFIC database at http://ispacsearch.nuffic.nl or use Study in Holland's database at www.studyinholland.co.uk/what_to_study.html.

> **"** I had to get used to a more concise way of writing, but it was more the workload that presented the real challenge for me. I did far more in my first few months in comparison to my friends at UK-based universities. I guess you are eased into it in the beginning but by the second month you are expected to be up to speed. Now that I'm in the second year, I would say that the course has now become more focused, whereas last year it was rather generalised. **"**
>
> *Simran Gill, Fontys University of Applied Sciences, the Netherlands*

Applying

In most cases, two or three A levels, or equivalent, should be sufficient to meet the requirements for most bachelor's degrees. If you studied an alternative qualification, you should discuss it with your chosen university. At postgraduate level, you will need a bachelor's degree to progress to a master's. It is likely that any offer you receive will require you to pass your courses, rather than achieve specific grades. Although getting a place at university may seem easier than in the UK, the university will need you to prove your capability in the first year. Students who can't cope academically will be asked to leave the course.

In some popular subjects like medicine or law, places may be restricted through a scheme known as *numerus fixus*. For these courses, the allocation of places is decided through a slightly complicated lottery system, which can vary according to the requirements of the university . According to studyinholland. co.uk, if you're applying to courses like medicine, psychology, economics, physiotherapy or law then you may be affected by *numerus fixus*. Talk to your chosen institution to gain an understanding of how to give yourself the best chance of success.

> As A level results are published after the qualification confirmation deadline for Dutch institutions, you should be asked to complete a late submission form. Your university will be able to tell you how and when to complete this.

Studielink

You can apply to public institutions at undergraduate and postgraduate level through Studielink (http://info.studielink.nl/en/ studenten/Pages/Default.aspx) from September or October onwards. You can choose up to four options, including one *numerus fixus* course. Requirements for supporting documentation vary, but could include:

- certificates
- academic transcript
- personal statement or letter of motivation indicating why you are applying
- copy of passport
- CV
- two letters of recommendation
- research proposal (where relevant).

For some postgraduate study, an admissions test like GRE (www. ets.org/gre) or Graduate Management Admission Test (GMAT; visit www.mba.com) will be needed. In all cases, your institution will be able to tell you whether they require application through Studielink and any supporting information they need.

Most courses have an application deadline of mid-May, although *numerus fixus* courses require an earlier application. You can find a helpful guide to Studielink at the Study in Holland website, www.studyinholland.co.uk/studielink.html. Some courses will require a direct application instead.

The application process at university colleges differs, in that it requires an earlier application that should be made direct; another key difference is that students are invited to an interview.

> **❝** I had to write a personal statement and an essay. I was out of Europe when I applied so they did the interview over Skype. They were also fine with me scanning and emailing a lot of the documents, which was a huge help. **❞**
>
> *Shanna Hanbury, Amsterdam University College,*
> *the Netherlands*

Costs

In the public universities, the annual fees started at around €1,835 (£1,586) for 2013–2014 at undergraduate level, and something similar at postgraduate level; the fees are expected to rise with inflation for 2014–2015 entry. This can be paid upfront or through an instalment system. Fees at university colleges are usually higher. EU undergraduate and postgraduate students can apply for a tuition fee loan from the Dutch government.

Undergraduate students under the age of 30 who work for at least 56 hours per month should be entitled to a basic grant of around €270 (£230) per month with the possibility of topping this up further with a supplementary means-tested grant. You can apply once you have been working for three months and you will also need to take out health insurance.

Access to grants at postgraduate level varies. You can find out more about loans and grants at DUO-IB-Groep (Department of Education), www.ib-groep.nl/International_visitors/EU_EEA_ students/Grant_for_tuition_or_course_fees.asp.

Scholarships are also available. You can search for a scholarship through NUFFIC's Grantfinder at www.studyinholland.nl/ scholarships/grantfinder.

At number 16 out of 102 countries on the 2013 Numbeo (www. numbeo.com) cost-of-living ranking, the Netherlands is not cheap; it is comparable in living expenses to the UK or France. You should budget for between €800 and €1100 (£683–£940) per month, according to studyinholland.nl.

> ❝ Living costs are relatively cheap. There are low price supermarkets which offer a wide variety of products at good prices. Food is pretty much the same here as it is in the UK. Supermarkets are tremendously accessible; I live above one. I'd recommend setting a budget and making food in bulk, if necessary. Going out to party is not too expensive, as drinks are cheap in Venlo and I rarely spend over €80 (£68) a week. ❞
>
> *Simran Gill, Fontys University of Applied Sciences,*
> *the Netherlands*

You could study . . .

BSc Psychology
Leiden University
Three years
Apply by 15 February

Annual fees €1,835 (£1,568)

Monthly living costs €800–€1,150 (£683–£982)

Master's degree in Human Geography

Radboud University Nijmegen

One year

Apply by 1 May

Annual fees €1,835 (£1,568)

Annual living costs of up to €10,000 (£8,547)

European Doctorate in Law and Economics

Erasmus University, Rotterdam (and University of Bologna and University of Hamburg)

Four years

Apply by 10 January

Annual fees €3,600 (£3,076), although scholarships are available

Monthly living costs €1,000 (£854) in Rotterdam

Useful websites

www.studyinholland.nl

Norway

With around 14,000 students from overseas, approximately 337 students from the UK and no fees at public universities, how about studying in Norway? It offers many postgraduate courses in English, although only a handful at bachelor's-degree level. Norway has high costs but one of the best standards of living in the world; it has been ranked top by the UN for the past eight years. It can be cold, but you will discover a great outdoor lifestyle.

> 66 Within the first month of arriving here, I'd been on
> fishing trips, hiking trips, whizzing around in a
> little rib boat on the Saltstraumen, swimming in some of the
> most beautiful lakes which are a 15-minute walk from the
> university, and even met the Norwegian Prime Minister. It's
> been quite something! 99
>
> *Megan Doxford, University of Nordland, Norway*

Higher education in Norway

Higher education takes place at universities, specialised university
institutions, university colleges or national colleges of the arts.
Universities have a research focus, while university colleges focus
on professional studies. It is possible to gain a master's degree and
sometimes even a doctorate at a university college. Most higher-
education institutions in Norway are state-funded, although
there are some private university colleges. In Norway, you would
generally study a three-year bachelor's degree, a two-year master's,
and a three-year doctorate. The academic year runs from mid-
August to mid-June.

It is common for students in Norway to take time out to work or
travel before university, so they may be a little older.

You can search for study opportunities through Study in Norway
at www.studyinnorway.no.

Applying

According to the GSU list (the list of minimum requirements for
admission to Norwegian higher education), you will need five
subjects in total, including two A levels (or one A level and two AS
levels); you could make up the other two or three subjects from
GCSEs. Students from Scotland will need to pass five Highers.

Some subjects will have additional requirements. You can find the GSU list at the Norwegian Agency for Quality Assurance in HE (NOKUT) website, www.nokut.no/en/Knowledge-base/Surveys-and-databases/GSU-list. Successful completion of a bachelor's degree is needed to progress to master's level.

You should apply direct to your chosen institution sometime between December and March for courses starting in August. Application deadlines vary, but your institution will be able to advise on specific deadline dates, as well as any supplementary information needed. This could include:

- academic transcript
- copies of certificates, for qualifications already gained
- CV
- research proposal, where necessary.

> **66** The application process was very simple and relatively hassle-free. Everything was done online and they only required a few documents such as my undergraduate transcripts, my CV and some essays I was required to write to apply for a scholarship. A GMAT score was also required. **99**
>
> *John Magee, BI Norwegian Business School, Norway*

Costs

Whether you are studying at undergraduate level or for a master's degree or a PhD, you are unlikely to have to pay fees at a state-funded university or university college. There is a small semester fee of NOK300–NOK600 (£32–£63), which gives you a student discount card along with membership of student welfare associations, access to campus health services, sports facilities and so on. Private institutions charge fees, although these should still be lower than those charged by universities in the UK, perhaps with the exception of some MBAs.

There are some scholarships available for study in Norway. See the Study in Norway website for details.

Living costs in Norway are high; in fact, it ranks number one out of 102 countries in a 2013 cost-of-living index, see www.numbeo. com. You should expect to have at the very least NOK8,900 (£935) per month for living expenses.

> **"** The price of living is very high, so the Norwegian government requests you have ample funds for the year ahead. You have to have NOK90,000 (£9,453) in a Norwegian bank account in order to be accepted. This is the amount of money needed to survive a year at university out here. It is possible to get work, which helps an awful lot financially, especially as the minimum wage is a lot higher than in the UK. **"**
>
> *Megan Doxford, University of Nordland, Norway*

You could study . . .

BSc Biology
University of Nordland, Bodø
Three years
Apply by 1 April
Tuition fees NOK0
Monthly living expenses NOK94,400 (£9,916)

Master's degree in Contemporary Art
University of Tromsø
Two years
Apply by 15 September
Tuition fees NOK0
Monthly living expenses NOK90,800 (£9,537)

PhD Marketing
BI Norwegian Business School
Four years
Apply by 1 April
Tuition fees NOK0
Annual living expenses NOK90,250 (£9,003)

Useful websites
www.studyinnorway.no

Spain
Although the option to study in Spain on an exchange programme is a popular one for UK students, with 1,009 university students based there according to latest figures, opportunities for a full degree are limited. Most options at public institutions are taught in Spanish though there are opportunities in private institutions, which make up around a third of the higher-education institutions in Spain. The number of courses taught in English is on the increase as a direct result of the Spanish government's interest in recruiting more international students, with plans for one in ten students to be from overseas by 2015.

Higher education in Spain
You can find information through the Ministry of Education at www.educacion.es. To search for courses, try Study Portals (studyportals.eu), EUNICAS (www.eunicas.co.uk) and A Star Future (www.astarfuture.co.uk).

Undergraduate degrees take from three years, master's degrees last one or two years, while doctorates take from two years. Some of the private universities offer accelerated programmes to reduce the length of study. The academic year runs from October to June.

> 66 It is a young university that is keen to keep growing with student participation; I was excited to influence and to be part of a new and growing institution. 99
>
> *Tudor Etchells, IE University, Spain*

Applying

Application deadlines tend to fall in early June for October start courses, but it is worth applying well in advance of this date as there are often more applicants than places. Some courses also offer a February intake.

As long as you have the general qualifications to access higher education (HE) in the UK, you should meet the general requirements for HE in Spain. Talk direct to your chosen university about their application procedures. You will need to register with UNED at http://portal.uned.es/portal/page?_pageid=93,932663&_dad=portal&_schema=PORTAL for evaluation of your qualifications or *credencial de acceso*. (Note: you may need to translate this page using a service like Google Translate.)

Completion of a bachelor's degree in the UK or the European Higher Education Area will satisfy the general requirements of a master's degree. Sixty ECTS credits are required to progress to research at doctoral level.

> **❝** The university application process explored your whole range of interest and motivations. It was personal and comprehensive, wanting to derive the best aspects from their applicants. **❞**
>
> *Esme Alexander, IE University, Spain*

Costs

Recent cuts in public spending have led to an increase in tuition fees. A bachelor's degree or *grado* at a public university now costs from around €800 (£683) per year, with some institutions charging three times this amount. At private universities, fees start at around €5,000 (£4,273), but can be considerably higher than this, although these institutions often have generous schemes of financial support.

Master's (*máster*) and doctoral (*doctorado*) degrees are paid for per credit, with the annual cost of a master's course ranging from €1,000 (£854) and with some public institutions charging up to €6,000 (£5,128). Private institutions set their own fees, but these must still fall within government limits.

Some scholarships are available and can be found through the Universidad website at www.universidad.es/en/spain/study-spain/scholarships. You can also ask the international office of your chosen university.

Living costs are lower than in a number of the European countries mentioned in this chapter. Spain is ranked number 28 out of 102 countries in a cost-of-living survey for 2013 (see www.numbeo.com), comparing favourably to the UK at number 18. Prices in the major cities, like Madrid or Barcelona, can be much higher.

You could study . . .

Bachelor's degree in Energy Engineering

Leganes campus, University Carlos III de Madrid

Four years

Apply by 5 July

Annual fees €1,860 (£1,589)

Monthly living costs €700– €800 (£598–£683)

Master's degree in Management, Organisation and Business Economics

Universitat Autònoma de Barcelona

Joint master's programme with Public University of Navarre and University of the Balearic Islands

Apply by 13 October

Annual fees €2,760 (£2,358)

Monthly living costs €700–€1,000 (£598–£854)

PhD Mental Health: Genetics and Environment

University Rovira I Virgili, Tarragona

Three years

Apply between 16 September and 10 October

Fees per module €536 (£458)

Monthly living costs €550 (£470)

Useful websites

www.universidad.es/en

Also worth considering . . .

Interested in studying in Portugal? Nearly all courses are in Portuguese, but you can find out more at DGES (General Directorate for Higher Education) at www.dges.mctes.pt/ DGES.

Sweden

As many as 30,000 international students currently choose Sweden for their studies and 620 of them are from the UK. With a strong focus on innovation and a forward-thinking, student-centred academic environment, Swedish higher education has much to offer.

Five Swedish institutions are in the Times Higher Education World University Rankings Top 200 2013–2014.

Higher education in Sweden

The academic year runs from late August to early June and is divided into two semesters. Three-year bachelor's degrees or *kandidatexamen* are the norm. A master's degree or *masterexamen* will take one to two years, while doctoral research or *doktorsexamen* takes at least four years.

Higher education takes place in universities and university colleges, with universities the only institutions with the automatic right to issue doctoral degrees. Local collaboration is widespread, so many institutions offer options reflecting the needs of local industries and businesses.

You can search for study options at Study in Sweden, www. studyinsweden.se/Course-search.

The name of the institution will not always reveal whether it is a university or university college; most university colleges will call themselves universities, while some universities are called *högskola* (or university college) in Swedish. Degrees awarded by both types of institution are equivalent to one another.

Applying

Any qualification that gives you access to HE in the UK should do the same for undergraduate studies in Sweden. Individual institutions then set their own procedures for selecting applicants; this might include grades, assessment of samples of work, interviews, admissions tests or work experience. Your institution's international office will be able to advise further about any special requirements.

For bachelor's and master's degrees, applications are made online through University Admissions at www.universityadmissions. se. Deadlines are generally mid-January for August start and mid-August for any courses starting in spring. At doctoral level, applications are made direct to the institution and often to the specific department, accompanied by copies of certificates, academic transcripts and letters of recommendation. Check any deadline dates with your academic department.

As the Swedish academic year begins in August, shortly after A level results come out, there may be insufficient time to confirm a place for the same academic year; applicants might need to consider a gap year.

Costs

In most cases, university courses in Sweden are free of tuition charges, although student-union membership fees are payable at SEK50–350 (£5–£34) per semester. A range of scholarships are available at Study in Sweden (www.studyinsweden.se/Scholarships). Ask your institution about any scholarships that they administer.

An average monthly budget for a student is around SEK7,070 (£691). Sweden is ranked number seven out of 102 countries in Numbeo's 2013 cost-of-living table at www.numbeo.com, which makes it cheaper than Denmark and Australia, but a bit more expensive than the UK.

You could study . . .

BA in Fine Art
Lund University
Three years
Apply via www.universityadmissions.se by 1 March
Tuition fees SEK0
Monthly living costs SEK7,800 (£762)

Master's degree in Bioentrepreneurship
Karolinska Institute, Stockholm
Two years
Apply via www.universityadmissions.se by 15 January
Tuition fees SEK0
Monthly living costs SEK8,000 (£782)

Useful websites
www.studyinsweden.se

Pros and cons of study in Europe

Pros

- Relatively close to home.
- Often cheaper for tuition fees than much of the UK.
- No visa restrictions.
- Able to work and to stay on after study.

Cons

- Language issues.
- Some countries have high costs of living.
- Pressure to do well in first year to remain on the course.

Student story
Tom Aitken, KU Leuven,
Belgium

Tom Aitken was no stranger to international study when he started to consider where he would take his master's degree. 'I previously studied abroad as part of my undergraduate degree in Washington, DC and it opened my eyes to the possibilities and ease of moving abroad.' Tom now finds himself in the unusual position of being able to compare university education in the UK, US and Belgium, after choosing an Advanced Master's degree in European Politics and Policies at KU Leuven.

'I decided to study in Belgium due to the opportunities to intern in Brussels alongside studying. KU Leuven fitted the bill perfectly: it has the best reputation both in Belgium and within EU institutions. There are very few graduate schemes for politically-minded students and therefore you are most likely going to be applying for jobs against people who have experience. In this market, a master's alone is not enough and therefore interning, and gaining work experience alongside, allows you to develop your CV.

'In the UK, politically-focused experience is generally in London where the cost of living is significantly higher. Belgium offered a world-renowned university at the heart of Europe for a fraction of the tuition price at American and British institutions. The proximity to Brussels meant that classes regularly utilise EU professionals as guest lecturers or actual course tutors. This was also something that was a particular advantage of studying in DC where you were able to engage with actual practitioners in your field of study. The opportunity to develop language skills was also particularly appealing.

'Due to the small class size there is great support for your academic studies. Especially when studying a selective course like an advanced master's, tutors are extremely keen to help you. Tutors are always willing to discuss, help you prepare your dissertation and also offer careers advice.'

Another benefit that Tom has experienced is increased flexibility in setting his own timetable. 'Modules have already been scheduled when you select them, so any clashes are your own fault, but the main advantage is that you can skew your timetable to favour the beginning of the week, or afternoons, or a particular semester. This is particularly useful to know if you are working or interning alongside studying, as you can plan your timetable around work. My experience in the UK is that you pick your modules based only on the topics and you don't find out your timetable until September which could limit your ability to work outside of study.'

Tom considered four main factors when deciding where to study: reputation, location, cost and course. 'KU Leuven ranks in the top 13 in Europe and top four on the continent (THE World Rankings 2013–2014). Speaking to EU professionals in Brussels it is clear to see that many have studied at KU Leuven, most prominently the President of the European Council, Herman Van Rompuy. The location, as mentioned, was ideal for career development. The cost was marginal in comparison to the UK: €2,800 (£2,400) for an advanced master's; €610.60 (£520) for an initial master's. Finally, the course at the institution was part of the EMPA (European Masters of Public Administration) structure, enabling me to possibly move to another university in the EMPA network for my second semester. Being accredited by EMPA also meant the course itself would be very academically rigorous and highly regarded. The course is also selective, meaning that you study as part of a small, close-knit class.

'I applied to a variety of universities across Europe and the application process seems a lot more relaxed than the UK, with deadlines being far later. Moreover, many Benelux (Belgium, the Netherlands and Luxembourg) universities do not require deposits on accepting a place and therefore it allows you to finish your undergraduate studies before spending money on something you will not begin for a further six months. In Belgium, they are not selective about undergraduate admissions and initial master's admissions, but they can be with advanced master's. Therefore the application process regularly asks for transcripts, motivational letters, a writing sample, TOEFL or IELTS scores (English language tests) and ideas for research upon entry to the programme.'

Tom has had to adjust to two different countries over the past few years, so he understands many of the challenges of settling in. 'Moving abroad for the first time is not easy; it can take some time to properly settle. Stick with it. The values and memories that studying abroad gives you are always worth it and it equips you with skills to do it again or adapt to similar alien situations in the future.'

Tom's top tips

Sources of information

'Expat websites can be extremely helpful in finding your way around cities and how things work. As official country websites sometimes overlook minor details which as a UK student you actually need, expat sites are particularly helpful.'

Housing

'The university provided a database for housing and the opportunity to apply for halls. Whilst halls primarily go to undergraduates, there is always a chance for postgraduate students. Housing in Leuven is a mixture of studios, rooms and shared apartments. The database is made up of registered landlords who sign up to a university-drafted contract, giving you full support if anything was to go wrong.

'If you can visit, go. It is always best to see it in person. Always begin by checking what their stance is with regards to guarantors. In America, many private apartments require guarantors with American bank accounts and certain levels of income, which you will be unlikely to have. You need to check if your visa can count as a guarantor. And try and get bills included, it is more common abroad than in the UK and it avoids utility company hassle.'

Food

'Finding British items such as PG Tips can be a welcome sight, but finding new favourites is equally rewarding.'

Living costs

'Remember that start-up costs are a lot. Whether it is desk lamps or mattresses, it soon spirals. Your first month's living costs will likely be twice as high as a normal month.'

Financial support for study

'Save up as much of your maintenance loan in your final year in the UK as you can. It is the best loan you will ever get! Allow two months if you're applying for a Professional and Career Development Loan as they can take some time.'

Working while studying

'Do it! Either you will be working to fund your studies and then it is necessary, or you are doing it for experience, and then it will give you the practical insight no academic course can.'

Making friends

'Whatever clubs and societies you are part of back home, they will be available abroad. Join them for the chance to meet like-minded people.'

Travel and transport

'Price comparison sites such as Skyscanner (www.skyscanner.net) allow you to view the cheapest days to travel each month. Unless you have a rewards card with an airline, there is no point sticking with one. Look out for airlines which offer student tickets, such as Brussels Airlines.

'Booking flights and trains in advance is the best way to cut the cost of travel. If you are bringing a lot of luggage, it may be worth looking at companies such as sendmybag.com. It ships luggage ahead of your arrival.'

For Tom, this next year will be an important year as he decides on his future direction. 'I hope to work for the EU in some capacity or in the field of international relations. This year will definitely define what my eventual career will be.'

And throughout Tom's experiences, the best and most important aspects of studying abroad have been the people. 'You can make some of your best friends being overseas, especially if they are non-natives like yourself. Even when they are not your friends, they may be a contact that can help you in your career.

'Studying abroad can help you in a career and socially, and it's the people that you meet that help create those opportunities.'

KU Leuven (www.kuleuven.be/english) is a Dutch-language university in Flanders, Belgium offering undergraduate and postgraduate opportunities taught in English. It appears at number 61 on the Times Higher Education World University Rankings Top 200 2013–2014 (the highest ranking Belgian university), just below the University of Manchester.

HAN University of Applied Sciences: Profile

Inspiring environment. Innovative and skilled professional staff. International student body. At HAN University of Applied Sciences, we make it our business to offer higher education of an outstanding quality to students across the globe.

HAN University of Applied Sciences is one of the largest providers of education in the Netherlands, with more than 30,000 students and almost 2,500 staff members spread over two campuses. With more than 3,000 international students, HAN excels at putting theory into practice in an international context throughout all four years of undergraduate study. Spread over the cities of Arnhem and Nijmegen close to the German border, HAN has modern buildings, state-of-the art multimedia centres, world-class laboratories and wireless internet access.

By following a bachelor's course at HAN University of Applied Sciences, students obtain a degree that will be an asset to any employee anywhere in the world. Fully accredited by the Dutch Ministry of Education and internationally recognized, the HAN bachelor's diploma is the starting point of graduates' successful careers and further studies in international postgraduate programmes.

The HAN bachelor's degree delivers its graduates high-powered credentials and marketable skills upon entering the global career market. It is our goal to prepare each of our students to meet the unique challenges found in today's working world. At HAN we ensure that our lectures and projects leave room for personal attention and student development.

Our students benefit from the experience and knowledge of foreign lecturers and international companies. Independence is stimulated and initiative rewarded by providing students with the opportunity to spend part of their education in more than one country. Students attend lectures in the Netherlands, do their work placement abroad, study at partner universities anywhere in the world and do their graduation assignment for an international company.

To maximize the learning process, classes are held only in English and in small groups of maximum 30 students, facilitating individual contact with teachers and fellow students. At HAN, personal development is just as important as professional education, therefore student guidance is offered throughout all four years of study. Joining the international student body means merging education with social networks. In the dynamic HAN community students are the heart of a multitude of activities: city trips, parties, thematic weeks etc.

The Faculty of Engineering and Arnhem Business School, two renowned institutes within HAN University of Applied Sciences, provide international courses in three different fields.

Bachelor courses taught in English:

* Automotive Engineering
* Communication
* Finance and Control
* International Business and Management Studies
* Life Sciences
* Logistics Management (Economics).

More information about course content and admission requirements can be found on www.han.nl/english.

HAN University of Applied Sciences: Case study

This world is at a constant state of change, evolving and changing towards a brighter future. Increased internationalism and the feeling of a smaller world is one important aspect of the future of the planet. HAN University of Applied Sciences is already a part of this international future. It's a place where you'll find people from all across the globe: from Australia to Canada and everywhere in between! The differences in cultures can be interesting, entertaining or scary, but will always manage to enlighten you further and better your perspective of the world.

A well-balanced course gives you both academic and practical skills essential to excelling in a professional environment. The learning environment itself is also great, with small class sizes and flexible teachers willing to spend extra time if you need the extra help. Smaller groups are also created for the purpose of set group projects which teach you great teamwork and leadership skills as you rotate through different assignments in the group.

Not only is the class internationally focused, but so is this course itself, with opportunities to do six months study abroad, along with six months internship abroad during your final two years, which make for great life and professional experiences. These international experiences, along with the practically focused parts of the course, are certain to make you more appealing and interesting towards prospective employers; it definitely gives you some good stories to tell!

By Ben Pyman (Third year Bachelor of Automotive Engineering, British student, currently doing his internship at Fontys in Helmond, near the Belgium border).

Amsterdam University College: Profile

$\underset{\text{UC}}{A}$

Amsterdam University College (AUC) offers a liberal arts and sciences programme, leading to a joint bachelor's (Honours) degree from the University of Amsterdam and VU University Amsterdam.

You can major in the sciences, social sciences or humanities. Discussions start from 'big questions' in science and society and lead to in-depth study in a wide range of disciplines. Six interdisciplinary themes provide an orientation to the choice of courses for your major:

- Energy, Climate and Sustainability
- Life, Evolution and the Universe
- Health and Well-being
- Information, Communication, Cognition
- Social Systems
- Cities and Cultures.

Substantial emphasis is placed on the sciences, offering a thorough in-depth training in disciplinary sciences such as physics, biology, informatics, earth and environmental sciences and (bio)medicine, but also requiring immersion in other fields of study.

All AUC students undertake community service or an internship, and AUC offers a wide range of study abroad opportunities.

As a residential and selective honours college, AUC attracts students from all over the world. Your time at AUC will become a true intercultural and social learning experience. AUC students live and study together on our modern international campus, located in the Science Park Amsterdam.

Would you like to know more? Visit the AUC website: **www.auc.nl**

187

Amsterdam University College: Case study

Aleksandra Arsova
Macedonia
Class of 2015

Building bridges between cultures

After finishing high school I knew that I wanted to gain global experience and shape myself as a cosmopolitan. Finding out about AUC was more than fortunate at that moment. The diverse curriculum, international environment, renowned professors and extraordinary facilities were just additional help for deciding to choose AUC as my further education. All this in one of the most amazing cities in the world – Amsterdam!

I had the opportunity to become the architect of my own curriculum, but living here also enriched me as a person. Besides getting my dream education, I found myself upgrading my knowledge of culture and diversity. People are friendly and eager to know about different cultures, and this is especially felt at AUC. All in all, choosing AUC was among the best decisions I have made so far and I am more than happy to pass on my experience to prospective students.

Zuyd University of Applied Sciences: Profile

Zuyd University
of Applied Sciences

ZU
YD

Zuyd University of Applied Sciences has more than 50 bachelor's and master's degree programmes. It is known for its highly rated education and applied research, with a strong orientation to professional practice. Zuyd is located in the south east of the Netherlands and is one of the larger universities of applied sciences in the country.

Programmes in English

At its campuses in Maastricht, Zuyd offers a number of bachelor's and master's degree programmes that welcome international students, both for a four-year study programme as well as for a study exchange. The subjects of study taught in English include International Business, Communication and Languages, Hospitality Management, Social Studies and Arts (Music and Design).

Educational approach

Despite the large student numbers (Zuyd has over 15,000 students of more than 40 nationalities) the study programmes feel comfortably small-scale and personal in set up. Students work in small groups with approachable lecturers, to stimulate interaction and active learning. The programmes offer a well-balanced mix of lectures, project work and group and individual assignments. All programmes taught in English have international classrooms where students are challenged to experience the values of cultural diversity.

Zuyd aims to teach its students using a practically oriented approach. The school co-operates extensively with other educational institutions and companies both in its region and abroad. Therefore, it offers all students the possibility to study or gain work experience abroad.

All campuses have a well equipped study infrastructure in an international environment.

City of Maastricht

Zuyd is located in the southernmost part of the country, where the borders of the Netherlands, Germany and Belgium meet. At this crossroads of countries, cultures and languages it offers an international and vibrant learning environment to its students.

Over 10% of Maastricht's residents are students, almost half of whom are from outside the country. It is one of the most popular destinations in the Netherlands for both national and international students. In the historic city centre you will find all a student needs: bars, restaurants and many shops. There is plenty of entertainment for an active student life with great theatres, cinemas, festivals and sports facilities for students. It is a relatively small and safe city with an international flair.

Chapter 6
Studying in the USA

The USA is an increasingly attractive destination for UK students; in the academic year 2011/2012, a record 9,186 UK students went to the USA according to the UK-US Fulbright Commission. The majority opted for undergraduate-level study, followed by postgraduate education, with the rest on non-degree programmes or post-study work schemes.

More and more students seem to want to discover the appeal of the American higher-education system: a system with a choice of over 4,500 universities and a broader, more flexible approach to university studies. Quality of education in the USA is unsurpassed; 77 of the 200 universities featured in the Times Higher Education World University Rankings 2013–2014 are from the USA. Some students are turning down places at the leading universities in the UK to take advantage of the breadth and quality of education on offer stateside.

> The academic year in the USA runs from mid-August or early September to late May or early June.

The education system

In the States, the terms 'university' and 'college' are generally used interchangeably. However, community colleges are different; they can only offer two-year associate degrees, rather than four-year bachelor's degrees.

Choosing where to study

When deciding where to apply, you need to consider which type of institution is right for you.

- Public universities are funded by the state and tend to have more students and lower fees. International students will end up paying more than state residents.
- Private universities tend to be campus-based, with better facilities and fewer students. They are funded by private donations, grants and tuition fees. Fees are higher, but the same fees are charged for all. More scholarships tend to be available.
- Community colleges offer associate degrees over two years (see page 194), with the possibility of transferring to a university to top up to a full bachelor's degree. They are often cheaper and less competitive.

The Ivy League is made up of eight prestigious private universities and colleges in the north-east of the USA. It started out as a sports league, rather than any kind of elite group or ranking system. For this reason, many top universities from across the country are not in the Ivy League, including Berkeley, which is a public university, and Stanford, which is on the west coast.

Keep an eye out for the public Ivy League which includes the universities of Michigan and California; these institutions offer a quality education without such extortionate fees.

American degrees offer a much wider choice of subjects to study than you would expect in the UK. They are made up of a range of types of courses.

- Core (or general education), providing the compulsory foundation for university study. Students will often be required to select from a broad range of courses including sciences, history, maths, English composition and literature and so on.
- Major courses, your main subject area; choose from options like English, engineering or history.
- Minor courses, taken in a secondary subject or allowing you to specialise within your main subject area. You could minor in a foreign language or consider adding a computer-science minor to a maths major.
- Academic track, a group of courses focused on a specific topic within a major; a student majoring in computer science could select a track in computer systems, for example.

Some universities offer co-operative education programmes, made up of paid work experience, rather like a sandwich course in the UK. In other cases, unpaid internships may offer degree credit.

Finding a course

You can use College Board (undergraduate), www.collegeboard. org, or College Navigator (undergraduate and postgraduate), www.nces.ed.gov/collegenavigator, to search for courses at public, private or community colleges. EducationUSA features a list of other college or course search sites on its '5 steps to study' web page, www.educationusa.info/5_steps_to_study.

The US system means it is essential to find somewhere that is a great match for you and what you have to offer. With this in mind and with so many institutions to choose from, why not start by writing a list of essential and desirable criteria relating to your preferred US state, size of institution, funding, diversity or activities on offer; whatever really matters to you. Use the information to filter your search at College Board or Peterson's (www.petersons.com). If you're looking for a student perspective, you'll find some useful information at Princeton Review (www. princetonreview.com).

Transfers

It is possible to transfer between universities. Transfers would normally take place after freshman year (Year 1), but (since you need a minimum of two years at a university to graduate) any later than sophomore year (Year 2) could prove tricky.

> The Sutton Trust runs a US Summer School Programme to encourage talented young people from low-income backgrounds to consider university in the USA. You can find out more at www.suttontrust.com/students/sutton-trust-us-programme.

Associate degrees

Associate degrees like Associate of Arts (AA) or Associate of Science (AS) are two-year programmes of general studies along with foundation courses in a chosen subject (a major or field of concentration). The qualifications often relate to vocational areas like hospitality management or health sciences. The programme might include core and concentration courses, electives, practical work, fieldwork and supervised study.

They are broadly equivalent to the first year of UK undergraduate study. After completion, students may wish to transfer to a US bachelor's degree by completing an additional two years of study.

Students who are only applying with GCSE qualifications could apply for an associate degree. Certain vocational qualifications might be accepted by community colleges, but not by the more competitive universities.

American college year names

Year 1   Freshman Year
Year 2   Sophomore Year
Year 3   Junior Year
Year 4   Senior Year

Bachelor's degrees

Bachelor's degrees generally take four years to complete, although there are some five-year courses in architecture, sciences and engineering. A US bachelor's degree is comparable in level to a British bachelor's degree. Unlike in the UK, where you choose your subject before you apply, you can apply for an undecided major, and decide on your chosen subject at the end of sophomore (or second) year. This has more in common with the Scottish system of education than with the rest of the UK. Much of the first year, and some of the second year, is spent on a range of introductory courses. Some of this core curriculum will relate to subjects you may wish to make your main subject choice (or major). For example, if you are considering majoring in psychology, you might opt for maths and quantitative reasoning, and social and behavioural sciences as your core subjects.

> ❝ I have had one-to-one support from the international student adviser who was fantastic in setting up my schedule and what I was going to study. ❞
> *Stuart Bramley, Scottsdale Community College, USA*

Entry requirements vary, but most would require a minimum of five GCSEs or National 5s at C or above, including maths and English. You would need to show that you are completing advanced-level study; the universities will be able to check your attainment from your academic transcript and any admissions tests you sit. Competitive universities will be looking for three A levels or equivalent. Less competitive universities may consider vocational qualifications, like a BTEC level 3 Extended Diploma, a vocational course broadly equivalent to three A levels. For more information on applying, see the following section.

Honours degrees

Gaining an honours degree in the USA tends to indicate that the student has defended an undergraduate thesis (or piece of original research) known in the UK as a dissertation. Confusingly, a degree with honours can also mean that someone has achieved with particular academic merit, although this is more usually known in the USA as *Cum laude* (with honour), *Magna cum laude* (with great honour) or *Summa cum laude* (with highest honour).

Graduate school

What we know as postgraduate education in the UK is described as graduate education or grad school in the USA. Master's degrees and PhDs gained in the USA are comparable to British master's degrees and PhDs. Certain subjects that you could start at undergraduate level in the UK can only be taken at graduate level in the USA; these include medicine and law. Pre-med and pre-law programmes are available at undergraduate level, although these programmes aren't a mandatory requirement for medical or law school.

Applying

The application process for undergraduate and postgraduate courses has some similarities to the UK system, although there is no admissions service like UCAS to coordinate applications. For the most part, applications are made direct to the chosen institution, although some universities use the Common Application for undergraduate programmes; see page 198 for more information.

As part of the application process, you will be required to send detailed academic records and official course information for qualifications you have completed. You may be required to submit your academic documents to an organisation that can convert your qualifications to a comparable level of study in the USA. Your university will give you further details of which organisation to use or, for a list of approved agencies, try the National Association of Credential Evaluation Services (NACES), www.naces.org.

Undergraduate applications

The timescale for applications is similar to that of UCAS, although there is a separate system if you are applying for a sports scholarship.

After Christmas in your first year at sixth form or college (Y13 in Northern Ireland or S5 in Scotland), you will need to start researching degree programmes and universities. It is suggested that you narrow down your choice to between three and seven universities, due to the time and costs involved.

Most applications comprise:

- application form
- fee (around $50 to $100 (£31–£62) per university)
- admissions test scores
- a few essays (of around 500 to 750 words)
- transcript (details of your academic performance)
- two or three recommendations

- financial statement
- possibility of an interview.

You will be applying to the university as a whole, so you will need to demonstrate why the university should consider you. Admissions staff will decide your fate, rather than academic staff from your chosen department. They will be looking at more than just success at A level; GCSEs, AS levels, your passion for learning, your love for your subject (if you have decided on a major), your extra-curricular activities and you as a person will all be considered. You'll need to demonstrate a match between what you have to offer and the type of institution you are applying to, so thorough research is essential.

Although you can apply for an undecided major, you will normally apply to a particular school within the university, for example, the School of Arts, School of Engineering or School of Management.

Application forms

From 1 August, the Common Application becomes available at www.commonapp.org. This is used by around 450 universities, although each university involved still retains its own deadlines, administration fees and requirements. All other universities require direct applications, so you may have a number of forms to complete. Even if you're not using the Common Application, most applications are similar, so you will not have to start completely from scratch with each one. There tend to be more sections to complete and more space available than on the UCAS application, so it can result in quite a lot of work. You will be able to copy and paste information, as long as you remember to amend and target it each time.

Universities tend to offer separate deadlines for early-decision and early-action applications, often sometime in November. The benefit of applying early is that you are being considered before the majority of applicants and competing with fewer students, so you might have a better chance of an offer. On the downside, you'll need to sit any admissions tests early. Most institutions offer either early decision or early action; some offer neither.

The main difference between the two is that early decision is binding, whereas early action gives you the comfort of knowing you have an offer, but with no strings attached. You can only apply to one university as early decision and you are committing yourself to that university if they offer you a place. This demonstration of commitment can have its benefits for consideration by the university and for scholarships. You might choose early decision if you have your heart set on one specific university, but it could be risky if the amount of scholarship or financial aid you are offered will play a part in deciding where you study.

Regular admissions deadlines come a little later, often in December or January. Check individual institutions for full details.

Undergraduate admissions tests

You will need to check whether an admissions test will be necessary. Many universities will be looking for both good grades and strong admissions-test scores; this is particularly so if you are applying for academic merit-based scholarships (see Help with finances on page 209). Where an admissions test is required, the amount of importance placed upon the test scores varies between universities.

Most universities ask for the American College Test (ACT) or the Scholastic Assessment Test (SAT) for undergraduate-level study; both tests are designed to assess academic potential. If the university accepts both, you will be able to choose which test to sit. Although the tests are both well-recognised and essentially achieve the same objective, the tests themselves are different and you may find that one will suit you more than the other. The SAT originally set out to measure aptitude, while the ACT was achievement-based, although both have changed since their inception.

The ACT includes more questions, so you end up with less time per question; it includes English, reading, science and higher maths. It comprises a single test, which may be more convenient, but is only available in limited locations across the UK. For the more competitive universities, you are likely to have to complete a supplementary 30-minute writing section (in addition to the nearly three-hour-long ACT test). It costs around $70 (£43), plus $16 (£10) for the written section.

The SAT comprises a reasoning test of nearly four hours, plus two or three subject tests for the more competitive universities. The test is widely available in the UK, but both tests are taken on different dates. It costs nearly $90 (£56) for the reasoning test, around $60 (£37) for the first subject test and $13 (£8) for subsequent basic subject tests.

It is essential to be prepared for these tests. Take a look at www.fulbright.org.uk/study-in-the-usa/undergraduate-study/admissions-tests/preparing-for-the-sat-act and www.collegeboard.org to help you prepare.

Sitting a test in early autumn of year 13 in England and Wales, Y14 in Northern Ireland or S6 in Scotland, is ideal, as it gives you time to resit, if necessary. Some candidates choose to take their first test as early as the previous spring. Candidates need to register sometime between spring and mid-September. It is worth registering early as places can quickly fill up. You can register and find a testing centre through the ACT website, www.act.org, and the SAT website, www.sat.collegeboard.org.

Essays

Essays are likely to be based on your response to specific questions set by the university; make sure that you answer the questions fully and directly. They may want to find out about your skills and personality traits; why you want to study at this university; what are your goals; and what inspires you. Although you might choose to write on a subject related to your area of interest, you do not normally have to do so. The Fulbright Commission (www.fulbright. org.uk/study-in-the-usa/undergraduate-study/applying/essays) has examples, video tips and useful handouts on this subject.

Sample questions for the Common Application essay (University of Virginia).

- Discuss some issue of personal, local, national or international concern and its importance to you.
- Indicate a person who has had a significant influence on you and describe that influence.
- Describe a character in fiction, a historical figure or a creative work that has had an influence on you, and explain that influence.

Transcripts

The transcript should include predicted grades from your current qualifications, but also your progress from year 10 (Y11 in Northern Ireland or S3 in Scotland) onwards. It could include GCSE or National 5s, details of any exams taken since then (AS levels and so on), results of mock exams or other internal assessments and any academic honours achieved. Where relevant, ask your school or college to include explanations for any anomalies in your academic record. Qualifications may also need to be explained and details of the institution incorporated.

The format of the transcript is generally chronological. It should be around a page in length and produced on official headed paper. You will need to work with your school or college to help them prepare this, directing them to sample transcripts, such as those on the Fulbright Commission website (www.fulbright.org.uk).

On the application form, you'll be asked for your GPA. The Grade Point Average cannot be officially converted from UK qualifications, so you should leave this section blank.

Recommendations

You will need to arrange two or three letters of reference or recommendations from staff who know you well; follow your chosen university's guidelines on whom to ask. The restrained and often modest tone taken in a UCAS reference might not be enough for a US university. Recommendations from US schools tend to be far more detailed and far more positive, so you will need to prepare your referee to really sell you. Refer potential referees to the Fulbright Commission website for tips and sample letters, www.fulbright.org. uk/study-in-the-usa/undergraduate-study/applying/reference-letters.

The EducationUSA website (www.educationusa.info) explains why you might choose to waive your right to see a copy of the recommendation

> " A recommendation form may include a waiver where you can relinquish your right to see what is written about you. If this option is offered, most admissions officers prefer you to waive your right so that recommenders may feel more comfortable when writing their evaluations. Admissions officers usually interpret waived recommendations as more honest. "

Financial statement

How will you fund your studies in the USA? Your university
will want to know, so you will need to complete any requests for
evidence. You can use the evidence again when applying for a visa.
You will need to show that you can at least cover the first year's
costs, maybe even the costs for the length of the whole course. If
you need financial assistance, you should include how much will
be required. In most cases, a 'need-blind' admissions system means
that your application will not be affected by this evidence.

Interview

These days, the internet and Skype are typically used for
interviewing. You may be surprised to find yourself being
interviewed by an ex-student. Alternatively, the interview may be
with a member of admissions staff. They may come to the UK or
may ask you to go to the States, in which case you could enquire
about help with travel expenses.

You could be asked why you have chosen this university, how you
will contribute and why you intend to study in the USA. They will
want to know about your subject interests, whether you have any
ideas about your major or what your strengths and weaknesses are.

To prepare, you should look over the research you did when
choosing this university. You can read over the essays you sent
and look at how you can expand upon what was written. You
should prepare questions to ask of the interviewer, but make sure
that any questions aren't already answered in the university's
prospectus or website.

Offers

Early-action applicants get an answer in December or January,
while regular applicants hear later in the spring. The response
could be one of three options: accepted, wait list, or not accepted.

Those accepted can choose to accept, decline or defer. (Deferring is rare, so you should always check the process with your university. Even if your university agrees, any offers for funding might not also be deferred.) A deposit of around $500 (£311) will secure your place.

If you are placed on a wait list, there is still a possibility that you will be offered a place; follow any instructions you receive about the wait-list process and keep your fingers crossed.

Your offer won't be conditional, but it is still important to work hard and do well. You may gain university credit or advanced standing from good UK qualifications.

Applying for graduate school

As with undergraduate admissions, students apply direct to their chosen universities. The Fulbright Commission suggests restricting applications to between four and six institutions.

The details of deadline dates, entry requirements and application fees will vary, although most will require some of the following:

- application form
- fee (around $50 to $100 (£31–£62) per university)
- admissions test scores
- a few essays (of around 500 to 750 words)
- research statement
- transcript (details of your academic performance)
- two or three recommendations
- possibility of an interview.

Each application may be different but, rather like a job application, you should be able to adapt the information you provide, rather than starting from scratch each time.

Most universities will be looking for at least a 2:2 from UK undergraduate study, with the more competitive universities looking for considerably more. They will be looking at your all-round offer, not just academic achievements, but also the way you demonstrate a good understanding of your chosen university and how this matches you as an individual. US universities are also keen to know about your involvement in extra-curricular activities. Contact the universities direct to discuss their requirements.

Much of the information in the previous section on applying for undergraduate study will also apply to postgraduate applications (see page 197). Notable differences include the research statement and the different admissions tests.

Research statement

The research statement allows you to outline your areas of interest, specialism and plans for how and why you intend to complete your research. Here are some of the key points that you need to consider when writing a research statement.

- Sum up your current plans for research, understanding that they may well change as you refine your ideas or as other developments occur.
- Relate your plans to your chosen university department and professors.
- Demonstrate your intellectual skills, but without alienating the admissions staff who may be considering your application.

Graduate admissions tests

Most postgraduate options require an admissions test and there are a number of different tests to consider:

- Dental Admissions Test (DAT), www.ada.org/dat.aspx
- Graduate Management Admissions Test (GMAT), www.mba.com
- Graduate Record Exam (GRE), www.ets.org/gre
- Law School Admissions Test (LSAT), www.lsac.org
- Medical College Admission Test (MCAT), www.aamc.org/students/applying/mcat.

The cost of these tests can be quite substantial, with DAT costing $385 (£239) and MCAT $355 (£220). Some tests are available across the country, with others restricted to London, and the DAT currently only being tested in the USA.

How the tests are used also varies, with some tests being a central factor in a successful application, while other tests are considered along with a variety of different aspects. In some cases, looking at how your scores compare to last year's averages can help to indicate your chances of success.

Preparation is vital, as the system tends to rely quite heavily on multiple-choice testing. Remember that you will be competing with US students who are used to this style of testing, so you need to know what to expect. See the individual test websites for sample papers or use the Fulbright Commission's 'Preparing for Admission Exams' page at www.fulbright.org.uk/study-in-the-usa/postgraduate-study/admissions-tests/preparation.

You could study . . .

Associate degree in Construction Management
Baton Rouge Community College, Louisiana
Two years
Apply by 18 August (financial aid applications by 15 April)

Annual fees $7,422 (£4,610)

Annual living costs $7,459 (£4,632)

Bachelor's degree in Mathematics

University of Virginia (public)

Four years

Apply by 1 January (early-action application by 1 November)

Annual fees $39,844 (£24,748), merit scholarships are available

Annual living costs $9,717 (£6,035)

Master's degree in Hispanic-American Studies

Rice University, Houston, Texas (private)

Two years

Apply by 1 January

Annual fees $38,941 (£24,187), financial aid available for
international students

Annual living costs $12,600 (£7,826)

Visas

If you plan to study in the USA and you aren't a US citizen or a
permanent resident in the USA, you will need a visa. Find out
about the rules and the procedures at Embassy of the US, London
(http://london.usembassy.gov).

You should apply for your visa at a US embassy or US consulate
before you leave the UK. There are two visa categories, F-1
Student Visa and J-1 Exchange Visitor Visa; F-1 is for students
undertaking a full-time programme in the USA, while J-1 is for
those on study-abroad programmes or exchanges. Your university
will tell you which one to apply for. There are differences in
restrictions on these two visas: whether you can work, for example
(see page 212).

> ❝ After you receive your visa you will need it upon
> entry to the USA and then again for opening
> accounts etc. After this you should store it carefully. Be
> aware of things that may impact on it, for example, if you
> decide to travel or get a job. ❞
>
> *Simon McCabe, University of Missouri, USA*

Once you have been offered a place at a university and provided
evidence as to how you will fund the first year of your studies,
your institution will prepare a Form I-20 (F-1 visa) or Form
DS-2019 (J-1 visa); you will need this to apply for your visa.
The university will also send instructions as to how to apply.
The process will involve a visa interview at the US Embassy in
London or the US Consulate in Belfast, as well as completion of
an online SEVIS I-901 form (requiring a $180 (£111) fee for J-1
or $200 (£124) fee for F-1) and an online visa application or MRV
(requiring a $160 (£99) fee).

If your application is successful, you will normally be admitted
for the duration of your student status. You should check any
visa restrictions and follow them to the letter, as breach of these
conditions is an offence.

Costs and help with finances

Tuition fees in the USA can be considerably higher than across
the rest of the world. However, weigh this up against a strong
tradition of financial aid and things might not always be
as expensive as first anticipated. One third of international
undergraduate students in the USA have a scholarship as their
main source of funding, while two-thirds of undergraduate
students receive some form of financial support.

Costs

According to the College Board (www.collegeboard.org), the following average annual tuition fees are reported for 2012/2013:

- four-year, public institutions (out-of-state students): $21,706 (£13,482)
- four-year, private institutions: $29,056 (£18,047).

Fees for out-of-state students at two-year community college should be around $8,000 (£4,969) per year.

> If you are looking at ways to make US education more affordable, you could consider taking a year or two at a community college before transferring to a university.

You should allow in the region of $10,000 to $12,000 (£6,211 to £7,453) per year for accommodation, food, books and materials, travel and so on. Costs could be higher than this as they will vary depending on where you live and the type of lifestyle you lead. Universities will provide an idea of local living costs on their websites.

The USA comes in at number 34 of 102 countries on a cost-of-living ranking from Numbeo (www.numbeo.com). This suggests that its living costs are more reasonable than the UK, Canada, Australia, New Zealand and much of northern Europe.

Help with finances

Research carried out by EducationUSA reveals that in 2010/2011 more than 1,000 universities supported their international students in the following ways: some awarded amounts of over $10,000 (£6,211); some offered options costing under $20,000 (£12,422) per year (including fees, accommodation, travel etc);

while others brought costs below $20,000 (£12,422) with financial aid or scholarships.

While you cannot access the UK student loans and grants for overseas study, there may be some alternative options available. You should be researching universities and investigating funding concurrently, since your choice of university will impact on your options for certain scholarships or financial aid. Start early and consider that support will often be pulled from a number of sources:

- scholarships from universities
- scholarships from external bodies
- sports scholarships
- savings or personal loans from the UK
- financial aid.

Much of the additional funding you may be applying for comes direct from US universities. Scholarships are allocated based on a range of criteria: merit, achievements, financial need, talents or personal background (country of origin, gender or ethnicity). Use the admissions or financial aid pages on the university's website to find out which institutions offer scholarships to UK students. Keep in mind that, even if you are lucky enough to get a scholarship, it is unlikely to cover all your costs.

The amount of financial aid varies between colleges. For example, if you have the brains to get into Harvard and your family income is under $65,000 (£40,373) per year, then you would not have to pay anything. The threshold is $75,000 (£46,584) at MIT (Massachusetts Institute of Technology). Further financial aid is awarded on a sliding scale for family income over these amounts up to around $150,000 (£93,168).

> You might be able to speed up your studies, and thereby reduce some of your costs, by taking additional courses each semester or gaining credit over the summer break.

Sports scholarships are a highly competitive option and you will need to start the process even earlier than for a mainstream application. Applicants must meet and maintain academic standards, while also having the sporting talent to participate at varsity (inter-university) level. Scholarships are awarded for a range of sports, with opportunities for UK students in soccer, golf, athletics or swimming, for example.

Certain sporting associations will require scores over a particular level on SATs or ACTs. You can make contact with university coaches direct or use the services of an agent, who will often charge a fee. Both EducationUSA and the Fulbright Commission have handouts on their websites taking you through each option.

There are a range of external bodies that offer scholarships, each with their own specifications and deadlines. Try this web page for more details of organisations you might want to contact: www.fulbright.org.uk/study-in-the-usa/undergraduate-study/funding/external-funding-bodies.

The following websites will help you get started on your search for funding:

- www.educationusa.info
- www.edupass.org/finaid/databases.phtml
- www.iefa.org
- www.internationalscholarships.com.

Cultural differences

If you have watched enough Hollywood films, you may feel that you already know the USA. You may have heard of Thanksgiving and Spring Break and you probably have some ideas about campus life. Therefore you might not expect to experience culture shock when leaving for this western, English-speaking country. Although the changes won't necessarily be too extreme, it may still take a little while to adjust and feelings of homesickness and uncertainty are normal.

Meeting new people and making friends are important to help you start to feel at home. It may be tempting to stick with other international students, but if you want to get to know the real America, you will need to meet some Americans. As a nation, they are much more open than the Brits, so introduce yourself to hall mates and classmates or get involved with activities.

> 66 Yale is, obviously, a top-class institution, but what drew me to it was the sense of community that I found there. Yale splits its students into colleges, akin to the ones at Oxbridge, which fosters a collaborative atmosphere for social and academic activities. 99
>
> *Stephanie Addenbrooke, Yale University, USA*

Drinking is less of a way of life than in the UK. The legal age is 21 and many university events, and even whole campuses, are dry.

Working while studying

It may be possible for you to work while you are studying in the USA, but it is essential to follow the rules to the letter. Remember that breaking employment law could lead to deportation. The information here should provide some of the basic details to get you started. For the latest rules and regulations, talk to the university's international office. You should check with them before taking on any work or voluntary commitments.

Full-time students on a Student Visa (F-1) can work 20 hours per week on campus. If you're on an Exchange Visitor Visa (J-1), you may request permission from your international office to work 20 hours per week on campus, but this is not guaranteed. You must have all appropriate paperwork, including SEVIS I-20, passport and Social Security Card – speak to your university for more information. Campus jobs might include library, cafeteria or office work. It makes sense to wait until you have had time to adjust to your new country before you start looking for work.

Paid, off-campus employment is possible on an F-1 visa through Curricular Practical Training (CPT), but it must be an integral part of your degree curriculum. If you are interested in CPT, look out for courses where an internship or practicum (practical work in a particular field) is required. Technical courses, like engineering, or vocational courses, like special education, might require this type of experience.

On an F-1 visa, you may be able to gain work experience during your studies in the USA and to work for up to one year on an Optional Practical Training (OPT) scheme; it is possible to do this during your studies, although most students opt to do it afterwards. The work is paid and at a professional level but must be related to your field of studies as listed on your SEVIS I-20. You will also need permission from the US Citizen and Immigration Services. If you have a J-1 visa, you could request permission for a period of Academic Training.

Staying on after study

Once your course has finished, unless you have further study or Optional Practical Training lined up, it will be time to return to the UK. You normally get 30 (if you have a J-1 visa) or 60 (if you have a F-1 visa) days' grace at the end of your studies, which you could spend tying up your affairs or seeing some of this vast country. If you have any queries about when you should leave, try your university's international office.

Occasionally, some students get job offers which mean that they can stay on and eventually apply for a green card, giving the right of permanent residence. Alternatively, if close family are permanent residents of the USA, they may be able to sponsor you to stay on permanently. Don't go to the States banking on the chance to stay; these opportunities are the exception, rather than the rule. You can find out more at the website for the US Citizenship and Immigration Services, www.uscis.gov.

Pros and cons of study in the USA

Pros

- Some of the most highly rated universities in the world.
- More international students choose the USA than anywhere else.
- Opportunities for financial aid or scholarships for international students.
- Great facilities and campuses.
- English-speaking country.

Cons

- Few opportunities to stay on permanently.
- High university tuition fees.

Student story
Stephanie Addenbrooke, Yale
University, USA

When it was time for Stephanie Addenbrooke to decide on her university subjects, she realised that it was going to be a difficult decision. 'The English higher education system asks students to decide on one subject for their studies, and solely study that subject for three or four years. While this was ideal for the majority of my friends, I felt constrained because I was interested in so much – I was not ready to make that decision. Also, the rise of tuition fees in England made me consider other options.

'The American liberal arts education is very broad and allows students to explore numerous interests. The colleges wish to graduate well-rounded students, and so there is a greater emphasis on getting involved outside of the classroom.'

Stephanie is studying a liberal arts degree and she hasn't had to decide on her major subject yet. 'The style of learning is very similar to A levels in that you are taking multiple subjects at once. Because of this, each of my classes feels very interdisciplinary. For example, there is a Math major in my English class, who brings a different perspective to the texts compared to a History major, for example.

'Yale is, obviously, a top-class institution, but what drew me to it was the sense of community that I found there. Yale splits its students into colleges, akin to the ones at Oxbridge, which fosters a collaborative atmosphere for social and academic activities. Also, Yale's admissions process is need-blind, which means that I was able to apply without worrying that my inability to pay would hinder my chances.

'Yale's grant system means that I am essentially only paying what I can afford to go to college. I have the opportunity to graduate with no or minimal debt – the complete opposite to my friends studying in the UK. Yale also includes a student job in its grant packet, which means I can work on campus in order to earn extra money. As well as the financial benefits of this, I will also have established a resumé and gained experience that will help me when looking for jobs post-graduation.

'The US university application process is very different to the system in the UK. It is considerably longer, involves standardised testing, and each school can ask their own application questions separate to the standard application. However, while this can be stressful and time-consuming, it means that your application is much more a representation of yourself. For the most part, US college admissions are holistic and consider you as a whole person, not just your grades. This was one of the most rewarding aspects of US college admissions – when I got admitted to Yale, I felt like they were admitting me, not my quantitative data.

'The process of applying for a visa was relatively stress-free – it was a lot of paperwork and involved a trip to the embassy, but in hindsight, it was not really something I felt like I needed to worry about.

'Yale is incredible in its support networks. All students, but freshman especially, have so many resources at their fingertips that it is sometimes difficult to keep track! As an international, I receive even more support. The most helpful support network that Yale offered was the Office of International Students and Scholars' five-day orientation programme at the beginning of the semester. The international students were acquainted with Yale's campus ahead of everyone else, were assisted in practical issues such as getting a cell phone or bank account, and we were prepped for life in America.

'Yale tries to link you with support for all outlets. I have a writing partner who is helping me adjust to US college essays. All freshmen have a freshman counsellor who is there to help us become acquainted with college and with Yale. We also have more formal academic advisors, and then less formal "older siblings" in our residential colleges.

'I have had minimal difficulty adjusting to life here, but I think that's due to Yale's community aspect. I genuinely feel like I've been welcomed into some sort of family that is looking out for me. Also, I guess that Britain and America aren't too different culturally, so that hasn't been too much of an issue. One of the hardest parts was Family Weekend – a tradition that Yale has where parents can come and visit. My parents weren't able to go, and it was kind of awkward to be surrounded by everyone and their parents. The same goes for breaks when people go home. That being said, I have been inundated with offers of places to stay and Thanksgiving dinners. I was spoilt for choice!'

Stephanie's top tips

Accommodation

'If you get the option, I would recommend living with American students. Some schools offer international houses that some people find benefit in, but I have found living with Americans made my transition easier because they were able to help me with cultural (and even language) differences.'

Food

'The food is different! It was actually one of the hardest cultural shifts I experienced, mainly because it is something you can't really shy away from. I do get my parents to ship over some of the British classics once in a while, which is not only exciting, but sometimes pretty helpful! Americans all assume the only thing British people drink is tea, so expect to be asked about it frequently.'

Making friends

'Get involved, especially early on! The first couple of weeks will be spent with everyone getting to know each other – there is no stigma about asking for someone's name and introducing yourself, because no one knows anyone. Extra-curricular activities and classes are also a great way to meet people with common interests.'

Best sources of information

'The Fulbright Commission was my first source of information. I was one of the students on their Sutton Trust programme, which obviously lends itself to an insane amount of support. The College Day that they offered was of great help to me – I was able to meet representatives from multiple

US colleges, and get a feel for what study in the USA, and at the individual schools, would be like.'

Stephanie has already begun to experience some of the benefits of studying abroad. 'You automatically have something special and interesting that no one else does. Your professor and friends will initially remember you as the "one with the British accent". Yes, this can be frustrating, but it also makes for interesting conversation starters – people want to hear all about your background, and will try and untangle some of their predetermined perceptions of your country. I also know that upon graduating, I will have something to make me stand out on my resumé. After all, not everyone has the courage to study away from home for four years.'

Yale University (www.yale.edu) is a prestigious Ivy League university which includes five US presidents amongst its alumni.

Chapter 7
Studying in Canada

If you're looking to get more for your money than in the UK and considering a country with a good quality of life where you may be able to stay on afterwards, Canada has a lot to offer. As many as 2,319 UK students are already out there enjoying the benefits (OECD Education at a Glance 2013).

The education system

The education system in Canada is run by a separate Ministry of Education in each province or territory. Each region has consistent standards and it is fairly easy to move between them. Courses are taught in English or French although some institutions teach in both languages.

The academic year runs from September to May and is divided into two semesters. Fall term runs from September to December and winter term follows from January to May. Some institutions offer a trimester system, with an additional summer term starting from May onwards, although there may be more limited programme choice at this time. Although it is possible to join courses in the second (and sometimes the third) term, September intake is the most common.

University study

More than 10,000 undergraduate and postgraduate degree programmes are available at a range of public and private (not-for-profit) universities and university degree-level colleges. The majority of universities in Canada are public. Canada's education system is considered to be of high quality, with investment in research and development at universities in Canada almost twice that of any other G8 nation. Canada can also boast seven universities in the 2013–2014 Times Higher Education World University Rankings Top 200. Bachelor's, master's and doctoral degrees are comparable in level to those from the UK.

How to find a course

The official Study in Canada portal is a good starting point for your research; it features a course finder for international students and links to information from the 10 provinces and three territories, as well as links to the individual institutions, www.educationau-incanada.ca.

The Association of Universities and Colleges of Canada (www.aucc.ca) features a course search, as well as university profiles, facts and figures, and information on quality assurance.

Accreditation and quality

You can check that your chosen institution is accredited by using the Directory of Universities, Colleges and Schools in the Provinces and Territories of Canada. You can find this at www.cicic.ca (Canadian Information Centre for International Credentials). The listing includes all public and accredited institutions, as well as some private establishments.

Undergraduate study

Bachelor's degrees from Canada take three or four years to complete. In some cases, an honours degree is part of the degree programme; in other cases, it is taken as an extra year of study. You will generally be looking at four years of study for an honours degree.

Four-year applied bachelor's degrees offer a more vocational option, combining academic study with the development of the more practical skills needed for employment. If you're looking to incorporate work experience, co-op programmes are similar to sandwich courses in the UK, providing the opportunity to work as well as gain academic credentials. It is worth noting that certain competitive fields, like medicine, may not always be widely available to international students; your university will be able to advise you of any issues.

Differences from education in the UK

A key difference in Canadian education is that the degrees tend to be much more general than you would expect in the UK, particularly when compared to England, Wales and Northern Ireland. Although there will be certain programmes you must study to achieve your major, you will have the option to study a range of additional subjects. For the first two years you might be choosing programmes from general sciences or general arts, for example, before starting to specialise.

> ❝ My best subject in school was maths and so that's what I decided to study. However, I have always had a wide range of interests so I wanted the flexibility to do other things as well. ❞
>
> *Lauren Aitchison, University of Waterloo, Canada*

Higher education in Canada takes place in universities, university colleges and community colleges. Some universities are research-intensive, with others focusing purely on teaching, in contrast to the UK, where all universities tend to carry out both teaching and research. The institution's website (or the institution's staff) should reveal what type of institution it is.

Associate degrees

Some students may choose to take their first year and second year
at a community college, studying for an associate degree, before
transferring to a university to achieve a bachelor's degree. In
some cases, community colleges and universities work together
to provide a joint programme. Colleges tend to offer applied
(rather than purely academic) studies, smaller classes (university
classes can be large, particularly in years one and two) and lower
tuition fees. There is some snobbery and colleges are sometimes
considered to be the second choice to university. Associate degrees
take two years on a full-time basis and are broadly equivalent to a
Certificate of HE in the UK.

Entry requirements

Much as in the UK, each university sets its own admissions
requirements and publicises the minimum qualifications required.
High-school graduation in Canada is at a similar level to A levels
or Advanced Highers in Scotland; universities will generally be
looking for applicants educated to this level. Community colleges
may have slightly lower entry requirements. Your institution will
be able to tell you more, including whether they have any additional
requirements, for example, for competitive or specialist subjects.

If you intend to study in French, the institution will talk to you
about the level of French they require and whether an assessment
of your skills will be necessary.

Postgraduate study

Postgraduate courses are available at some, but not all,
universities in Canada and include master's and doctoral degrees.
Postgraduate study in Canada includes coursework, although less
than at undergraduate level, alongside research. The courses tend
to be based around seminars and will involve large amounts of
structured reading, particularly in the early years.

Most master's degrees take two years to complete and don't always require completion of a thesis. Doctoral degrees (for example, PhDs) last between four and seven years, with a dissertation forming an essential component of the qualification. It is sometimes possible to move straight from an undergraduate honours degree to a doctoral degree. In these cases, the doctoral degree will often incorporate the master's degree.

What we know as 'postgraduate study' in the UK is more commonly known as 'graduate study' in Canada and the USA.

For those intending to follow a regulated profession like law, medicine or social work, a licence to practise is granted following success in academic study and a relevant internship.

Entry requirements

Institutions will normally require an honours degree for progression to postgraduate study, although some exceptions are made for those with substantial work experience. Three-year degrees from the UK (and other parts of the European Higher Education Area) should meet the general entry requirements for postgraduate study in Canada.

Academic recognition

Your chosen institution may already know and understand the qualification you are applying with; in which case, they may accept your certificates without further evaluation. If the qualification is unfamiliar, or if they are less experienced at dealing with international qualifications, you may need to pay to have your qualification evaluated. Talk to the admissions staff to see whether evaluation is required, as you may save yourself some money if you don't need this service. The Canadian Centre for International Credentials (www.cicic.ca) will provide further information on how to proceed.

Applying

Your first step when applying should be to contact the international office requesting application documentation. They should send you information about the application procedure and timescale, along with requirements for the evaluation of qualifications, the costs of study and the visa-application processes.

Alberta, British Columbia and Ontario each have a centralised application service, while Quebec has a number of different regional systems. You will find that many individual institutions require direct application. Applications may be paper-based or online. Applications will incur a fee, often well in excess of the £23 required by UCAS. If you are applying to a number of universities in various provinces, you may have to pay more than once. Remember to factor in this cost when working out the costs of study. Careful research and narrowing down your choices should help to reduce these costs, and the additional work required by multiple applications.

Application deadline dates vary between provinces and between individual institutions. International applicants are normally required to apply between December and early spring for September start, in the autumn for January start, and around January for start dates in the summer. Graduate application deadlines may be earlier, particularly for the more competitive courses.

Start planning for your application a good year in advance. Bear in mind that evaluation of qualifications, the need to sit admissions tests and the time taken for international post may slow the process down considerably. You should expect a decision around four or five months after the deadline date, although this will also vary between institutions.

The application form

The application form itself is likely to be quite a small part of the application process, requiring basic information about the applicant's:

- personal details
- contact details
- education
- test scores
- relevant professional experience (where applicable)
- referees.

Further documents required in support of an application could include:

- transcript
- letter of intent/statement of purpose
- essay or sample of writing
- letters of reference
- proof of immigration status.

A CV, medical form and portfolio may be required for certain courses. Similarly, a criminal records check will only be required in certain cases.

There will be an initial deadline date for the application and a later date for the provision of the supporting documentation. Some institutions won't consider an application until all documents are received, so send all documents promptly to improve your chances.

Transcript

A transcript is an academic record produced by your school, college or university. It might include details of your education and progress from year 10 in England and Wales, year 11 in Northern Ireland or S3 in Scotland. It will include exam and mock-exam results, internal assessment results and predicted grades; it should include any special awards or recommendation, as well as an explanation of any problems or anomalies in your educational attainment.

Letter of intent or statement of purpose

This is a key part of the application and may determine whether you are accepted. Use the statement to explain your interest, any relevant experience and what you hope to achieve with the qualification. You need to demonstrate your suitability and your potential. Try to analyse your experiences and remember to back up any claims you make about your strengths with examples. Explain any discrepancies or gaps in your education.

At postgraduate level, you should incorporate an outline of the research you intend to undertake. Consider what interests you about this area of work, how you intend to approach the research and illustrate how the research will fit in with the focus of the department.

The statement needs to be well written and free from spelling and grammatical errors. Two typed A4 pages should be sufficient.

Letters of reference

A letter of reference should be a positive document that provides details of your skills, strengths and achievements; a detailed, targeted letter is much more helpful than a general one. You will need to find two or three academic staff who know you well and can comment on your capabilities and really sell you.

Provide your referee with details of the courses you are applying for, along with a copy of your statement and transcript. You could suggest some of the key skills you would like them to draw attention to.

The referee will need to illustrate their own academic competence and background. The referee should provide specific examples of your strengths, since any claims should be backed up by relevant evidence. It may be useful for your referee to compare your achievements and skills to others that they have taught.

Give your referees around one month to compile the letters. It is helpful to gently follow them up to check that the letters have been completed. Thank them for their efforts; you may need to use their services again.

Tips, sample references and standard reference forms are available on university websites. See the University of British Columbia, www.grad.ubc.ca/prospective-students/application-admission/letters-reference, and McGill University, www.mcgill.ca/law-admissions/undergraduates/admissions/documents/#LETTERS, for some examples.

Admissions tests

Canada does not have a standardised university entrance exam; universities have their own admissions requirements. In most cases, UK students shouldn't need to take admissions tests for undergraduate courses.

Entrance exams required by Canadian graduate schools include the GRE (Graduate Record Examination), which can be taken across the world (www.cts.org/gre). It is available as a computer-based test in the UK and costs US$185 (£109). Other tests include the Graduate Management Admissions Test (GMAT) for business studies (www.mba.com), LSAT for Law School (www.lsac.org) and MCAT for Medical School (www.aamc.org/students/applying/mcat).

Different universities use the results from these tests in different ways. In some cases, the result will be a deciding factor; in others, the result will be just one of a number of considerations. Ask your chosen institution how they use the results and what kinds of scores previous applicants have achieved.

You are likely to do better in these tests if you are prepared for the style of questioning and any time limits for completion. Books and courses are available to help you prepare. You can take tests like the GRE more than once, but the costs can end up being quite substantial if you do so.

What next?

If you are successful in gaining a place at a Canadian college or university, you will be provided with a letter of acceptance. The next step will be to apply for a study permit.

You could study . . .

Associate of Arts degree Creative Writing
Camosun College, Victoria, British Columbia
Two years
Apply by 1 August
Annual fees C$13,000 (£7,692)
Monthly living costs of around C$1,000 (£592)

Bachelor of Arts and Sciences (Hons)
McMasters University, Hamilton, Ontario
Four years
Apply by 1 April via OUAC International (www.ouac.on.ca)
Annual fees C$20,988 (£12,419)
Annual living costs C$11,000 (£6,509)

MSc Biochemistry (research)

University of Alberta, Edmonton, Alberta

Two years

Application deadline dates vary by department

Annual fees C$8,220 (£4,864)

Annual living costs C$900 (£533)

Visas

A study permit is required for anyone who will be studying for more than six months in the country; you will need to apply to the Canadian High Commission in London. To gain a study permit, you will need to prove that you can pay your tuition fees plus living costs of around C$10,000 (£5,917) per year. You will also need to be in good health and without a criminal record. Follow all instructions carefully and allow around 10 weeks for processing. There is a processing fee of C$125 (£74).

There are different immigration requirements if you study in Quebec, where a *certificat d'acceptation du Québec* (CAQ) from the Immigration Service of Quebec is required prior to entry to Canada. See www.immigration-quebec.gouv.qc.ca/en/immigrate-settle/students/index.html.

If your chosen university or college welcomes lots of international students, the staff should be experienced in supporting applicants through the immigration procedures.

Further information on the procedures and how to apply can be found at www.cic.gc.ca/english/study/index.asp.

Costs and help with finances

Canada promotes itself as being more affordable for international students than the USA, Australia and New Zealand.

Costs

Tuition fees across the provinces and territories of Canada
vary. According to Imagine Studying in Canada (the Council of
Ministers of Education), university tuition fees range from around
C$8,000 to C$26,000 (£4,733–£15,385) per year, with college fees
of between C$5,500 and C$15,000 (£3,254–£8,875) per year.

Overall, international undergraduate students paid annual
tuition fees averaging C$19,514 (£11,547) per year in 2013/2014.
The average fees varied across subject area: C$18,365 (£10,867)
for humanities degrees, C$21,810 (£12,905) for engineering
and C$29,198 for medicine (£17,277). International full-time
postgraduate students paid an average of C$13,628 (£8,064) per
year (www.statcan.gc.ca).

> ❝ The cost of study has been a lot more expensive but
> now that the fees in the UK have gone up, the
> difference is much less. The fees are approximately C$8,000
> (£5,037) per semester. I also received an entrance scholarship
> and a second scholarship in my second year. ❞
> *Alex Warren, University of British Columbia, Canada*

Some research-based postgraduate study is subsidised and the fees
can be lower than undergraduate fees. To calculate more specific
costs for the courses and institutions you are interested in, the
Imagine Studying in Canada website has a useful cost calculator
at www.educationau-incanada.ca/educationau-incanada/template-
gabarit/education_cost-cout_education.aspx?view=d.

To compare the cost of living in Canada to the rest of the world,
try the Numbeo Cost of Living Ranking at www.numbeo.com.
Canada is ranked number 20 of 102 countries, suggesting that it
is cheaper than the UK, Australia and New Zealand.

Help with finances

If you're looking for a scholarship to help offset the costs of international study, be prepared to start your research early, more than a year ahead. Consider how you will support yourself, as scholarships are limited, highly competitive and may not cover the full costs of your studies.

Talk to your chosen university about any scholarships they offer and take a look at the Canadian government's website as a starting point, www.scholarships-bourses.gc.ca/scholarships-bourses/index.aspx?view=d.

Scholarships include the Canadian Commonwealth Scholarship Program, Vanier Canada Graduate Scholarships and Trudeau Scholarships. There are more opportunities for postgraduate than undergraduate study.

Other sources of information include:

- Commonwealth Scholarships: http://cscuk.dfid.gov.uk/apply/scholarships-uk-citizens
- Scholarships Canada: www.ScholarshipsCanada.com.

Cultural differences

Canada is considered to be a tolerant and multicultural society and it welcomes students from across the world. Canadian culture shares much with its neighbour, the USA, but there are differences. The province of Quebec is French-speaking and culturally quite different from the rest of the nation. Parts of Canada show a particularly British influence, including Toronto and Victoria.

Adjusting to the sheer size of Canada can be a shock, as well as getting used to the long, cold winter in much of the country.

> **"** I knew it was cold in Canada but the UK really doesn't prepare you for a Canadian winter. I wish I knew to invest in a good winter coat and pair of snow boots! **"**
>
> *Lauren Aitchison, University of Waterloo, Canada*

Citizenship and Immigration Canada has some helpful information on culture shock, as well as on adjusting to life and the weather in Canada at www.cic.gc.ca/english/newcomers/after-life-shock.asp.

Working while studying

Full-time degree-level students can work on campus at their university or college without any special permission. You will need a work permit to work off campus; the permit allows you to work up to 20 hours per week during term-time, and full-time in the official holidays. If you are taking a spouse or partner with you, they can apply for a work permit too.

Citizenship and Immigration Canada should tell you all you need to know about working while studying, co-op programmes and internships, and working after graduation, www.cic.gc.ca/english/study/work.asp.

Staying on after study

The Canadian authorities have a number of programmes that allow students to stay on in Canada after completion of their studies. Remember that these schemes change from time to time and may even have changed by the time you complete your studies.

Post-graduation work permit programme

Graduating students can apply for a permit of up to three years, depending on the length of their studies, see www.cic.gc.ca/ english/study/work-postgrad.asp.

Canadian experience class

Graduating students have the opportunity to apply to stay on in Canada permanently; you will need to meet various conditions including at least one year's Canadian work experience in a managerial or professional occupation or the skilled trades. See www.cic.gc.ca/english/immigrate/cec/index.asp for details.

Provincial nominee programme

If you are considered to offer the skills, education and experience to make an immediate economic contribution to your province, you may be able to gain residence under this scheme, www.cic.gc.ca/ english/immigrate/provincial/index.asp.

If you are leaving Canada, you can still remain connected through the Global Canadian Alumni Network. The nearest Canadian embassy or High Commission will be able to tell you more.

Pros and cons of study in Canada

Pros

- Good quality of education.
- High investment in research and development.
- Opportunities to stay and work after graduating.
- Possibility of emigrating after graduating.

Cons

- Certain competitive fields may not always be widely available to international students.
- Different systems in place in the different provinces.

Student story
Lauren Aitchison, University of
Waterloo, Canada

Lauren Aitchison spent her childhood in the UK, but decided to venture further afield for her university education. 'I decided to study overseas because I wanted a change. I wasn't excited about the courses and universities in the UK but I was about Canada. It was also an opportunity to meet new people and get out on my own. It's really improved my confidence in my decisions.'

It turns out that Canada was the obvious choice for Lauren. 'I have Canadian citizenship and my parents also studied at Canadian universities so it made sense to at least check it out. You get a great education for a cheaper fee. Also with extended family in the country, I have been coming here for holidays all my life, so it wasn't a massive culture shock. My grandma lives an hour from my university so I try to visit her as much as possible.

'My best subject in school was maths and so that's what I decided to study. However, I have always had a wide range of interests so I wanted the flexibility to do other things as well. University of Waterloo is known for its maths and engineering faculties and is one of the top universities in Canada. They also have the only mathematics faculty in North America. This means that I graduate with a Bachelor of Mathematics instead of a Bachelor of Arts or Science like at most other universities. I am getting a good education here where I take mostly maths courses but, for my course, I have to take a certain amount of breadth courses or electives. This way I can take other subjects that interest me like psychology, economics, and history.

'I think my heart was always set on going to Canada. I only visited one university in the UK despite applying to five. The courses didn't really excite me. I then went on a trip to Ontario with my mum to visit some of the universities. I also did some research online. In Canada, there is a magazine called MacLeans that ranks the universities under different categories such as teacher quality and student happiness. I went to this for information first. From there, I just used the university websites to look at courses offered.

'Ontario has a similar application process to UCAS in the UK. It is called OUAC (Ontario Universities' Application Centre). My careers adviser at school didn't know anything about the application process so I just threw myself into it and figured it out as I went along.

'I applied to three universities in Ontario: Toronto, Western, and Waterloo. Waterloo was the first university that sent me an information package and the others followed after. From there it was all about the waiting. No one wants to get rejections but in a way I was hoping that I would get some so it would narrow it down for me. I ended up getting into seven of the eight universities I applied to.

'One major factor in choosing my university is what we call the co-op programme. Waterloo has the biggest co-op programme in the world that we know of. Co-op is a chance for students to take what they learn in the classroom and apply it to the workplace, much like an internship but better. Students alternate four-month work terms with four-month study terms and complete up to six work terms in maths. During your work terms you are like a normal employee, not simply an intern. You have a high level of responsibility and are expected to bring something to the table. You are also paid during your term. Students can earn between C$25,000 and C$80,000 (£14,793 and £47,337) if they are employed for all of their work terms, and then they come out with up to two years' work experience. It's something different for the CV.

'The high-school education system in Canada seems to be a bit more relaxed than that in the UK. I think, because of this, students coming from Canadian schools find university more of a shock. I found the transition pretty easy. The professors teach with similar methods to teachers in school using things such as PowerPoint and writing on the board. In maths, we get weekly assignments from each class for the first two years, which is just like school. The obvious difference is the class sizes are a lot bigger. Coming from the UK, I had studied some areas of maths that were covered in first year (this was nice because the first few lectures weren't as daunting) but there were also some things that I hadn't learnt that others from Canada had. The first year is about getting everyone on the same page, which I can imagine is similar in the UK.'

There is plenty of support on offer too, should you need it. 'Academically there is lots of support available. There are upper-year tutors for help with assignments, and professors are very approachable. I also like to use my advisers. There are advisers for each course and for the co-op programme who can answer your questions or direct you to the person who can.'

Lauren is finding Canada to be the cheaper option for her studies, but this won't necessarily apply to every student. 'With the increase in UK university fees, Canada is actually cheaper for me. I pay on average C$7,000 (£4,142) for eight months of tuition. However, I am a Canadian citizen so I do not need to pay international fees that are considerably higher. They vary depending on programme but can be around C$20,000 (£11,834). This is a bit more expensive than education in the UK.'

She didn't experience too many challenges when adjusting to life overseas. 'Adjusting wasn't too hard. Everyone is starting university new in the first year and I wasn't the only international student either. It's easy to meet new people. The only bit I find difficult is keeping in contact with family and friends back home. With the time difference, it's especially difficult.

'In Canada we have additional holidays to those in the UK, like Thanksgiving and Family Day, which give us some long weekends. These are hard sometimes because everyone goes home and I don't get to see my family as much as others.

'I haven't had any negative experiences as such, more like difficulties that I've had to adjust to. For example, I have a car here and when it breaks down, I can't call my dad to help. I need to take it to the garage myself. Little things like that aren't too hard but make you realise that you are growing up. It's scary sometimes.'

Lauren's top tips

Accommodation

'Stay in a traditional-style accommodation residence. You share a bathroom with maybe 10 people and have small rooms but it's all about the experience. It's a great way to meet lots of people when you first arrive at university, and people who are all new to the experience surround you.'

Keeping healthy

'We have something at our university called the "Frosh 15" (or Freshers 15). It is said that, as a first year, you put on 15 lb staying in residence because there is so much food and not all of it is good for you. So stay healthy, so you are in the best condition to enjoy school!

'University of Waterloo has a health-insurance policy for all students, unless you opt out of it. Lots of things are covered such as dentist visits and contact lenses so I would definitely investigate the insurance plans that your university might have.'

Living costs

'Living costs vary depending on the area in which you are going to be living. Waterloo has lots of student housing so there are a range of prices depending on what you are willing to pay. Our local grocery store has a 10% off for students on Tuesdays, so you'll need to find out things like this to save some money. Every little bit counts!'

Scholarships

'Waterloo offers a lot of entrance scholarships for students coming in with high grade averages and for students who maintain high averages throughout their studies. You need to look into what is offered where you decide to go.'

Part-time work

'I wouldn't get a job until you know your workload. If you have the extra time, then a part-time job is a great way to earn a little bit of spending money and have something extra to add to your CV! It shows that you have good time management as you are able to be in school and hold down a job. See if there are jobs available on campus. I work part-time as a student ambassador for the university and it's really nice to give something back.'

Lifestyle

'Look into what makes your university town or campus unique. In Waterloo, there are lots of shops and places to eat but there are also cute little places like the town square, which is converted into an ice rink in the winter. And we have a local market where you can buy locally grown food for cheaper prices. Also join clubs or sports teams if you have time. I am on the varsity hockey team and it's given me an automatic group of friends and a good stress relief and break from school.

'I knew it was cold in Canada but the UK really doesn't prepare you for a Canadian winter. I wish I knew to invest in a good winter coat and pair of snow boots!'

Travel

'If you are going to study in a different country, find the time to travel around the country outside of the university bubble. It helps to broaden your knowledge and gives you a change of scenery from libraries and lecture halls.'

Plan for the future

'Find your university's career services. Ours helps with CVs, postgraduate studies, entrance into professional schools and advice on what to do after finishing studies. Start thinking about what you want to do early, so that you're not stuck after university without a plan. My course is five years' long so I have two years left to decide. Through co-op I am hoping to find an area I like working in, or at least decide what I don't want to do. In the long term, I would like to come back to London because of its central location in the world but if I find a job I love here, maybe I'll stay in Canada for a few years. It's still up in the air.'

Lauren has many positive things to say about the whole experience. 'One of the best bits is the opportunity to meet new people of all different cultures. The Canadian people are so friendly and open that it really makes you smile. Also you can travel and go to places you've never been before. I've visited Toronto multiple times and taken trips to places like Ottawa. You can get your local friends to show you around. I've been in Canada so long now it feels like home. I like having two places I can call home.'

University of Waterloo (www.uwaterloo.ca) is based in the 'Silicon Valley of the North' and is considered to be one of Canada's most innovative universities. It is ranked among the top 250 universities in the world, according to the 2013–2014 Times Higher Education World University Rankings.

Seneca College: Profile

With more than 3,500 international students from 111 countries, Seneca College has a proud history of welcoming the world. Located in Toronto, Canada's largest city, Seneca offers a diverse, multicultural college community. Our four main campuses across the Greater Toronto Area offer modern, cutting-edge learning facilities.

Seneca's four-year bachelor's degrees, two-year and three-year diplomas and one-year graduate certificate programmes are designed with input from business and industry leaders to help lay the foundation for your success. Choose from over 140 full-time programmes, each offering unique theoretical and applied learning opportunities.

Our reputation for excellence is supported by many partnerships with universities throughout Canada and around the world. These partnerships represent exciting pathways to further education and academic opportunities. As a Seneca student, you'll also have the chance to gain valuable work experience through the co-operative education programme.

The Seneca experience is unique and there's lots of flexibility while you're in your programme, both in class and in your co-op work placement. Once you've completed your programme, you can keep studying at Seneca, you can go on to university, or you can start working.

Transitioning to life in Toronto and at Seneca is easy with the help of International Student Services. The friendly staff will assist you with housing and accommodation, academic advice, study and work visa inquiries, orientation sessions, trips and activities. Our aim is for our students to be as comfortable as they can while still enjoying the independent experience of being away from home.

STUDYING ABROAD

Studying abroad is an incredible and lasting experience. Whether you decide to return home after graduation or stay in Canada to pursue a career, Seneca will help you to become the person you want to be. To find out more visit www.senecacollege.ca/international or contact seneca. international@senecacollege.ca.

Seneca College: Case study

UK student graduates top of her class from one of Canada's largest colleges

Ekta Tachkani from Surrey, England recently graduated from the eight-month Fraud Examination and Forensic Accounting Graduate Certificate programme at Toronto's Seneca College.

After completing her honours bachelor's degree in Business Management in the UK, Ekta decided to advance her career in the specialised financial area of forensic accounting and fraud investigation. Ekta chose Seneca because of its world-renowned reputation for providing high-quality education. She also wanted the experience of studying and staying in Canada, a country full of diversity and vibrant culture. Ekta says the programme was exceptional and attributes her success to the encouragement she received from her professors.

During her time at Seneca she excelled in her studies and was very involved campus life, serving as a Student Ambassador during college events and working part-time in the Student Services and Career Services offices.

Ekta's passion and determination did not go unnoticed by the faculty. She was nominated as the Valedictorian for the Class of 2013 by the Chair of Seneca's School of Accounting and Financial Services.

At the Convocation Ceremony last June, Ekta addressed the graduating class, as well as their family and friends.

'I came to Canada to study not so long ago from the United Kingdom. Whilst I adore my country, I have come to love and admire your beautiful country. I am amazed by your respect for diversity and the equal educational opportunities offered to people wishing to learn – even international students like myself,' she said to the audience of more than 1,000 people.

'This great institute has proved that no matter where one comes from or who they are, it has trained us to become future leaders and we all can achieve brilliance together.'

Ekta also thanked her mum who was seated in the front row for all the support and encouragement she provided as a single parent.

'We are forever grateful because Seneca is the place that has made our dreams come true. My education from the Fraud Examination and Forensic Accounting programme has taught me so much for a lifelong rewarding career,' Ekta continued. 'I have enjoyed every moment of my time with my fellow classmates, including the laughter and struggles we each endured on our path to success.'

Ekta now plans to study for the Certified Fraud Examiner exam and gain some valuable work experience in Canada.

With campuses across the Greater Toronto Area, Seneca offers degrees, diplomas and certificates renowned for their quality and respected by employers. Combining the highest academic standards with practical, hands-on learning, expert teaching faculty and the latest technology ensures Seneca graduates are career-ready.

For more information, please visit www.senecacollege.ca/international.

Chapter 8
Studying in Australia

What makes UK students choose to travel halfway around the world to experience study in Australia? Perhaps it's down to the combination of good-quality education, great lifestyle and reasonable entry requirements. Many UK students are already convinced, with 1,540 of them enrolled in Australia when the last checks were made (OECD Education at a Glance 2013); that's a 26% increase since 2002.

The education system

A significant difference between the UK and Australia is the academic year, in Australia, this runs from February to November. Universities tend to run a two-semester year with semester one running from February to June and semester two from July to November. It is possible to start most courses in July, although some courses, including medicine and dentistry, are only available to start in February. The long summer holiday runs from December to February.

University study

The style of teaching tends to be slightly different from that in the UK, focused on practical learning to encourage independent thought and discussion. The approach is less formal, but equally challenging. You will need to share your views on subjects and may even be assessed on your class participation. In fact, you will probably be assessed in a range of different ways, in recognition of the fact that individual students learn in different ways.

Independent study and the development of critical thinking are encouraged, much as in the UK. You might find that you have more contact hours and a closer link with the lecturers than you would generally get in the UK.

Nearly all of Australia's universities are public, with only a few private universities. Undergraduate and postgraduate study can be offered at both pass and honours level.

How to find a course

You could start your search with the official Australian government site, www.studyinaustralia.gov.au. Use the handy study wizard to research courses or institutions, check entry requirements and create a shortlist. Study in Australia also includes a mini-site for students from the UK at www.studyinaustralia.gov.au/uk.

Accreditation and quality

It is fairly straightforward to ensure that you will be studying with an approved provider. The institutions that are approved to offer degrees and other higher-education qualifications can be found on the AQF Register at www.aqf.edu.au/register/aqf-register.

Australia also has an Act in place to ensure that institutions taking on international students support them adequately; this might include helping students adjust to life in Australia as well as helping them to meet their learning goals. Go to www.cricos.deewr.gov.au to discover the list of institutions that meet these requirements.

> 66 I find it seems to be more personal than at UK
> universities. Our class is quite large, but somehow
> you still manage to feel a personal connection with the
> lecturers; they really try to get to know you and give you
> great feedback on assignments and how you're going
> throughout the year. 99
>
> *Kadie O'Byrne, Murdoch University, Australia*

Academic recognition

If your institution takes lots of international students, they may
understand your UK qualifications and accept you without the
need to compare their standard to those offered in Australia. If
the qualification is not known to them, they may ask you to have
your qualifications assessed. There is no need to get an assessment
done until your institution tells you to; you will have to pay for the
service and it might not be needed. If required, they will put you
in touch with AEI NOOSR (Australian Educational International,
National Office of Overseas Skills Recognition), see www.aei.gov.
au/Services-And-Resources/Pages/AEINOOSR.aspx.

Undergraduate study

Undergraduate study tends to take three to four years in
Australia, with a strong emphasis on coursework. Certain courses,
like medicine, can take as long as six years. Unlike the UK,
ordinary or pass degrees are the norm, generally taking three
years. Access to an honours degree is reserved for those who
have achieved particularly well. A bachelor's degree (honours)
would normally take at least four years and requires independent
research and the completion of a thesis.

The system allows for more flexibility than you get in much of the UK. You choose a major and study a fixed number of relevant courses, but you will also have the chance to study a range of elective courses in different subjects. You might start off majoring in one subject and end up graduating with a major in a different subject, based on your interests and abilities as you proceed through your studies.

A degree with honours is achieved after completing an ordinary bachelor's degree with high achievement. It is different from an honours degree.

Vocational education

TAFE (Technical and Further Education) and VET (Vocational Education and Training) colleges may also offer some higher-education courses. They tend to offer more vocational courses that prepare you for an industry or trade. Vocational higher-education qualifications include associate degrees and AQF (Australian Qualifications Framework) advanced diplomas, both of which are similar in level to HNDs or foundation degrees in the UK.

Entry requirements

If you have passed three A levels or equivalent study, then you should meet the general entry requirements for degree-level study in Australia. Certain university courses require particular grades and specific subjects to have been studied previously, while some courses will require a selection test or audition. On the whole, grade requirements tend to be slightly lower than in the UK. Programmes like medicine and dentistry are competitive, requiring high-achieving applicants with some relevant experience. Associate degrees or advanced diplomas may have lower entry requirements, although they may require specific experience or relevant previous study.

> **❝** The grading process is different. Instead of getting a first, 2:1, 2:2, you are awarded high distinction, distinction, credit or pass on each of your assignments, exams or units. **❞**
>
> *Vicky Otterburn, Murdoch University, Australia*

Postgraduate study

A range of different graduate qualifications are available, including graduate certificates and diplomas, master's degrees and doctorates.

- Graduate certificates (one semester) and diplomas (two semesters) are the shortest postgraduate options. They are of a similar level to postgraduate certificates and diplomas in the UK and can be used as a bridge to the study of a new subject at postgraduate level.
- A master's degree by coursework (or taught master's) tends to take two years. It may include a minor thesis.
- A master's degree by research generally takes one year after a bachelor's (honours) degree, or two years after an ordinary or pass degree.
- Doctor of Philosophy (PhD) takes from three years.

The length of your postgraduate study depends on your academic background and the subject you choose to study.

Entry requirements

The successful completion of an undergraduate degree is the standard entry requirement for postgraduate study in Australia. For some courses, you may also be required to demonstrate relevant work experience or previous research.

Entry requirements vary between institutions and their departments. The institution will be able to tell you more or you can browse institutions, using the study wizard, at www.studyinaustralia.gov.au.

Applying

There are some centralised admissions services in Australia, but in the vast majority of cases, international offices require direct applications. Alternatively, some students opt to apply via an Australian educational agent (see page 106).

Closing dates fall in the autumn for courses starting in February. You need to apply to university in good time to give yourself a chance to get a visa and to sort out all the other aspects of a move overseas. Certain courses, like medicine and dentistry, require a much earlier application; likewise, if you're applying for a scholarship as well, you may need to start the process much earlier. Ideally, you should be preparing for your application a good year in advance.

The application form

Contact your chosen institution requesting information about the application process and an application form. Application forms can often be completed online. If paper-based, the application might be sent direct to the institution. Alternatively, you may choose to deal with an agent or local UK representative, depending on the requirements of the university or college.

The application process is more straightforward than the UK system. When applying direct to an institution, you will choose a first preference for your course, along with second and third options. The institution may charge you a fee to apply, ranging from around A$50 to A$100 (£30–£60). Certain fees may be waived when applying online or through some educational agents.

Other documents

Alongside the application, you will be asked to provide an academic transcript with details of any qualifications gained, as well as details of units and unit grades. Proof of existing qualifications will be needed. If you are applying before your qualifications have been completed, you are likely to receive a conditional offer and will have to provide proof of qualifications once the results come out.

Some courses, but not all, require a personal statement and an accompanying academic reference.

Admissions tests

In some cases, an admissions test will be required. Your institution will tell you more.

If a test is required, please make sure that you are prepared. Although you may not be able to revise, preparing yourself for the style and time constraints of the test can make a big difference.

Undergraduate admissions tests

Applicants to medicine, dentistry and health-science courses at certain universities may be required to sit either the UMAT (Undergraduate Medicine and Health Sciences Admission Test, www.umat.acer.edu.au) or the ISAT (International Student Admissions Test, www.isat.acer.edu.au). Both are available in the UK.

Postgraduate admissions tests

Postgraduate tests used in Australia include:

- the Law School Admissions Test (LSAT), www.lsac.org
- the Graduate Australian Medical Schools Admissions Test (GAMSAT), www.gamsat.acer.edu.au.

> If an interview is required as part of the admissions process, you may be interviewed online or over the phone.

What next?

If your application is successful, you will receive an offer letter. Once the offer is accepted and the required tuition fees are paid (generally the fees for one semester), you will be sent an electronic confirmation of enrolment (eCoE). You will need this document to apply for a visa.

You could study . . .

Bachelor of Antarctic Science
University of Tasmania, Hobart
Three years
Apply up to 4 weeks before semester start date
Annual fees A\$22,226 (£13,151)
Annual living costs A\$12,000–A\$14,500 (£7,100–£8,580)

Master of Environment (coursework)
Australian National University, Canberra
1 year
Apply by 12 December for February start
Annual fees A\$30,000 (£17,817)
Annual living costs A\$19,812 (£11,723)

PhD Disaster Response and Resilience
University of Western Sydney
Three years
Apply by 15 November for February start
Annual fees A\$12,380 (£7,325)
Annual living costs A\$18,610 (£11,012)

Visas

In order to apply for a student visa, you will need your eCoE and the ability to financially support yourself throughout the course; this includes the cost of tuition fees, return air fare and A$18,610 (£11,012) living costs. Remember, you may need more money than this to live on.

A further condition is adequate health insurance whilst you are in Australia. You will also need to meet certain health requirements and may be required to show evidence of your good character.

> The new streamlined visa process (SVP) means that applications for degrees at participating universities require less evidence and are processed more quickly.

This information is a basic introduction to the visa process; contact the Australian High Commission in London (www.uk.embassy.gov. au) for the latest application procedures and fees information. You should be able to apply online and fees are currently set at A$535 (£317). You shouldn't apply more than four months in advance and should normally expect your application to be processed within four weeks. Ask your institution if you need further support; they are likely to have experience in this process.

Further information on applying for a study visa can be found at www.immi.gov.au.

Costs and help with finances

Even the cheapest Australian undergraduate degrees cost more than those on offer in England, while the most expensive courses far exceed English fees. Scottish, Welsh and Northern Irish students will pay more in Australia than at home. So Australia is not a cheap option, but it does have some great benefits in terms of quality of education, lifestyle and opportunities.

Costs

Fees vary between different universities. According to www.studyinaustralia.gov.au, you can expect to pay annual tuition fees as follows:

- bachelor's degree – A$15,000 to A$33,000 (£8,875–£19,527)
- master's and doctoral degree – A$14,000 to A$37,000 (£8,284–£21,893).

Lab-based courses and those requiring specialist equipment are likely to be at the higher end of the fees' scale, with courses in arts or business towards the lower end. Courses such as medicine and veterinary science will be significantly higher. Remember to consider the cost of books, materials and field trips too.

All students in Australia pay a student-service fee of up to A$273 (£162) for campus services and student societies. Some universities incorporate this within tuition fees for international students, so check with your institution whether an additional payment is necessary.

The strong Australian dollar means that the cost of living in Australia is currently higher than in the UK, although it also means that earnings are higher too. Australia is currently listed at number three out of 102 countries on a cost-of-living ranking for 2013 at www.numbeo.com.

It is a requirement of the visa that you have adequate health insurance; the cost of overseas student-health cover (OSHC) starts at a few hundred pounds per year. According to the Australian Department of Health and Ageing, the average cost of minimum cover is A\$437 (£259) for 12 months. Visit www.studyinaustralia. gov.au/en/Study-Costs/OSHC/Overseas-student-health-cover for more details.

The following average weekly costs are provided by www. studyinaustralia.gov.au:

- accommodation: A\$80 to A\$400 (£47–£237)
- groceries and eating out: A\$80 to A\$200 (£47–£118)
- utilities (including internet): A\$80 to A\$150 (£47–£89)
- public transport: A\$10 to A\$50 (£6–£30)
- entertainment: A\$50 to A\$100 (£30–£59)

The Australian Trade Commission quotes average monthly living costs of A\$1,400 to A\$1,900 (£828–£1,124). To find out about finances and budgeting in Australia, go to www.moneysmart.gov. au/managing-my-money.

Help with finances

If you're hoping for a scholarship to help fund your studies in Australia, you need to start early and get ready to prove yourself, as competition is fierce. Scholarships are hard to come by and often don't cover all the costs, so think about how you will support yourself.

You can make a start by using the scholarship database on www.studyinaustralia.gov.au. You should talk to your university about any scholarships that they offer.

You could also take a look at the following websites:

- www.australiaawards.gov.au
- www.kcl.ac.uk/artshums/ahri/centres/menzies/ scholarships/index.aspx
- http://cscuk.dfid.gov.uk/apply/scholarships-uk-citizens.

Cultural differences

You will soon discover how multicultural Australia is; with one in four of its population born overseas, you are sure to come across other British people. Adjusting to Australia includes adjusting to its extremes of weather and its vast size. Find out about the climate in the different states and territories when you are deciding where to study.

The way of life in Australia is a bit different too; things are generally more informal and the good weather means that there is more time to enjoy life outdoors.

“ The Australian lifestyle is great! Everyone is so friendly, welcoming and laid back. Sport is a big part of the Aussie lifestyle; there are heaps of regular sports clubs and great facilities to use all year around. In the summer, people have BBQs regularly; you don't rush around because of the heat and spend a lot of time at the beach or around a pool with friends. There are lots of music festivals and events on offer. **”**

Vicky Otterburn, Murdoch University, Australia

Working while studying

The opportunity to start working as soon as you start your studies is a definite benefit of study in Australia. For new students gaining a student visa, there is no need to apply for extra permission to work 40 hours per fortnight in term time. You are permitted to work unlimited hours during holiday periods. Remember: there will be serious consequences if you break the conditions of your visa. The Australian Government Department of Immigration and Citizenship (www.immi.gov.au) has the most up-to-date and detailed information.

There are a range of opportunities in pubs, bars, restaurants and shops, but you will need to balance your study and your work. The national minimum wage is A$16.37 (£9.69) per hour, although some junior employees may get paid less than this.

You will need a Tax File Number (TFN) from the Australian Tax Office (www.ato.gov.au) to work and to open a bank account.

Staying on after study

Australia is keen to welcome international students and has introduced a number of changes to make it even more attractive. In early 2013, a new post-study work visa was launched. International students with a bachelor's degree or master's degree by coursework from an Australian university, and who are granted a visa, are now able to work for two years in Australia in any type of job. Students with a master's degree by research are able to sign up for three years' work and doctoral students for up to four years.

For those considering staying on a more permanent basis, Australia has a skilled migration programme targeting those who can contribute to the economy. The requirements and occupations needed vary, so choosing a course of study because it is on the skilled-occupation list is not a guarantee of success; the list may well have changed by the time your course is completed. For the latest details, see the Department of Immigration and Citizenship website at www.immi.gov.au/skilled/general-skilled-migration.

> **❝** There are many ways to stay after you have finished studying: applying for residency, applying for a work visa or a sponsorship by a company based on an employment opportunity. The studying is the easy part, finding the job is much harder, so many more people are going to university these days and it is much more competitive for places in the workforce. **❞**
>
> *Vicky Otterburn, Murdoch University, Australia*

Pros and cons of study in Australia

Pros

- Strong reputation for higher education.
- Reasonable entry requirements.
- Good pay for part-time work.
- Possibility of emigrating if you have the right skills.

Cons

- High cost of fees.
- High living costs (while the Australian dollar is strong and the pound is weak).

Student story
Joshua Jackson, SP Jain School of Global Management (Singapore and Sydney, Australia)

Josh Jackson took a big step when he decided to study abroad. 'I wasn't sure what I wanted to do for university. The headmistress of my school announced one morning in assembly that an institution was offering the possibility of 100% scholarship on fees and accommodation for four years. The new Global Bachelor's of Business Administration course required two years study in Singapore and ended with two years in Sydney, Australia.'

Getting a scholarship to cover his tuition fees resulted in a huge saving. 'The full cost of study would be about US$20,000 (£12,400) a year.'

Josh found the application process to be fairly straightforward. 'I had to write a short essay about myself. After that there was a written task with three questions that I needed to complete in a certain amount of time. Following that, I had an interview on Skype with one of the professors. The interview was very short and informal as I had met the professor around six months before on a week-long "bridge to BBA" event the university ran. This was a five-day event where students were invited to stay in university accommodation, meet the staff and spend some time in SP Jain and Singapore.

'The university sorted out the visa for Singapore for me. A few days after we arrived, the university staff took us to the immigration office where we were given the visa. For Australia, we had to apply for the visa ourselves but the university provided us with a code we needed once we had paid the tuition fees. A few days after the application went through, I was instructed to have a medical at one of a small number of panel doctors in the UK. Around seven working days after the medical, my visa was granted and I was able to fly over.

'Sorting out of the Singapore visa was the single most useful thing the university did. They also put me in touch with a current student who could answer my questions and the head of the student council emailed all the new students to give them some information before they came.

'Since I arrived, I feel the university does not help very much. They helped us get health insurance in both countries and the former dean and student counsellor were very helpful to the students in every way possible, but other than that we are very much on our own. The most important aspect of this is that although the master's degree graduates often get 100% placement, there is currently no facility in place to help us get jobs when we graduate, which many find very concerning.'

Josh has coped well with adjusting to life on two new continents. 'In the two and a half years I have been away I have had about two nights where I felt homesick, but other than that I have enjoyed the experience greatly. Some of my peers have felt very out of their comfort zone and struggled somewhat, but there are people from almost all round the world so finding someone quite similar to you is not too hard.'

He explains about some of the differences in teaching and learning that he has experienced. 'Due to the small size of the institution I actually have a very close relationship with all of my professors.

Classes rarely, if ever, exceed 30 students whereas I have friends in the UK who have lectures with 400 or more students. I think this is a huge benefit, as well as the fact many professors teach master's degree students as well and so are very highly qualified and knowledgeable.'

Joshua's top tips

Accommodation

'Staying on-campus is always useful at first for making friends. Staying off-campus is usually cheaper, sometimes by quite a long way, but normally less convenient.

'I have stayed on-campus in both countries. In Singapore, the city is so small and transport so cheap it doesn't matter where you stay, but in Sydney the city is very expensive. I stay in Wentworth Point, near the Olympic Park, and it is very removed from the city centre. Travelling up to central Sydney takes over an hour, and almost two hours to reach the east coast of the city.'

Food

'The cuisine in Singapore is a huge mix of different cultures, mostly traditional Asian Chinese but also influenced by Indian and western food. They also have most of the large fast-food chains as well (McDonald's, Subway, KFC etc). Traditional Singapore hawker centres were a great place to go to eat like the locals. The food was cheap and quick but good and tasty as well, almost like a Singaporean version of fast food!'

Insurance

'Our school provided us with health insurance policies in both Singapore and Sydney. In Sydney it was mandatory to have health insurance to get the visa.'

Living costs

'Singapore was very cheap compared to where I live in England. At the time I was there, it was around two Singapore dollars to one British pound, but you could get a fast-food meal for around S$5. Going out to the movies and drinking was also cheaper.

'Australia is about as expensive as London as far as I can tell, though I have only been here for a few months. I buy almost everything non-branded, eat at home every day and rarely go out drinking.'

Financial support for study

'I have a 100% scholarship on my tuition fees but pay for accommodation. This is conditional on the basis that I get within the top 25% of the class throughout the year.'

Working while studying

'In Singapore I did not have to work, but I was told the pay was not very good as there is no minimum wage. Working in Australia is pretty good though. I am able to work 20 hours a week during term time and an unlimited amount during the holidays. The pay is far better than England for unqualified jobs. However, there do seem to be a few licences around that you need to get before working. For example, I needed to pay A$100 (£60) to get a "Responsible Service of Alcohol" (RSA) licence.'

Making friends

'Making friends was never that hard. Everyone is in the same position, away from home and starting a new chapter of their life. Many had never studied away from home before, and almost everyone had never studied in a different country to their home.'

Lifestyle and culture

'The lifestyle in Singapore is very metropolitan, busy, and Asian; they are more traditional, hierarchical and family oriented. It is definitely a hybrid between typical Western and Eastern lifestyles, a good stepping stone between England and Malaysia, for example.

'Australian lifestyle and culture is very like England's, but more relaxed and with a slightly heavier influence on sport and relaxation.'

Travel and transport

'Public transport in Singapore was very good and cheap. Taxis were cheap as well and very useful when you couldn't use public transport.

'In Sydney, though, the transport is not as good and quite expensive. The buses are still quite costly, especially for a student. Getting to the city is quite a hassle and taxis are very expensive.'

Options for after you finish your studies

'I am not very sure about options after I finish, though both places seem a little easier to get a job after graduation than England. The pay in Singapore is not that great in comparison, but in Australia you get paid very well and there are more job opportunities than in England.

'The best things about studying overseas have been experiencing a new culture and travelling; seeing a completely different way of life, cuisine and society has been truly amazing. As I am in each place for two years, I really get a feel for it as opposed to going on holiday somewhere for a few weeks. The travelling has been amazing as well. Going from Singapore to Indonesia, Malaysia and Thailand is as simple as visiting France, Germany or Spain from England, and often cheaper! There are so many travel opportunities in Australia as well that I am very much looking forwards to experiencing.

'Overall, studying abroad is completely what you make of it. You really have to go out there and immerse yourself in the place you are studying to fully enjoy it. If you keep yourself to yourself and only look at why it is worse than home, you won't enjoy it.'

SP Jain (www.spjain.org) was originally established in Mumbai, India in 1981 and now has campuses in Dubai, Sydney and Singapore and achieves high global rankings for its MBAs.

Chapter 9
Studying in New Zealand

New Zealand might seem like a long way to go for an education, but many international students choose the country for its safety, quality of life and the option to settle after studies. According to a 2013 survey, over 6,500 UK students are already studying there.

New Zealand is a little larger in area than the UK, but with a population of only 4.5 million.

The education system

Much as in Australia, New Zealand's academic year runs from late February to November. The academic year incorporates two semesters, each lasting 12 weeks. You can expect breaks mid-semester and at the end of semester one, with a longer summer break after semester two (from November to February). It may be possible to join certain courses in July or as part of a summer school between November and February.

At all levels, students in New Zealand are encouraged to develop independent thought and defend their ideas in discussion and debate. Most taught courses are assessed by means of exams and classroom activities, which could include essays, assignments, presentations, projects and practical work. Make sure that you get involved in class activities; your participation may be assessed here too.

All eight of New Zealand's universities are publicly funded. There are also a range of other institutions with degree-awarding powers: polytechnics, colleges of education and wānanga.

- Polytechnics, or institutes of technology, originally specialised in technical or vocational studies, but now offer a range of subjects and research activities.
- Colleges of education, for the most part, offer studies in the fields of early-years, primary and secondary education.
- Wānanga provide mainly vocational educational opportunities that include Māori tradition and culture.

There are also private training establishments offering degree-level education.

How to find a course

Take a look at New Zealand Educated (www.newzealandeducated. com) to search for programmes at universities, institutes of technology, and polytechnics. The site also features a scholarship search option, as well as useful information about study and life in New Zealand.

For more detailed information on options at postgraduate level, try New Zealand Postgraduate at www.newzealondpostgraduate.com.

Accreditation and quality

New Zealand has strong quality systems for education. In order to verify that your course or provider is accredited, you can search for approved qualifications and recognised institutions at the

New Zealand Qualifications Authority website (www.nzqa.govt.nz/ search).

Five of New Zealand's eight universities can be found in the 2013–2014 Times Higher Education World University Rankings Top 400, with one of its universities featured in the Top 200.

As an international student so far from home, you need to know that you will be well supported. The New Zealand Ministry of Education has a code of practice that all institutions accepting international students must adhere to. The code requires clarity and accuracy in the information you receive before you apply; ensures that international students have access to welfare support and information on life in New Zealand; and explains grievance procedures, should things go wrong. It should help you to make an informed choice on where to apply and give you a realistic idea of the support you can expect once you arrive. For more details, go to www.minedu.govt.nz/NZEducation/EducationPolicies/ InternationalEducation/FourInternationalStudentsAndParents. aspx.

Undergraduate study

Bachelor's degrees in New Zealand tend to take three years to complete, although some subjects take longer, up to six years for a Bachelor of Medicine. Students must successfully complete each year before moving on to the next. High achievers may opt for an additional year of study to gain an honours degree, or choose a course of at least four years with honours already incorporated.

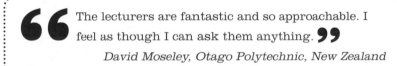

66 The lecturers are fantastic and so approachable. I feel as though I can ask them anything. 99
David Moseley, Otago Polytechnic, New Zealand

You can often be flexible in the direction your academic studies take you, having the opportunity to try out a range of subjects. It is not unusual for the major subject you choose when you apply to end up being different from the major subject you graduate in. Your university will guide you through the process of choosing the right core and elective subjects to achieve a major in your desired subject.

Stage 1 or 100-level courses are taken in the first year, stage 2 or 200-level courses in the second year, and stage 3 or 300-level courses in the third year.

It is possible to transfer credit and move between different institutions at tertiary level.

Vocational education

Qualifications in technical and vocational education are available at polytechnics, institutes of technology or in the workplace; some opportunities are available through universities and wānanga. Level 6 national diplomas could be compared to qualifications like HNDs or foundation degrees in the UK. If you decide to move from a national diploma to a relevant degree, it may be possible to transfer credit or to gain exemptions from the initial stages of the degree programme.

Entry requirements

Entry requirements in New Zealand tend to be lower than in the UK, as the smaller population means less of a demand for places. The grades required tend to reflect the academic level you will need to cope with the demands of the course. In most cases, you will need to have gained three A levels, or equivalent; some universities ask for three Cs at A level and there are additional grade requirements for certain courses.

At the University of Auckland, New Zealand's highest-ranking university, students need to achieve a minimum of CCC at A level to be considered for entry in 2014. There are additional course-specific requirements, for example, a minimum of CCC for Bachelor Education (Teaching), BBC for Bachelor Architectural Studies, and BBB for Bachelor (Hons) Engineering. They are not currently accepting international applicants to Bachelor Pharmacy, or for direct entry to Bachelor Medicine. If you are applying with alternatives to A levels, contact the university's international office via www.auckland.ac.nz/uoa/is-contact-auckland-international.

Postgraduate study

At postgraduate level, you might choose to study for a:

- postgraduate certificate
- postgraduate diploma
- master's degree
- doctoral degree.

All of these are of a comparable level to the same qualifications in the UK. Postgraduate certificates take one semester to complete, with postgraduate diplomas taking one year. Master's degrees tend to take two years (or less, if you have achieved an honours degree) and can be based on the completion of a thesis or have more of a focus on coursework. Doctorates would normally take three years to complete.

> If you are not ready for postgraduate study, perhaps because of your achievements at undergraduate level or maybe because you are changing subject, you could consider a graduate diploma.

Entry requirements

An undergraduate degree from a recognised institution is required to undertake postgraduate study in New Zealand. You generally need a master's degree to join a doctoral degree, although applicants with a bachelor's (honours) degree with a first or upper-second classification may also be considered.

Distance learning

New Zealand has a range of distance-learning providers offering education at degree level, including the Open Polytechnic of New Zealand (www.openpolytechnic.ac.nz) and Massey University (www.massey.ac.nz/massey/learning/distance-learning). Most tertiary institutions offer blended learning, delivering their education in a range of different ways (including online) to meet their students' needs.

Applying

Institutions in New Zealand require direct application, so the first step should be to contact the international office at the universities where you would like to study. They will provide all the information you need on how to apply and show you how to access the relevant application forms. They may charge an application fee. Some students choose to use the services of an agent, rather than dealing direct with the institutions.

Ideally, you should start the research process more than a year in advance, to allow time to apply for scholarships, apply for a visa and make the arrangements to move. You should plan to make contact with the universities at least six to eight months beforehand. Closing dates for applications to start in semester one (February) normally fall between September and December; to join programmes in semester two (July), you should apply by April or May. Restricted-entry or competitive courses often have an earlier closing date and some may only have a February intake.

The application form

The application forms tend to be a lot shorter and simpler than the UCAS form in the UK. You will need to provide personal details, information on your previous and current academic studies and your career plans. You will be asked for a first and second choice of degree, along with details of your intended major(s).

Applications are paper-based or online. If they are online, you will still need to allow time for certified or witnessed documents to be posted or couriered to New Zealand.

Other requirements

Other documents required include academic transcripts (with details of education and qualifications) and certificates. Academic references and written statements may be requested, along with portfolios and other evidence for certain courses. The institution will also ask for a copy of your passport. Copied documents often need to be certified or witnessed by someone in the legal profession or in another position of responsibility.

In addition, postgraduate applicants may need to provide two references and a CV, and may be asked to submit a research proposal.

In some cases, an interview over the phone or online may be necessary for undergraduate and postgraduate applicants.

Academic recognition

If your qualifications are unfamiliar to the international office, you may need to pay for an International Qualifications Assessment through the New Zealand Qualifications Authority: www.nzqa.

govt.nz/qualifications-standards/international-qualifications/apply-for-an-international-qualifications-assessment.

What next?

If your application is successful, you will receive an offer of admission. The next step will be to apply for a visa.

You could study . . .

BSc Geology

University of Otago, Dunedin

Three years

Apply by 31 October for February start

Annual fees NZ$26,565 (£13,623)

Annual living costs (term-time only) NZ$15,000–NZ$17,000 (£7,692–£8,718)

Master of Pacific Studies

University of Canterbury, Christchurch

Two years

Apply from October for February start

Annual fees NZ$26,100 (£13,385)

Weekly living costs NZ$300–NZ$350 (£154–£180)

Doctor of Mechanical Engineering

University of Auckland

Three to four years

Applications accepted throughout the year

Annual fees NZ$6,013 (£3,084)

Weekly living costs NZ$380–NZ$480 (£195–£246)

Visas

Once you have accepted an offer of admission and paid your tuition fees (or the appropriate deposit), you can start to apply for a student visa. You are also likely to have to provide a chest X-ray, police certificates (or criminal records check) and accommodation details, along with evidence of funds for living costs and air fare home. For courses of over nine months, you will need access to NZ$15,000 (£7,692) (as at November 2013) per year to cover your living costs alone; you may need more than this to live on. You will also need to take out adequate health insurance to cover you during your stay in New Zealand.

> **"** I found the experience of applying for a visa for New Zealand a little daunting at first, especially as there were several different types of visa which you could apply for. However, with helpful advice from my tutor at the University of Birmingham and from properly reading through the information provided on the website, the process was pretty simple. You had to prove that you had enough money to fund yourself for the year, which could be challenging for some, but because I had savings from a part-time job it was fine for me. I applied for my visa quite early on and it took about three weeks for it to arrive; however I know of some people who had some problems such as the date of return on the visa being wrong and the visa not actually being placed in the passport! So it is really important to make sure that you apply for your visa well ahead of leaving for the country, but also to check the visa information once you get it back.**"**
>
> *Madeleine Prince, Cawthron Institute, New Zealand*

When you apply for a visa for an undergraduate or postgraduate degree lasting over two years, if you hope to work, tick the boxes under 'variation of conditions' requesting permission to work up to 20 hours a week during the academic year and full-time during the Christmas and new-year holidays.

For full details of how to apply, rules and regulations and the latest fees, go to Immigration New Zealand (www.immigration. govt.nz). Further information can be found at the New Zealand High Commission in London (www.nzembassy.com/united-kingdom). You should allow four to six weeks for processing, although many applications are processed within 25 days. The fee is currently £135.

Most international offices have lots of experience in helping students through these processes. They will know the problems that previous applicants have encountered and should support you to make a successful application for a visa.

Once you have a visa, you will need to follow certain requirements in order to retain it, such as attending your course and achieving certain standards. Your visa will only last for a maximum of one academic year, so you will need to reapply for subsequent years of study. You may be able to renew it online through your institution in subsequent years.

Costs and help with finances

New Zealand is unlikely to offer a cheaper option for education at undergraduate level; some of the cheapest university undergraduate fees in New Zealand are comparable in cost to the most expensive in the UK. At postgraduate level, the costs can be higher than in the UK, although there is an incentive to study PhDs, making New Zealand a very attractive proposition.

Costs

Individual tertiary institutions set their own fees, which will vary depending on the course you choose. According to New Zealand Educated (www.newzealandeducated.com), annual tuition fees for undergraduate study range from NZ$18,000 to NZ$25,000 (£9,230–£12,820). Fees for courses at polytechnics or institutes of technology may be lower than NZ$18,000 (£9,230) per year, making them a more affordable option.

Postgraduate tuition fees for international students can be as much as NZ$40,000 (£20,513) per year. However, international PhD students pay the same fees as students from New Zealand, starting at around NZ$5,000 (£2,564) per year.

Although you will be required to prove access to NZ$15,000 (£7,692) per year for visa purposes, New Zealand Educated suggests allowing as much as NZ$20,000 (£10,256) for living costs. In comparison to the rest of the world, New Zealand is ranked number eight of 102 countries on a 2013 cost-of-living ranking at www.numbeo.com; the UK is listed just below at number 18.

Remember to budget for medical and travel insurance; international students are legally obliged to hold this throughout their period of study in New Zealand.

Help with finances

A range of scholarships are available, although you will need to compete with other applicants. Apply early, follow all the guidelines and be prepared to supplement any scholarship with other sources of funding; most scholarships will not cover all costs. Scholarships include the Commonwealth Scholarship and Fellowship Plan, and international doctoral research scholarships.

You can search for scholarships at www.newzealandeducated.com/int/en/institutions_courses/scholarships. This searches options including national and university-specific awards. Talk to your university or polytechnic about the range of scholarships they administer.

Take a look at the Commonwealth Scholarships website for details of their scholarships, awards and fellowships, http://cscuk.dfid.gov.uk/apply/scholarships-uk-citizens.

Cultural differences

New Zealand is a multicultural nation with an informal way of doing things. One in seven New Zealanders is Māori, so their language and culture forms an important part of the national identity. In New Zealand, you can expect an outdoor lifestyle with the opportunity to get involved with sports and a range of cultural activities.

Although there will be similarities to the UK, don't assume that life will be the same; there will be cultural differences. It is helpful to find out about the culture and way of life in New Zealand in order to prepare yourself for a successful transition. Talking to other people who have already made the transition can be helpful. There are many websites for expats that might help in this process. Your university's international office may be able to help too.

Working while studying

If you have ticked the relevant boxes on the student visa application (variation of conditions), you may be allowed to work up to 20 hours per week during academic term, and full-time during the summer holidays. Make sure you have permission before you start working and follow the visa requirements to the letter. Your right to work can normally be found on your student visa. You can apply for a variation of conditions at a later date, if necessary.

> **❝** Obviously getting a part-time job is useful; however, the reason you are on this year abroad is to study. I would advise making studying your top priority; make sure that the part-time job doesn't get in the way of that (or even in the way of socialising with your new-found friends). Sometimes a part-time job can hinder other exciting opportunities such as visiting other parts of the country at the weekend. It all depends which you feel is more important.**❞**
>
> *Madeleine Prince, Cawthron Institute, New Zealand*

Don't assume that you will find work immediately. It can be hard to find the right job to fit in with your studies and your visa requirements. You will also need to consider how you balance your academic studies and your working life. Take a look at Student Job Search for opportunities in your area, www.sjs.co.nz. You will need an Inland Revenue Department (IRD) number too. Find out more at www.ird.govt.nz/how-to/irdnumbers.

Staying on after study

If you hope to stay on in New Zealand after finishing your studies, there are a number of schemes currently in operation. The government is keen to retain young people with the right skills and knowledge to contribute to the New Zealand economy. If you hope to emigrate, you may decide to choose your subject based on skills-shortage areas at the time you apply; don't forget that these lists are subject to change and may well be different by the time you complete your studies.

If you don't have a job offer, you have the following options.

- **Graduate job search work visa**
  Recent graduates from tertiary institutes in New Zealand can apply for a visa of up to 12 months giving them time to search for a skilled job (and to work on a temporary basis while searching). Amongst other requirements, you will need to provide evidence that you can support yourself financially. On finding a skilled, long-term job, you can apply for a graduate work experience visa for two to three years.
- **Skilled migrant category visa**
  This is a points-based residence visa, with points gained for a job offer, experience, qualifications and so on.

There are a number of options if you are offered a job considered to be in a shortage area.

- **Essential skills visa**
  The essential skills visa allows those with a job offer to work in New Zealand on a temporary basis (provided a New Zealander cannot be found to do the job).
- **Long term skills shortage list (LTSSL) work category**
  If offered a job on the LTSSL, you can apply for a 30-month work visa; after two years, holders of this visa can apply for a resident visa.

- **Skilled migrant category visa**

  A job offer will enhance the points you can gain on this
  points-based residence visa.

For information on all these options and more, see www.
immigration.govt.nz/migrant. The information is complex and
subject to change. Your university may be able to put you in touch
with relevant sources of support for this process.

Pros and cons of study in New Zealand

Pros

- Range of internationally recognised qualifications.
- Support for international students.
- Reasonable entry requirements.
- Possibilities to stay on and work afterwards.

Cons

- Current costs of living.
- Far from home.

Student story
David Moseley, Otago Polytechnic, New Zealand

David Moseley is a passionate outdoor enthusiast. So much so, he packed his bags and travelled from the United Kingdom to picturesque Otago in New Zealand, to experience an area that is packed full of activities for the adrenaline junky.

'University fees in the UK tripled, so I thought "why not come to New Zealand for around the same amount?" ' David says.

The 19-year-old is based in the city of Dunedin, a coastal beauty spot and education hub, home to about 125,000 people. Because 25,000 of those residents are students, Dunedin offers a study experience unlike many other cities in New Zealand. Most students live in the north of the city around the campuses of Otago Polytechnic and Otago University, creating a truly unique student community.

David is in his second and final year of a Diploma in Outdoor Leadership and Management at Otago Polytechnic's Otago Institute of Sport and Adventure. This hands-on programme allows students to tackle a range of outdoor pursuits, and allows them to strengthen and develop technical, professional instruction and leadership skills relevant to adventure sports.

'I have always loved the outdoors and have quite a lot of experience in mountaineering, rock climbing and kayaking. This programme is just perfect for me because it encompasses everything I want,' David explains.

'I absolutely love it and can't say a single bad word about it. It doesn't feel as though I'm actually studying, I'm just having loads of fun!'

But at the same time, David admits he is learning a lot – and he has nothing but praise for the teaching staff at Otago Polytechnic. 'The lecturers are fantastic and so approachable,' he says. 'I feel as though I can ask them anything.'

Between a buzzing student social life and a raft of adventure opportunities in Dunedin, nearby Queenstown and Central Otago, David has no problems keeping his weekends full. 'I live in student accommodation in Dunedin so there's always something going on there! And town is so accessible, you can just walk everywhere.

'I love getting out amongst the breathtaking scenery. As part of the course we spend a lot of time in Central Otago, and it's amazing. The rugged landscape and the mountains are just beautiful.'

David is starting to plan for life after study and he already has a job lined up with a New Zealand sea-kayaking company once he completes the two-year programme.

'I love New Zealand – it's the adventure capital of the world!'

Otago Polytechnic (www.otagopolytechnic.ac.nz) prepares learners for successful and fulfilling careers in a wide range of trades, industries and professions. Offering a combination of theory and real-world learning, the institution works closely with industry and business. The polytechnic has a 91% student-success rate – the highest in New Zealand.

Chapter 10

The rest of the world

You might imagine that you wouldn't find students from the UK studying right across the globe; well, prepare to be surprised. Although a less common choice than Australia or the States, some UK students opt for South Africa, Qatar or Singapore as their place of learning. This chapter introduces you to some of the countries you might not have considered for your studies.

Countries where English is an official language

Hong Kong

Hong Kong is a special administrative region of China, offering a cosmopolitan lifestyle and a gateway to China. As Hong Kong was under British rule for many years, English is still an official language. Street signs and announcements on public transport are in English, Cantonese and often Putonghua (Mandarin).

Now under Chinese rule, Hong Kong has its own currency and political system and a separate identity from the rest of China.

Higher education in Hong Kong

Hong Kong offers a four-year bachelor's degree. Both ordinary and honours degrees are available, along with associate degrees at a lower academic level. Master's degrees will take one to two years, and doctorate degrees a minimum of three years to complete.

If you are interested in opportunities in China, you will
find that degrees from Hong Kong are compatible with
Chinese qualifications. Beginners' courses in Cantonese and
Putonghua will be available; some programmes even offer the
chance of a year in Beijing or Shanghai.

The academic year runs from early September to May, with
orientation activities taking place in late August. The year is split
into two equal semesters. Hong Kong features 15 degree-awarding
institutions made up of a combination of public and private
establishments. Higher education is split between universities,
polytechnics and technical institutes.

To find out more about studying in Hong Kong or to search for a
course or an institution, go to Study HK (http://studyinhongkong.
edu.hk/eng).

Applying

Entry requirements vary, but satisfactory performance at A level
should meet the general requirements for undergraduate-level
study. For example, the University of Hong Kong (currently
placed above University of Manchester and University of Bristol
on the 2013–2014 Times Higher Education World University
Rankings Top 200) asks for a minimum of three passes at A
level (not including English or Chinese language) to meet the
general academic requirements. However, that is not the full
story, as the International General Academic Requirements
document (www.als.hku.hk/admission/applying-or-admission-info/
hong-kong-students/non-jupas/entrance-requirement) indicates:
'Competitive applications should have good or excellent grades in
all three subjects. Actual grades will be dependent on the degree
programme and the number and quality of applications that year.'
There may be additional subject requirements and you will need

GCSE English Language at grade C. The University of Hong Kong also looks for evidence of second-language ability (evidenced by a grade E or better at GCSE) and state that they 'value all-roundedness'.

An honours degree is required for entry to postgraduate study.

Application deadlines vary, but may be as early as December or as late as May for a September start. Applications should be made direct to your chosen university and are likely to include:

- personal statement
- reference
- predicted grades plus previous educational achievement
- research statement (for postgraduate research).

Costs

According to Study HK, annual tuition fees on government-funded programmes range from HK$75,000 to HK$120,000 (£5,990–£9,585).

Accommodation in university halls of residence is reasonably priced, but space is at a premium in Hong Kong and private rental can be astronomical. As Study HK explains, 'If you live in university-provided residence halls or hostels, you'll pay a modest HK$5,000 to HK$20,200 (£399–£1,613) per semester; expect to pay that much per month if living off-campus.' Most institutions prioritise accommodation for international students; some universities even guarantee it.

> **"** Accommodation is small (this is Hong Kong after all, where space is in short supply); however, you get used to it and it is all the space you need.**"**
>
> *Warren Mitty, Hong Kong Polytechnic University*

When weighing up living costs, Study HK estimates, 'HK$30,000–HK$60,000 (£2,396–£4,792) per year for additional costs, including food, leisure, transportation, and personal items, depending on how extravagantly you plan to live.' Hong Kong comes in at number 37 of 102 countries on a cost-of-living ranking for 2013. Compare that to the UK, which is listed at a pricier number 18 (www.numbeo.com).

Scholarships are available, although opportunities are limited and most, although not all, are restricted to those displaying academic excellence. See Study HK for a list of scholarships or talk to your institution for further details.

Three of Hong Kong's 15 degree-awarding institutions can be found in the Times Higher Education World University Rankings Top 200 2013–2014.

You could study . . .

BBA (Hons) Financial Services
Hong Kong Polytechnic University
Four years
Apply by 17 January
Annual fees HK$120,000 (£9,585)
Monthly living expenses from HK$4,075 (£325)

Master of Laws (Chinese Law)
University of Hong Kong
One year
Apply from 30 April
Annual fees HK$135,000 (£10,782)
Annual living expenses approximately HK$64,200 (£5,128)

Visas

Once you have been accepted and have found a place to live, you can then apply for a student visa. This should be arranged through the university which will normally act as your local sponsor to support the visa application. You'll need to provide proof of academic qualifications, proof of accommodation and proof of finances. There is no specific amount required by the Hong Kong Immigration Department; your university will be able to give you an idea of appropriate amounts to cover academic and living costs.

For more information on visas, go to www.immd.gov.hk. The application can take up to eight weeks to be processed and will need to be renewed every year. Your institution will be able to support you through the process.

Working while studying

Although a student visa doesn't normally allow work alongside study, there may be opportunities to take internships, campus-based work or work during the holidays. Talk to your university about these procedures and whether you can apply for a 'no objection letter' allowing certain conditions of employment.

After you complete your degree, you can apply for a 12-month stay without a job offer.

Pros and cons of study in Hong Kong

Pros

- High proportion of highly ranked institutions.
- A gateway to China.
- English as an official language.
- Chance to experience a different culture.
- Modern, efficient and cheap public transport.

Cons

- Private accommodation is small and expensive.
- Air pollution and humidity.
- Densely populated.

South Africa

Why South Africa? The Rainbow Nation offers diversity, culture and an outdoor lifestyle combined with a great climate and low cost of living. According to the most recent figures, more than 150 UK students are currently taking advantage of what the country has to offer.

Higher education in South Africa

Higher education is offered at universities, universities of technology, and comprehensive universities. Traditional universities offer academic study, while universities of technology focus on practical or vocational options; comprehensive universities offer both. There are a variety of private universities in South Africa. The languages of English and Afrikaans are both used.

Bachelor's degrees take at least three years (up to six years for medicine), with an additional year of study to achieve an honours degree. A master's degree takes at least one year, while doctorates require a minimum of two years' research.

The academic year runs from February to November. Higher Education South Africa (www.hesa.org.za) has links to all the public universities, where you can browse the courses on offer.

South Africa has one university in the 2013–2014 Times Higher Education World University Rankings Top 200, and three in the top 400.

Applying

Applications should be made direct to your chosen institution by the deadline date they specify. The institutions will often charge an application fee. They will advise you how to get a certificate of exemption to validate your international qualifications. Two A levels plus three GCSEs at grades A* to C (or four Scottish Highers plus one National 5) should meet the general requirements for undergraduate programmes in South Africa. For further details, see the South African Matriculation Board website (www.he-enrol. ac.za/qualification-country). There will be additional requirements for specific subjects. A bachelor's (honours) degree should meet the general entry criteria for a master's degree.

While postgraduate-research programmes may be flexible about when you can apply, you will need time to apply for a study permit and to prepare for the move. South African post can be slow, so you should apply as early as possible. Deadline dates for undergraduate and taught postgraduate courses vary; expect to apply in the autumn if the course starts in February, maybe earlier if you're also applying for a scholarship.

Costs

Fees vary depending on what you study and where. For example, the University of Western Cape charges between ZAR40,000 and ZAR50,000 (£2,516–£3,145) per year for its undergraduate courses, plus an additional ZAR35,000 (£2,201) international supplement. For a room on campus at University of Western Cape, you should expect to pay around ZAR5,500 (£345) per semester, plus ZAR2,000 (£126) per month on food and from ZAR4,400 (£277) on books and stationery. The international office will be able to tell you more about the costs at your chosen university.

> **❝** My tuition fees were more than in the UK as I was an international student. However, that was more than compensated for by the relatively low cost of living in Cape Town compared to London. For this reason, my overall cost of living and studying in Cape Town for a year and a half was about 50% less than it would have been had I studied in London. **❞**
>
> *Nick Parish, master's student, South Africa*

In a 2013 cost-of-living ranking produced by www.numbeo.com, South Africa is listed at number 62 of 102 countries, making it one of the cheapest countries featured in this book.

You could study . . .

BA Cultural and Heritage Tourism
University of KwaZulu-Natal, Durban
Three years
Apply by 30 September for February start
Annual fees US$8,950 (£5,560)
Annual living expenses around ZAR70,000 (£4,403)

Master's in City Planning and Urban Design
University of Cape Town
Two years
Apply by 30 September for February start
Annual fees ZAR89,270 (£5,614)
Monthly living expenses ZAR11,000 (£692)

Visas

Once you have received a written offer, you will need to apply for a study permit at the South African High Commission (www. southafricahouseuk.com). There is a £35 processing fee and an expected turnaround time of 30 working days. You will need to prove that you can support yourself financially and will be asked for a medical report and a police certificate (or criminal records check), as well as proof of medical cover. The study permit will need to be renewed every year.

Further information

If you need further information, you'll find Study South Africa, a helpful guide for international students, on the International Education Association of South Africa website (www.studysa. co.za).

Pros and cons of study in South Africa

Pros

- Great climate.
- Low cost of living.
- Outdoor lifestyle.

Cons

- Crime rate.

Malaysia

Malaysia has hundreds of higher-education institutions to choose from and strong links with the UK. Many overseas universities have chosen to base campuses there, including institutions from the UK such as the University of Nottingham, Newcastle University (Medicine) and, from 2015, University of Reading.

Other institutions offer degrees incorporating UK qualifications. For example, BEng (Hons) Electrical and Electronic Engineering from INTI International College, Penang is awarded by University of Bradford.

Higher education in Malaysia

The academic year in Malaysia has changed to a September start to bring it into line with the northern hemisphere; certain courses also have intakes in January or May. In Malaysia, a bachelor's degree takes three to four years to complete, with the exception of courses like medicine and dentistry, which take five years. A master's degree will take between one and three years and can be coursework-based, research-based, or a combination. A minimum of two years' subsequent study can lead to a doctorate.

Courses taught in English tend to be restricted to private or international universities at undergraduate level. At postgraduate level, there should be English-medium options at public universities too. Only selected private institutions approved by the Ministry of Home Affairs are open to students from overseas; you will need to check that your chosen university has the appropriate permissions to recruit international students. All public universities can recruit from overseas.

Study Malaysia (www.studymalaysia.com) has a course search, along with useful information about education, costs and the country itself.

Applying

International applicants will need to apply direct to their chosen institutions, either online or via a paper application. A personal statement will be a key component of the application. You should apply by the required deadline date and at least six months before you are due to commence your studies.

You could study . . .

BA (Hons) Finance, Accounting and Management

University of Nottingham Malaysia Campus, Semenyih

Three years

Application deadline not provided

Annual fees RM37,950 (£7,500)

Monthly living expenses RM1,500–RM2,000 (£296–£395)

MSc Philosophy of Science

University of Malaya, Kuala Lumpur

From one year

Apply by 30 July for February intake

Annual fees RM8,496 (£1,679)

Monthly living expenses RM700–RM1,000 (£138–£198)

Visas

Your university will apply for a student pass on your behalf. Processing fees of up to RM2,500 (£494) are payable, although the full amount won't be required in advance. Once the student pass is granted, you will then be able to apply for a visa. Following some recent changes to immigration rules, you may need to obtain a visa in advance, rather than on arrival in the country. More information is available from the Malaysian High Commission in London at www.kln.gov.my/perwakilan/london or Study Malaysia at www.studymalaysia.com.

Costs

Tuition fees vary from institution to institution. Study Malaysia suggests that undergraduate fees range from RM33,000–RM140,000 (£6,522–£27,668) (for pharmacy) at private universities and from RM50,000–RM450,000 (£9,881–£88,933) (medicine) at overseas university branch campuses. These costs are for the entire programme, not per year. The annual average undergraduate tuition fee is RM20,000 (£3,953).

Postgraduate research degrees at public universities cost from RM1,800–RM6,000 (£355–£1,186) per year at master's level, and RM2,700–RM8,000 (£534–£1,581) for PhDs.

The fees for a UK degree might be only slightly lower in Malaysia, but if you choose to study overseas, you will benefit from the lower cost of living and the international experience. Living costs are considerably lower than in the UK, with an average cost of living of RM15,000 (£2,964) per year. Malaysia is rated number 71 out of 102 countries on a cost-of-living index for 2013 (www.numbeo. com), making it the cheapest country featured in this book. Information on funding and scholarships can be found at www. studymalaysia.com, Commonwealth Scholarships (http://cscuk.dfid. gov.uk/apply/scholarships-uk-citizens) and from your institution.

Pros and cons of study in Malaysia

Pros

- Reasonable tuition fees for Malaysian degrees.
- Opportunity to gain degrees from USA, UK and Australia in a country with a low cost of living.
- Chance to experience a different culture.
- Tropical climate.

Cons

- No world-renowned Malaysian universities.
- Need approval of your institution before you can work during term-time.
- Not all universities are open to international students.

Singapore

Neighbouring Singapore may be small, but it is a hot spot for financial services, an important trading centre in the heart of Asia and home to the world's busiest port. Its education system is well recognised around the world and comparable in level to education in the UK. English is widely used, particularly for education and business, and most courses are taught in the language.

Higher education in Singapore

The academic year runs from the beginning of August to early May and is divided into two semesters. Bachelor's degrees are available at ordinary level (after three years' study) and with honours (after four years). Most master's degrees take one year, with a minimum of three years required to complete a PhD.

Singapore has four autonomous public universities:

- National University of Singapore
- Nanyang Technological University
- Singapore Management University
- Singapore University of Technology and Design.

As an alternative, Singapore Institute of Technology, a publicly funded institute of technology, provides an industry-focused university education.

You will find one private university, SIM University, along with a number of other private institutions and international universities with a campus in Singapore.

> Singapore might only have a handful of universities, but two of them can be found in the Times Higher Education World University Rankings Top 200 2013–2014.

To find out about university options, you could start with
Ministry of Education Singapore, www.moe.gov.sg/education/
post-secondary, where you'll find a handy guide to post-secondary
education. Contact Singapore (www.contactsingapore.sg) has a lot
of information on living in Singapore.

Applying

At undergraduate level, universities will be looking for good
passes in three A levels, so you should be aiming to apply with
grades at C or above. In some cases, particularly if you're
applying before you know your results, the universities will
require the SAT or ACT admissions tests. (For more information
on the SAT and ACT, see the US-UK Fulbright Commission website,
www.fulbright.org.uk/study-in-the-usa/undergraduate-study/
admissions-tests.)

At postgraduate level, you are likely to need a 2:1 in an honours
degree combined with GMAT (www.mba.com) or GRE (www.ets.
org/gre) admissions tests for specific subjects. See individual
universities for entry criteria and test requirements.

Applications should be made direct to the university's admissions
or international office. Undergraduate applicants can select up
to five potential courses. As part of the application, you might
have to write a short essay on your achievements or reflect on
any positions of responsibility. Postgraduate-research applicants
will need to write a research proposal. At both undergraduate and
postgraduate level you will need to provide references.

The university will charge you an application fee from around
S$20 (£10). You can apply from September or October.

At the National University of Singapore, you will not be eligible for competitive courses like dentistry and medicine if you apply with predicted grades. If this is the case at your chosen university or with your chosen course, wait until you have your actual grades to make the application; this might mean waiting for the next intake, but can also result in exemption from certain admissions tests.

Costs

Tuition fees in Singaporean universities are high, but are subsidised by the government through the tuition-grant scheme. This scheme is open to international students on the condition that you work for three years after graduation for a Singaporean company; this can be deferred for specific reasons including further study. You can find out more at the Ministry of Education website (www.moe.gov.sg) or from your university.

The National University of Singapore (ranked above the London School of Economics and Political Science and the University of Edinburgh on the Times Higher Education World University Rankings Top 200 2013–2014) charges fees for undergraduate degrees ranging from S$27,900 to S$123,050 (£13,950–£61,525) (for medicine and dentistry). These fees fall to between S$15,300 and S$46,100 (£7,650–£23,050) when the tuition grant is included.

At postgraduate level, Nanyang Technological University will charge S$11,700 to S$37,500 (£5,850–£18,750) for master's degrees in 2013/2014; this includes the tuition grant (or service obligation). Without a tuition grant, you would be looking at fees of S$27,800–S$51,800 (£13,900–£25,900). Additional fees may be payable for the students' union, exams and health services.

Scholarships are available and can be searched for at the Ministry of Education website (www.moe.gov.sg) or discussed with your university. Some loans may be available.

> **❝❝** Singapore was very cheap compared to where I live in England. At the time I was there, it was around S$2 to £1, but you could get a fast food meal for around S$5 (£2.50). Going out to the movies and drinking was also cheaper, though drinking was only marginally so.**❞❞**
>
> *Joshua Jackson, SP Jain Global School of Management,*
> *Singapore and Australia*

The Nanyang Technological University website estimates living costs of S$1,000 to S$1,700 (£500–£850) per month.

It falls at number 15 of 102 countries listed on a cost-of-living ranking (www.numbeo.com), so is considered slightly more expensive than the UK at the moment.

You could study . . .

Bachelor's degree in Public Policy and Global Affairs
Nanyang Technological University
Four years
Apply from 1 October
Annual fees S$15,300 (£7,650) with tuition grant, S$27,980 (£13,990) without
Estimated annual living expenses S$8,850 (£4,425)

Master of Chemical and Pharmaceutical Engineering (dual degree)
National University of Singapore/Massachusetts Institute of Technology
18 months (split between Singapore and Boston, USA)
Apply by 16 December
Full scholarship awarded covering tuition fees and monthly allowance

Visas

You will need a Student's Pass to study in Singapore. Your university will register you on the Immigration and Checkpoints Authority online registration system (SOLAR) and you will then need to complete an online application. There is no required amount of money that you need to provide evidence of, so you should talk to your university about an advisable amount. You won't receive the student pass until you arrive in Singapore, so you will first be granted a social-visit pass at the airport.

Find out more at the Immigration and Checkpoints Authority (www.ica.gov.sg) or the High Commission for the Republic of Singapore in London (www.mfa.gov.sg/london).

Working while studying

International students can work up to 16 hours per week under certain conditions and with the approval of the university or polytechnic that you are studying in. You would need to talk to your institution to request a letter of authorisation.

On graduating, if you are successful in finding a job, you will need to obtain an employment pass before you can start working. For more details, see the Ministry of Manpower (www.mom.gov.sg).

Pros and cons of study in Singapore

Pros

- Chance to experience another culture.
- Modern city-state with a high standard of living.
- Tropical climate.

Cons

- Densely populated.
- Competitive entry.
- Need approval of your university before you can work in term-time.

The Caribbean

A number of UK students head off to the Caribbean for their studies, particularly for medical or dental programmes, with over 60 medical schools listed there. Many opt for international universities with a base in the Caribbean that prepare students for a medical or dental career in countries like the USA, Canada or the UK. This list might include St George's University Grenada, Ross University, the American University of the Caribbean, and Saba University School of Medicine. St George's recruits from the UK and prepares students for medical practice in a number of countries, including the UK, whereas the other institutions tend to have more of a North American focus.

At St George's University, you could be looking at average tuition fees of around £30,000 per year for medicine and £20,000 for veterinary medicine. In addition, you'll need to budget for living expenses of £11,000 to £14,000 per year. The university has intakes in August and January and you should apply direct.

There are also local universities offering courses, most notably the University of the West Indies (UWI), a regional university representing 15 countries with four sites across the Caribbean. Its fees at undergraduate level are around US$15,000 (£9,317) per year, with the exception of medicine, which is around US$28,000 (£17,391).

Undergraduate degrees tend to take three to four years, followed by a two-year master's degree and a three-year PhD. Make sure you check the validity of any professional qualification with the relevant professional body. If you intend to practise medicine in the UK, you should check requirements with the General Medical Council. For a list of the relevant professional bodies in the UK, see the website of the National Contact Point for Professional Qualifications in the UK at www.ecctis.co.uk/uk%20ncp.

Unfortunately, there isn't one single source of information to find other recognised universities. You could use the High Commission websites in the UK; for example, the Jamaican High Commission in the UK, at www.jhcuk.org/citizens/universities, lists UWI, University of Technology, and Northern Caribbean University. You could also use accreditation organisations like the University Council of Jamaica, the Barbados Accreditation Council, and the Accreditation Council of Trinidad and Tobago. Find contact details for these and other accreditation bodies at CANQATE (Caribbean Area Network for Quality Assurance in Tertiary Education), www.canqate.org/Links/RelatedLinks.aspx. Once you are sure that your university is recognised and accredited, you can go to their website for the latest information on courses, fees and how to apply.

You could study . . .

BA History

University of the West Indies, Mona Campus, Jamaica

Three years

Annual fees US$15,000 (£9,317)

Living expenses not provided, hall fees from JA$124,000–
JA$235,500 (£738–£1,400) per academic year

Master of Science in Biology

Northern Caribbean University, Manchester, Jamaica

Two years

Annual fees approximately US$10,000 (£6,211)

Living expenses not provided, accommodation with meal plan from
US$3,300 (£2,049) per academic year

Pros and cons of study in the Caribbean

Pros

- Tropical climate.
- Low cost of living.
- Chance to gain medical training relevant to more than
  one country.

Cons

- A range of education systems on offer with no single
  reliable source of information.
- High costs for medical and dental studies.

Countries where English isn't widely used

Across the rest of the world there are options for those wanting
to study in English. Even in places where English is not widely

spoken you will find pockets of opportunity for UK students. We will explore a few of those countries here.

China

The Chinese government is investing heavily in its higher education and is keen to attract international students; around 35,000 European students were studying in China in 2012 according to information from the China Scholarship Council. The growth of China as an economic force means that awareness of Chinese culture and language is likely to be an important asset.

The British government is also keen that UK students develop their understanding of China; its Generation UK project offers internships and scholarships towards short-term study in China. Fine out more at www.britishcouncil.org/china-education-generationuk.htm.

How to find a course

You could start your search at Campus China (www.campuschina. org). You can also search for degree programmes on the CUCAS (China's University and College Admission System) website, www. cucas.edu.cn. Once your search brings up a list of courses, you can select those taught in English. The Chinese Ministry of Education also holds a list of English-taught programmes in Chinese higher education, as well as information on scholarships; visit www.moe. edu.cn/publicfiles/business/htmlfiles/moe/moe_2812/200906/48835. html. You'll find more opportunities at postgraduate level rather than at undergraduate level.

Only two of China's universities feature in the Times Higher Education World University Rankings Top 200 2013–2014.

Higher education in China

The academic year runs from September to mid-July and international students should apply between February and April.

Bachelor's degrees normally take four years to complete, master's degrees take two to three years, and doctorates take from three years; all are similar in level to those offered in the UK.

Traditionally, the style of teaching in China has been more teacher-centred than in the UK. You may find that this is less of an issue on English-taught courses aimed at international students.

Applying

A level study is generally required for undergraduate courses, with a bachelor's degree (plus two references) required for master's study, and a master's degree (plus two references) for doctoral study.

Applications can be made direct to universities or online through CUCAS. If applying through CUCAS, additional documentation (copy of passport, academic transcripts and police certificates (or criminal records check), for example) can be scanned or clearly photographed for submission. CUCAS charges a service fee of US$50 to US$135 (£31 to £84) for up to six applications. The exact fee depends on your chosen institution. Institutions also charge an application fee before they will issue the school-admission notice required for a visa; they will normally take a further four to eight weeks to process an application.

You could study . . .

Bachelor's degree in Food Quality and Safety
Jinan University, Guangzhou
Four years

Apply by 1 July

Annual fees RMB26,000 (£2,648)

Annual living expenses RMB20,000–RMB40,000
(£2,037–£4,073)

Master of Law

Peking University, Beijing

Two years

Apply by 20 March for September start

Annual fees RMB80,000 (£8,147)

Annual living expenses approximately RMB50,000 (£5,092)

Visas

For study in China of over six months, you will need an X-
visa. You can apply through the Chinese Embassy. Go to www.
visaforchina.org for more details.

Costs

CUCAS advises of tuition fees around US$2,000–US$4,000
(£1,242–£2,485) per year and living expenses of around US$6,000–
US$9,000 (£3,727–£5,590), although other organisations suggest
that more money will be needed. Costs will vary depending on the
type of lifestyle you want to lead. China is listed as number 60
of 102 countries on the Numbeo cost-of-living ranking for 2013;
making it one of the cheapest countries for cost of living featured
in this book.

> **"** The city of Ningbo itself was much cheaper than the
> UK and the cost of living was a fraction of what I
> would spend in the UK. **"**
> *Lewis McCarthy, University of Nottingham Ningbo, China*

Full and partial scholarships are available through the China Scholarship Council (www.csc.edu.cn/Laihua). If you are proficient in a Chinese language, you may be eligible for a Chinese Government Scholarship. Search for scholarships on the Ministry of Education website (www.moe.edu.cn) and through CUCAS (www.cucas.edu.cn).

There are age restrictions for international students hoping to study higher education and apply for certain scholarships in China.

- Undergraduate applicants should be under 25.
- Master's degree applicants should be under 35.
- Doctoral applicants should be under 40.

Pros and cons of study in China

Pros

- An increasingly powerful world economic force.
- Investment in higher education.
- Chance to experience a new culture.

Cons

- Language barrier outside the classroom.
- A new setting for international students.
- Issues around censorship and political restrictions.

Saudi Arabia

Although most courses are in Arabic, there are opportunities in English at certain Saudi universities and over 100 UK students are already studying in the country (OECD Education at a Glance

2013) Saudi Arabia's first international university, King Abdullah University of Science and Technology (www.kaust.edu.sa), opened in 2009 and offers postgraduate courses taught in English.

Higher education in Saudi Arabia

Public and private universities in Saudi Arabia are overseen by the Ministry of Higher Education. Bachelor's degrees run for a minimum of four years, master's degrees take two years, and doctorates from three years. Qualifications are of a similar level to those in the UK. For a list of universities, go to the Ministry of Higher Education website at www.mohe.gov.sa. Some institutions are not open to women.

Life in Saudi Arabia

Saudi Arabia is a Muslim country where Islamic law is strictly enforced. Life differs greatly from that in the UK; mixed gatherings are not customary and alcohol is not permitted. Recreation activities for men centre on sport, with many activities for women restricted.

Applying

Applications should be made direct to your chosen university.

Costs

Tuition fees vary, with individual universities setting their own. Scholarships and fellowships are available; talk to your chosen university about what is on offer.

Saudi Arabia is listed at number 42 of 102 countries on the Numbeo cost-of-living ranking for 2013 (www.numbeo.com). The UK is at number 18.

You could study . . .

Master's degree in Applied Mathematics and Computational Science
King Abdullah University of Science and Technology, Thuwal
Two years

Apply by 15 January

Full fellowships awarded covering tuition fees and living expenses

Visas

Once you have been offered a place, you should then start the process of applying for a visa or entry permit. For details, go to the Ministry of Foreign Affairs website at www.mofa.gov.sa or www.saudiembassy.org.uk.

Pros and cons of study in Saudi Arabia

Pros

- Investment in higher education.
- Chance to experience a new culture.

Cons

- Saudi universities (and Middle Eastern universities in general) are not well represented on the world university rankings.
- Social and recreational activities may be restricted, particularly for women.

Qatar

If you're interested in the Middle East, but prefer the familiarity of a UK or US degree, you could take a look at Qatar. Qatar's Education City is a huge complex of education and research facilities and includes universities from the USA, France and the UK. Find out more at the Qatar Foundation for Education, Science and Community Development at www.qf.org.qa/education/universities or at Education City at www.myeducationcity.com.

As it is a hub for elite international universities, your experience will vary according to which institution you choose. You can opt for a UK degree or choose a degree from another country. The

tuition fees, style of teaching and who will award your degree will
be determined by your chosen university.

> **66** My visa was organised by UCL Qatar and was very
> straightforward, apart from some mandatory health
> checks and appointments, which all expatriates moving to
> Qatar must undertake after they arrive in Doha. Support
> upon arrival was particularly helpful, starting with a "meet
> and greet" at Doha airport, and followed by lots of induction
> activities.**99**
>
> *Benedict Leigh, UCL Qatar*

Student life is likely to be different in Qatar, where the sale of
alcohol is limited and modest dress is expected. Social activities
might be more focused on campus activities, cultural events and
shopping malls rather than all-night clubbing.

You could study . . .

MA Archaeology of the Arab and Islamic World
UCL Qatar, Doha
Two years
Apply by 31 May
Annual fees QAR123,900 (£21,107)
Approximate monthly living expenses QAR1,500 (£256)

Pros and cons of study in Qatar
Pros

- Investment in higher education.
- Chance to experience a new culture.

Cons

* Different student life.

Japan

At the last count, 487 UK students had chosen Japan as their study destination (OECD Education at a Glance 2013). The Japanese government is keen to attract more international students and is investing in higher education and extending the study options available in English.

A group of universities known as Global 30 has been set up to boost the number of international students in Japan. They receive extra funding and are developing an increasing number of degrees taught in English.

* Doshisha University
* Keio University
* Kyoto University
* Kyushu University
* Mciji University
* Nagoya University
* Osaka University
* Ritsumeikan University
* Sophia University
* Tohoku University
* University of Tokyo
* University of Tsukuba
* Waseda University.

Find out more, including links to all these universities, at Japanese Universities for Motivated People (JUMP), visit www.uni. international.mext.go.jp/global30.

Higher education in Japan

Currently, most institutions in Japan require proficiency in Japanese, but there are some exceptions. A number of Japanese universities offer master's and doctoral degrees in English, although the options are more limited at undergraduate level. JASSO (Japan Student Services Organisation) has a list of university degree courses offered in English, see www.jasso.go.jp/study-j/schinfo-e.html.

There are far more private than public universities. Japan has some international universities and overseas universities with campuses in Japan.

Five of Japan's universities have made it into the Times Higher Education World University Rankings Top 200 for 2013–2014.

The academic year starts in April and is run as a two-semester system, April to September, and October to March, with holidays at intervals throughout the year. It should take you four years to complete a bachelor's degree; the first two years offer more general studies, while the final two years allow you to specialise. Study at master's level tends to take two years, with a further three years required for a doctorate.

You should apply direct to your chosen university; you may be required to sit an entrance exam.

Costs

Study in Japan (www.g-studyinjapan.jasso.go.jp) suggests average monthly costs, including fees, of JPY138,000 (£875). The cost of living in Tokyo will be higher, so you should check individual universities for local costs. The Study in Japan website also has lots of information on scholarships, living and accommodation costs.

University accommodation is substantially cheaper than private rented accommodation, so check whether your chosen university will guarantee accommodation for you. In private accommodation, in addition to rent, there are deposits and 'thank you' money to be paid, which can be around four months' rent (and sometimes more).

Japan has a reputation for being expensive; it is ranked number 6 out of 102 countries on the cost-of-living ranking (www.numbeo.com).

You could study . . .

BA Liberal Arts (Japanese Society and Global Culture)
Doshisha University's Institute for the Liberal Arts, Kyoto
Four years
Rolling admission (early deadline of 24 August for April entry)
Annual fees JPY1,109,000 (£7,031) (including admission and facilities fees)
Monthly living expenses JPY100,000–JPY120,000 (£634–£761)

MA International Development
International University of Japan, Niigata (private)
Two years
Apply by 17 February for April entry
Annual fees JPY2,200,000 (£13,949) (including admission fees)
Minimum monthly living expenses JPY94,000 (£596)

Visas
You will need a student visa in order to study in Japan; your university will act as a sponsor for the visa process and should obtain a certificate of eligibility for you. This will need to be processed at the Embassy of Japan (www.uk.emb-japan.go.jp) in the UK (or the country where you are resident). Student-visa

holders need the approval of their university and the immigration office to be able to work.

For information on study in Japan, go to www.studyjapan.go.jp/en.

Pros and cons of study in Japan

Pros

- A culture which combines tradition and cutting-edge technology.
- Drive to increase numbers of international students.

Cons

- Language barrier outside the classroom.
- Relatively few western students at present.
- The need to factor in additional fees for study and accommodation.

Hopefully, the information about these countries will have whetted your appetite and given you a starting point for your research. Of course, the countries profiled here are not the only options open to you; many other countries are keen to attract students from the UK. If you are interested in studying elsewhere in the world, you can use the information in this book (see Chapters 2, 3 and 4) to help ensure that the education you opt for is the right step for you.

Student story
Justin Axel-Berg, University of São Paulo, Brazil

'I originally left the UK two years ago during the financial crisis after I had graduated and was unable to find a job that I wanted. Instead, I qualified as an English teacher and started travelling. I always had the intention of returning to study and when the opportunity arose I took advantage of the fact that there was a top-class university on my doorstep.

'I decided I wanted a change from Asia, which I know well and have lived in before, and Australia, in which I studied during my degree. Brazil has a dynamic and exciting economy with lots of opportunity for foreigners. It has a deserved reputation for being friendly, exciting and warm.'

With a first degree from University of Sussex, Justin is now enrolled to a Mestrado (master's degree) in International Relations. 'The Universidade de São Paulo (USP) has consistently been rated the best institution in Latin America, with a very strong research tradition and excellent reputation. All degree courses in federal and state universities in Brazil are completely free to all applicants, with a good chance of receiving a scholarship for living expenses while you study through one of the funding bodies.'

However, there is a downside to study in Brazil. 'In order to do anything in Brazil, Portuguese language is a pre-requisite, and that includes, for the time being anyway, university. The university offers language courses to foreign students while you study, which are of good quality, and they are also currently launching an online distance-learning programme, so you will be able to pick up some Portuguese at home before you leave. It's not an insurmountable challenge, but it is a challenge nonetheless. People are always willing to help you out with it and will happily share class notes with you in case you missed anything. Essays can be submitted in English if you prefer.'

Justin found the application process to be fairly straightforward. 'I had to sit the GRE exam, which I did in London, although it is also possible at other locations across the UK. I then wrote up a research proposal and a CV and sent it via email along with the application form. The procedure does vary from course to course, so it's best to check their website.

'While I was waiting for my documents to arrive I was in constant contact with the university by phone and by email, and they took a real personal interest in getting me to Brazil safe and well.

'The process of applying for a visa was quick, but a little bit complicated. Firstly you must register and complete a form on the federal police's website before booking an appointment at the consulate. Unfortunately, my university acceptance letter was caught in a postal strike so I was rather delayed in getting documents sorted, but once I got to the consulate they were friendly and helpful and the whole process took well under a week from giving them my passport to receiving my visa. Once you arrive in Brazil you then have to go to the police to register and get your Brazilian ID card (RNE), which takes about six months to arrive.'

Justin praises the academic support he has experienced since starting at the university. 'My academic advisor is excellent, and here they tend to take a much more hands-on approach to support than in the UK. He is constantly sending me interesting events to attend or things to read. I would say that education in Brazil is much more tutor led; Brazilian students have their hands held much more than in the UK. There is also more of a focus on personal and career development alongside research than in the UK.'

Although he is an experienced traveller and has studied overseas before, Justin did have to make some adjustments. 'There are always little things that surprise me. Although Brazil is superficially very European, in reality it most definitely isn't. People's outlook on life is different, what people say versus what they mean is very different. Also the fact that, in a polite way, Brazil functions in a kind of irrational bureaucratic chaos can be difficult to adjust to; things simply don't work in the way that you expect.'

On the whole, there have been very few negative experiences. 'Perhaps a few too many afternoons sitting in the *policia federal* trying to register my documents. Despite São Paulo's violent reputation, it's really quite a safe place. I've lived here for three years now, travelling all over the city at all times of night and day and never come to harm anywhere.'

Discovering the latest information about study in Brazil can be a challenge. 'The information is unfortunately a bit scattered at the moment as UK and international students are so few. It's best to contact the university and ask for information. Gringoes (www.gringoes.com) is a good guide to living in Brazil with a very supportive forum.'

Justin's top tips

Accommodation

'USP cannot guarantee accommodation because of the size of the student body, but private sector provision is excellent and catered towards students in either "republicas" (shared houses) or individual kitchenettes or studio flats both next to the campus and further into the city. It'll be very hard to sort anything out before you arrive though, so plan on starting in a hostel for a couple of weeks'.

Food

'Brazilian food is delicious, heavy on meat and beans, as represented by the famous feijoada (bean and meat stew). Fresh fruit juices are everywhere and made of a vast array of things you'll never have heard of. São Paulo also has the best sushi outside of Japan as a result of the huge Japanese population, and the Italian food and especially the pizzas are fantastic.'

Insurance

'As a student you may use the public healthcare system. It is probably recommended to have your own private insurance too, but personally I haven't bothered, and every time I've needed the doctor I've been well looked after.'

Living costs
'São Paulo is not a cheap city to live in. People come to Brazil expecting the third world and finding the first. Expect to spend up to BRL700–BRL1000 (£198–£283) per month on a room. I pay more than this because I live in my own apartment in the city. Food is often roughly the price of the UK, although savvy shoppers buy in street markets where it is much lower. Alcohol is reasonably priced. All electronics and other non-consumables are absurdly expensive (200–300% of UK price); bring your iPhone and laptop with you from home.'

Financial support for study
'Both CAPES and FAPESP give generous scholarships which will go a long way towards supporting you as you study. They are widespread and not terribly difficult to get. The university also offers postgraduates the opportunity to monitor and assist courses in return for money.'

Working while studying
'Working is not possible on a student visa, although there is a burgeoning market for international students tutoring English privately all over the city.'

Making friends
'It's Brazil: everyone wants to stop and chat with people passing by. It's extremely easy to make friends and Brazilians are very welcoming warm people who treat foreigners very well.'

Lifestyle and culture
'Brazil is a lot more laid back than the UK and a lot more informal and relaxed. People live for the beach, and it is easily accessible from SP at the weekends. São Paulo is the cultural capital of Brazil and the amount of art, especially street art, is phenomenal, as is the range of music and fashion available in the city. There is something here for everyone, but you might have to search for it.'

Travel and transport

'The traffic is terrible. Really bad. However, the buses are very regular, clean, safe and cheap (BRL1.50 or 40p for 2 hours travel as a student) and the metro, although limited, will cover everywhere you will want to go as a foreigner. It is also cheap, quick, safe and very clean.'

Options for after you finish your studies

'Brazil is expanding rapidly, and has technical needs in almost every field at the moment. It also has a specific need for bilingual people with some expertise. If you're planning to do almost anything in Brazil, a qualification from USP will get you there.

'I am getting married here in Brazil this year, and planning afterwards to either look for a job in an NGO, in university administration or carry on and do a doctorate. Possibly a combination of the above.'

So how would Justin reflect on his experiences so far? 'Living in beautiful Brazil, being exposed to another culture in a deep way not open to most travellers or even expats and learning to view the world through another culture is fascinating and an experience I wouldn't trade for the world.'

University of São Paulo is the highest ranked university in South America according to the Times Higher Education World University Rankings 2013 2014. It has 86,000 students and over 15,000 staff.

Chapter 11

Further research and resources

Before you go

British Council UK Students Abroad
www.britishcouncil.org/uk-students-abroad

Prospects Country Profiles (postgraduate focus)
www.prospects.ac.uk/country_profiles.htm

UK National Academic Recognition and Information Centre
(NARIC)
www.ecctis.co.uk/naric/individuals
Information on the comparability of international qualifications

National Contact Point for Professional Qualifications in the
United Kingdom (UKNCP)
www.ecctis.co.uk/uk%20ncp

Foreign and Commonwealth Office
www.fco.gov.uk
Find an embassy or seek travel advice by country

iAgora
www.iagora.com/studies
Students review and rate their international universities

SteXX

www.stexx.eu

Students review and rate their European universities

Association of Commonwealth Universities

www.acu.ac.uk

Citizens Advice

www.citizensadvice.org.uk

For information on how studying overseas might affect your status in the UK

HM Revenue and Customs

www.hmrc.gov.uk

Information on tax when you return to the UK

International course search

Find a master's/MBA/PhD

www.findamasters.com

www.findanmba.com

www.findaphd.com

International Graduate

www.internationalgraduate.net

Search for postgraduate opportunities worldwide

International university league tables

The Times Higher Education World University Rankings

www.timeshighereducation.co.uk/world-university-rankings

QS Top Universities

www.topuniversities.com/university-rankings

Academic Ranking of World Universities
www.shanghairanking.com

Financial Times Business School Rankings
http://rankings.ft.com/businessschoolrankings/rankings

Costs and funding

Numbeo
www.numbeo.com
Cost-of-living comparison

Expatistan
www.expatistan.com
Cost-of-living comparison for cities worldwide

Professional and Career Development Loans
www.gov.uk/career-development-loans/overview

International Student Identity Card (ISIC)
www.isic.org
Student discounts worldwide

Student Finance England
www.gov.uk/student-finance/overview

Student Awards Agency for Scotland
www.saas.gov.uk

Student Finance Wales
www.studentfinancewales.co.uk

Student Finance Northern Ireland
www.studentfinanceni.co.uk

Marie Curie Scheme

www.ukro.ac.uk/mariecurie/Pages/index.aspx

Fellowships and grants for research

Commonwealth Scholarships

http://cscuk.dfid.gov.uk/apply/scholarships-uk-citizens

Insurance

European Health Insurance Card (EHIC)

www.ehic.org.uk

Endsleigh Insurance

www.endsleigh.co.uk/Travel/Pages/study-abroad-insurance.aspx

STA Travel Insurance

www.statravel.co.uk/study-abroad-travel-insurance.htm

Blogs and diaries

Third Year Abroad, The Mole Diaries

www.thirdyearabroad.com/before-you-go/the-mole-diaries.html

Samuel Knight in Groningen

www.samstudyingabroad.tumblr.com

Residence Abroad Blogs (University of Manchester)

www.llc.manchester.ac.uk/undergraduate/residence-abroad/blogs

Maastricht Students

www.maastricht-students.com

The Student World Blog

www.thestudentworld.com/news_and_blog/article/preparation_for_
studying_abroad#.UFrwCK6Dfcs

From Turbans to Clogs
http://fromturbanstoclogs.blogspot.co.uk

The University of Nottingham in North America
http://universityofnottinghamnorthamerica.blogspot.co.uk/

Leon's Overseas Adventures and Muddled Thoughts
http://hungryleon.blogspot.co.uk

Short-term study overseas

Study China
www.studychina.org.uk

INTO China
www.intohigher.com/china

IAESTE
www.iaeste.org

Fulbright Commission
www.fulbright.org.uk
Summer schools at US universities

EducationUSA
www.educationusa.info/pages/students/research-short.php

Third Year Abroad
www.thirdyearabroad.com

Distance learning

International Council for Open and Distance Education (ICDE)
www.icde.org

Study Portals (search for a distance-learning course in Europe)
www.studyportals.eu

Distance Education and Training Council (USA)
www.detc.org/search_schools.php

Educational agents and marketing consultancies

A Star Future
www.astarfuture.co.uk

Study Options
www.studyoptions.com

Degrees Ahead
www.degreesahead.co.uk

Mayflower Education Consultants
www.mayflowereducation.co.uk

PFL Education
www.preparationforlife.com

M & D Europe
www.readmedicine.com

Pass 4 Soccer Scholarships
www.pass4soccer.com

Outreach Education
www.outreacheducation.co.uk

Study International
www.studygo.co.uk

Admissions tests

Scholastic Assessment Test: SAT
www.sat.collegeboard.org

American College Test: ACT
www.act.org

Undergraduate Medicine and Health Sciences Admission Test: UMAT
www.umat.acer.edu.au

International Student Admissions Test: ISAT
www.isat.acer.edu.au

Special Tertiary Admissions Test: STAT
www.acer.edu.au/tests/stat

Graduate Management Admission Test: GMAT
www.mba.com

Graduate Record Exam: GRE
www.ets.org/gre

Dental Admissions Test: DAT
www.ada.org/dat.aspx

Law School Admissions Test: LSAT
www.lsac.org

Medical College Admission Test: MCAT
www.aamc.org/students/applying/mcat

Graduate Australian Medical Schools Admissions Test: GAMSAT
www.gamsat.acer.edu.au

Health Professions Admission Test (Ireland): HPAT
www.hpat-ireland.acer.edu.au

Studying in Europe

Study Portals
www.studyportals.eu
Search for courses and scholarships in Europe

PLOTEUS (Portal on Learning Opportunities throughout the
European Space)
www.ec.europa.eu/ploteus/home_en.htm

A Star Future
www.astarfuture.co.uk/what_to_study.html
Search for courses taught in English in Europe and beyond

EUNICAS
www.eunicas.co.uk
Search for courses taught in English

GES Database
www.study-info.eu/index.htm
Search for courses taught in English

EURAXESS
www.ec.europa.eu/euraxess
Research opportunities in the EU

PromoDoc
www.promodoc.eu/study-in-the-eu
Doctoral study in the EU

European Commission, University in Europe

www.ec.europa.eu/youreurope/citizens/education/university

European Commission, Study in Europe

www.ec.europa.eu/education/study-in-europe

Eurodesk

www.eurodesk.org.uk

Information on European work, study, travel and volunteering

Europass

www.europass.cedefop.europa.eu

Documents to make your qualification and skills easily understood across Europe (CVs, diploma supplements and so on)

Erasmus

www.britishcouncil.org/erasmus-about-erasmus.htm

Erasmus Mundus

www.britishcouncil.org/erasmus-programmes-erasmus-mundus.htm

Austria

www.oead.at/welcome_to_austria/education_research/EN

Belgium

www.highereducation.be (Flemish community)

www.studyinbelgium.be (French community)

Czech Republic

www.studyin.cz

www.msmt.cz (Scholarships)

Denmark

www.studyindenmark.dk

www.en.iu.dk/education-in-denmark (Danish Agency for Universities and Internationalisation)

www.optagelse.dk/vejledninger/english/index.html (Danish Co-ordinated Application System, KOT)

www.su.dk/English/Sider/foreign.aspx (State Educational Support, SU)

Estonia

www.studyinestonia.ee

Finland

www.studyinfinland.fi

www.universityadmissions.fi (applications to university)

www.admissions.fi (applications to polytechnic or university of applied sciences)

France

www.campusfrance.org/en

www.cnous.fr (National Centre for University & Student Welfare, student life and student costs)

Germany

www.study-in.de/en

www.hochschulkompass.de (HochschulKompass, institution search)

www.daad.de (German Academic Exchange Services, DAAD)

www.uni-assist.de/index_en.html (uni-assist, application service for international students)

Hungary

www.studyhungary.hu

Ireland

www.educationireland.ie

www.hetac.ie (Higher Education and Training Awards Council)

www.icosirl.ie (Irish Council for International Students)

www.qualifax.ie (course search)

www.postgradireland.com (postgraduate search)

www.cao.ie (Central Applications Office)

www.pac.ie (Postgraduate Applications Centre)

Italy

www.study-in-italy.it

Latvia

www.studyinlatvia.lv

Lithuania

www.lietuva.lt/en/education_sience/study_lithuania

www.skvc.lt/en/content.asp?id=235 (Lithuanian Centre for Quality Assessment in Higher Education)

The Netherlands

www.studyinholland.nl

www.studyinholland.co.uk

http://info.studielink.nl/en/studenten/Pages/Default.aspx

(Studielink for applications)

www.ib-groep.nl/International_visitors/EU_EEA_students/Grant_for_tuition_or_course_fees.asp

(Department of Education, grants and loans)

Norway

www.studyinnorway.no

www.nokut.no (Norwegian Agency for Quality Assurance in HE, NOKUT)

Poland

www.studyinpoland.pl

Portugal

www.dges.mctes.pt/DGES/pt (General Directorate for HE)

Slovakia

www.studyin.sk

Slovenia

www.slovenia.si/en/study

Switzerland

www.swissuniversity.ch

www.crus.ch/information-programme/study-in-switzerland.
html?L=2

Spain

www.universidad.es/en

www.educacion.es (Ministry of Education)

www.uned.es (UNED, for evaluation of qualifications)

Sweden

www.studyinsweden.se

Studying in the USA

Fulbright Commission
www.fulbright.org.uk

EducationUSA
www.educationusa.info

College Board
www.collegeboard.org

College Navigator
www.nces.ed.gov/collegenavigator

National Association of Credential Evaluation Services (NACES)
www.naces.org

Common Application
www.commonapp.org

Hobsons Virtual Events
www.hobsonsevents.com
US virtual student fairs

Scholarships and financial aid

Edupass
www.edupass.org/finaid/databases.phtml

International Education Financial Aid
www.iefa.org

International Scholarships
www.internationalscholarships.com

US Citizenship and Immigration Services
www.uscis.gov

Studying in Canada

Study in Canada
www.educationau-incanada.ca

Association of Universities and Colleges of Canada
www.aucc.ca

Canadian Information Centre for International Credentials
www.cicic.ca

Citizenship & Immigration Canada
www.cic.gc.ca/english/study/index.asp

Immigration Québec
www.immigration-quebec.gouv.qc.ca/en

Statistics Canada
www.statcan.gc.ca

International Scholarships
www.scholarships-bourses.gc.ca/scholarships-bourses/index.
aspx?view=d
www.cbie-bcei.ca/?page_id=1692
http://cscuk.dfid.gov.uk/apply/scholarships-uk-citizens
www.ScholarshipsCanada.com

Studying in Australia

Study in Australia
www.studyinaustralia.gov.au
www.study-in-australia.org/uk

Australian Qualifications Framework
www.aqf.edu.au

Australian Good Universities Guide
www.gooduniguide.com.au

Australian Educational International, National Office of Overseas
Skills Recognition (AEI NOOSR)
www.aei.gov.au/Services-And-Resources/Pages/AEINOOSR.aspx

Australian High Commission in London
www.uk.embassy.gov.au

Department of Immigration & Citizenship
www.immi.gov.au

International Scholarships
http://cscuk.dfid.gov.uk/apply/scholarships-uk-citizens
www.australiaawards.gov.au
www.kcl.ac.uk/artshums/ahri/centres/menzies/scholarships/index.
aspx

Finances and budgeting
www.moneysmart.gov.au/managing-my-money

Australian Tax Office
www.ato.gov.au

Studying in New Zealand

New Zealand Educated
www.newzealandeducated.com

New Zealand Postgraduate
www.newzealandpostgraduate.com

New Zealand Qualifications Authority
www.nzqa.govt.nz/search

Universities New Zealand
www.universitiesnz.ac.nz

Immigration New Zealand
www.immigration.govt.nz

New Zealand High Commission in London
www.nzembassy.com/united-kingdom

Student Job Search
www.sjs.co.nz

Inland Revenue Department
www.ird.govt.nz/how-to/irdnumbers

Studying in the rest of the world

Hong Kong
Study in Hong Kong
http://studyinhongkong.edu.hk/eng

Hong Kong Immigration Department
www.immd.gov.hk

South Africa
International Education Association of South Africa
www.studysa.co.za

South African Matriculation Board
www.he-enrol.ac.za/qualification-country

South African High Commission in London
www.southafricahouseuk.com

Malaysia
Study Malaysia
www.studymalaysia.com

Singapore
Contact Singapore
www.contactsingapore.sg

Ministry of Education
www.moe.gov.sg

Immigration and Checkpoints Authority
www.ica.gov.sg

High Commission for the Republic of Singapore in London
www.mfa.gov.sg/london

Ministry of Manpower
www.mom.gov.sg

The Caribbean

Jamaican High Commission in London
www.jhcuk.org/citizens/universities

Caribbean Area Network for Quality Assurance in Tertiary
Education (CANQATE)
www.canqate.org/Links/RelatedLinks.aspx

China

Campus China
www.campuschina.org

China's University and College Admission System
www.cucas.edu.cn

Chinese Ministry of Education
www.moe.edu.cn

China Scholarship Council
www.csc.edu.cn/Laihua

Chinese Embassy
www.visaforchina.org

Saudi Arabia

Ministry of Higher Education

www.mohe.gov.sa

Ministry of Foreign Affairs

www.mofa.gov.sa

Royal Embassy of Saudi Arabia in London

www.saudiembassy.org.uk

Qatar

Qatar Foundation for Education, Science and Community Development

www.qf.org.qa/education/

Education City, Qatar

myeducationcity.com

Japan

Study in Japan

www.studyjapan.go.jp/en

JUMP (Japanese Universities for Motivated People)

www.uni.international.mext.go.jp/global30

JASSO (Japan Student Services Organisation)

www.jasso.go.jp

Embassy of Japan in the UK

www.uk.emb-japan.go.jp

Glossary

Academic transcript

A record of academic progress from around Y10 (Y11 in NI, and S3 in Scotland) onwards, including exam results, unit grades, internal assessments, academic honours and explanations for any anomalies.

American College Test (ACT)

The ACT is used to determine academic potential for undergraduate study.

Associate degree

A two-year programme of higher education, often in a vocational subject such as hospitality or health.

Bologna process

A system to make higher education comparable and compatible across the EHEA, through use of mutually recognised systems and a clear credit framework.

Community college (USA)

These colleges offer two-year associate degrees, with the possibility of transferring to a university to top up to a full degree; a cheaper option than going straight to a US university.

Co-op programme

Period of paid work experience linked to a university course, rather like a sandwich course in the UK.

Core

The compulsory foundation for university study (used in North America and a number of other countries); students choose from a broad range of subjects.

Diploma mobility

Taking an entire degree overseas, as opposed to a study-abroad or exchange programme.

Diploma supplement

A detailed transcript of attainment in higher education, recognised across the EHEA and beyond.

eCoE (electronic confirmation of enrolment)

The eCoE is issued by Australian colleges and universities as proof of enrolment and is required to apply for a student visa.

ECTS

European Credit Transfer and Accumulation System, aiding the transfer of students between institutions.

EHEA

European Higher Education Area; the countries where the Bologna process is utilised.

Elective

An optional course taken at university.

English medium

Education with English as the language of instruction.

Europass

Helps people to study, work or train across Europe, by presenting skills and qualifications in a standardised format that is easily understood in a range of countries.

Freshman year

First year (USA).

Frosh

Another name for a fresher or freshman. Frosh week is similar to freshers' week in the UK.

Graduate Australian Medical Schools Admission Test (GAMSAT)

Used to determine academic potential for postgraduate medical courses.

Graduate Record Exam (GRE)

Used to determine academic potential for postgraduate study.

Junior year

Third year (USA).

Letter of intent

A statement demonstrating why you should be considered for your chosen course, used by the universities to distinguish between applicants. It may also be described as a letter of motivation, a statement of purpose or a personal statement.

Letter of motivation

A statement demonstrating why you should be considered for your chosen course, used by the universities to distinguish between applicants. It may also be described as a letter of intent, a statement of purpose or a personal statement.

Letter of recommendation

Reference letter to a potential university, most often (but not always) from a member of academic staff who can comment on your ability and potential.

Major

Your main subject area, for example, history, engineering or nursing.

Mid-term

An exam taken midway through the academic term.

Minor

A secondary subject area or a specialism of your major.

Nollning (Sweden)

The introduction of new students to university life, much like freshers' week in the UK.

Numerus clausus (Germany)

A competitive system for courses that have more applicants than places.

Numerus fixus (the Netherlands)

A fixed number of places are available on a course.

OECD

Organisation for Economic Co-operation and Development.

Orientation

Events and activities for new students, like freshers' week in the UK.

Personal statement
A statement demonstrating why you should be considered for your chosen course, used by the universities to distinguish between applicants. It may also be described as a letter of intent, a letter of motivation or a statement of purpose.

Polytechnic (New Zealand; Finland)
An institution providing professional or work-related higher education, in conjunction with business and industry; also known as a university of applied sciences.

Research-intensive or research-based university
An institution involved in extensive research activity and doctoral education.

Research proposal or research statement
The outline of an applicant's plans for research, including area of interest and rationale.

Scholastic Assessment Test (SAT)
Used to determine academic potential for undergraduate study.

Semester
The two periods into which the academic year is divided in some countries.

Senior year
Fourth year (USA).

Sophomore year
Second year (USA).

Statement of purpose
A statement demonstrating why you should be considered for your chosen course, used by the universities to distinguish between applicants. It may also be described as a letter of intent, a letter of motivation or a personal statement.

Study-abroad programme
A term often used to describe an exchange programme or short-term overseas study.

Tertiary education
Education following secondary level; it includes university education, as well as other post-18 education such as vocational training.

UNESCO
United Nations Educational, Scientific and Cultural Organization.

University college (Denmark, Norway and Sweden)
An institution providing professional undergraduate degrees in areas like engineering, teaching or business.

University of applied sciences (Finland and the Netherlands)
See Polytechnic.

Wānanga
An educational establishment in New Zealand that teaches degree-level courses in a Māori cultural context.

Index of advertisers